ENERGY: SUPPLIES, SUSTAINABILITY, AND COSTS

ISSN 1534-1585

ENERGY: SUPPLIES, SUSTAINABILITY, AND COSTS

Kim Masters Evans

INFORMATION PLUS® REFERENCE SERIES
Formerly Published by Information Plus, Wylie, Texas

GALE
CENGAGE Learning·

Farmington Hills, Mich • San Francisco • New York • Waterville, Maine
Meriden, Conn • Mason, Ohio • Chicago

GALE
CENGAGE Learning®

Energy: Supplies, Sustainability, and Costs

Kim Masters Evans

**Kepos Media, Inc.: Steven Long and
Janice Jorgensen, Series Editors**

Project Editors: Tracie Moy, Laura Avery

Rights Acquisition and Management: Ashley M.
    Maynard

Composition: Evi Abou-El-Seoud, Mary Beth
    Trimper

Manufacturing: Rita Wimberley

For product information and technology assistance, contact us at
Gale Customer Support, 1-800-877-4253.
For permission to use material from this text or product,
submit all requests online at **www.cengage.com/permissions.**
Further permissions questions can be e-mailed to
permissionrequest@cengage.com

Cover photograph: ©Lisa S./Shutterstock.com.

Gale
27500 Drake Rd.
Farmington Hills, MI 48331-3535

ISBN-13: 978-0-7876-5103-9 (set)
ISBN-13: 978-1-57302-650-5

ISSN 1534-1585

This title is also available as an e-book.
ISBN-13: 978-1-57302-676-5 (set)
Contact your Gale sales representative for ordering information.

Printed in the United States of America
1 2 3 4 5   19 18 17 16 15

TABLE OF CONTENTS

PREFACE

Energy: Supplies, Sustainability, and Costs is part of the *Information Plus Reference Series*. The purpose of each volume of the series is to present the latest facts on a topic of pressing concern in modern American life. These topics include today's most controversial and studied social issues of the 21st century: abortion, capital punishment, child abuse, crime, the economy, health care, immigration, national security, race and ethnicity, social welfare, women, youth, and many more. Although this series is written especially for high school and undergraduate students, it is an excellent resource for anyone in need of factual information on current affairs.

By presenting the facts, it is the intention of Gale, Cengage Learning, to provide its readers with everything they need to reach an informed opinion on current issues. To that end, there is a particular emphasis in this series on the presentation of scientific studies, surveys, and statistics. These data are generally presented in the form of tables, charts, and other graphics placed within the text of each book. Every graphic is directly referred to and carefully explained in the text. The source of each graphic is presented within the graphic itself. The data used in these graphics are drawn from the most reputable and reliable sources, such as from the various branches of the U.S. government and from private organizations and associations. Every effort was made to secure the most recent information available. Readers should bear in mind that many major studies take years to conduct, and that additional years often pass before the data from these studies are made available to the public. Therefore, in many cases the most recent information available in 2015 is dated from 2012 or 2013. Older statistics are sometimes presented as well, if they are landmark studies or of particular interest and no more-recent information exists.

Although statistics are a major focus of the *Information Plus Reference Series*, they are by no means its only content. Each book also presents the widely held positions and important ideas that shape how the book's subject is discussed in the United States. These positions are explained in detail and, where possible, in the words of their proponents. Some of the other material to be found in these books includes historical background, descriptions of major events related to the subject, relevant laws and court cases, and examples of how these issues play out in American life. Some books also feature primary documents or have pro and con debate sections that provide the words and opinions of prominent Americans on both sides of a controversial topic. All material is presented in an evenhanded and unbiased manner; readers will never be encouraged to accept one view of an issue over another.

HOW TO USE THIS BOOK

The United States is the world's largest consumer of energy in all its forms. Gasoline and other fossil fuels power its cars, trucks, trains, and aircraft. Electricity generated by burning oil, coal, and natural gas—or from nuclear or hydroelectric plants—runs Americans' lights, telephones, televisions, computers, and appliances. Without a steady, affordable, and massive amount of energy, modern America could not exist. This book presents the latest information on U.S. energy consumption and production and compares it with years past. Controversial issues such as U.S. dependence on foreign oil and government subsidies for the fossil fuel industries are explored.

Energy: Supplies, Sustainability, and Costs consists of nine chapters and three appendixes. Each of the major elements of the U.S. energy system—such as coal, nuclear energy, renewable energy sources, and electricity generation—has a chapter devoted to it. For a summary of the information that is covered in each chapter, please see the synopses that are provided in the Table of Contents. Chapters generally begin with an overview of the basic facts and background information on the chapter's topic, then proceed to examine subtopics of particular interest. For example, Chapter 9: Energy Conservation describes various national indicators of energy efficiency, including energy consumption per capita (per person) and energy consumption per dollar of gross domestic product. The chapter notes that the United States has improved its energy efficiency over time through a variety of means, including government interventions in the energy markets. Energy consumption and energy conservation measures are described for the following energy-use sectors: electric power, transportation, industrial, and residential and commercial. In addition, international energy conservation measures are examined. The chapter ends with a discussion of energy conservation in relation to global warming, which is believed to be driven in large part by carbon emissions from the combustion of fossil fuels (i.e., coal, natural gas, and oil). Readers can find their way through a chapter by looking for the section and subsection headings, which are clearly set off from the text. They can also refer to the book's extensive Index, if they already know what they are looking for.

Statistical Information

The tables and figures featured throughout *Energy: Supplies, Sustainability, and Costs* will be of particular use to readers in learning about this topic. These tables and figures represent an extensive collection of the most recent and valuable statistics on energy production and consumption—for example, the amount of coal mined in the United States in a year, the rate at which energy consumption is increasing in the United States, and the percentage of U.S. energy that comes from renewable sources. Gale, Cengage Learning, believes that making this information available to readers is the most important way to fulfill the goal of this book: to help readers understand the topic of energy and reach their own conclusions about controversial issues related to energy use and conservation in the United States.

Each table or figure has a unique identifier appearing above it, for ease of identification and reference. Titles for the tables and figures explain their purpose. At the end of each table or figure, the original source of the data is provided.

To help readers understand these often complicated statistics, all tables and figures are explained in the text. References in the text direct readers to the relevant statistics. Furthermore, the contents of all tables and figures are fully indexed. Please see the opening section of the Index at the back of this volume for a description of how to find tables and figures within it.

Appendixes

Besides the main body text and images, *Energy: Supplies, Sustainability, and Costs* has three appendixes. The first is the Important Names and Addresses directory. Here, readers will find contact information for a number of organizations that study energy. The second appendix is the Resources section, which is provided to assist readers in conducting their own research. In this section, the author and editors of *Energy: Supplies, Sustainability, and Costs* describe some of the sources that were most useful during the compilation of this book. The final appendix is the Index. It has been greatly expanded from previous editions and should make it even easier to find specific topics in this book.

COMMENTS AND SUGGESTIONS

The editors of the *Information Plus Reference Series* welcome your feedback on *Energy: Supplies, Sustainability, and Costs*. Please direct all correspondence to:

Editors
Information Plus Reference Series
27500 Drake Rd.
Farmington Hills, MI 48331-3535

CHAPTER 1
AN ENERGY OVERVIEW

In scientific terms, energy is the capacity for doing work. Humans have learned to harness and use multiple energy sources to get work done. A perfect energy source would be widely available, safe, easy to procure and use, environmentally friendly, provide tremendous amounts of energy, and never run out. As yet, such an energy source has not been found. Instead, there are multiple energy sources with varying levels of suitability. This book will examine the various sources in terms of their availability (supplies), sustainability, and costs.

ENERGY CONVERSIONS

An important law of nature is that energy cannot be created or destroyed, it can only change forms. The most common form of energy conversion facilitated by humans is the conversion of chemical energy (e.g., the energy stored within fuels by virtue of their chemical structures) to thermal energy (heat). For example, the energy that is stored within wood and other combustible fuels is transferred to heat and light when the fuel is burned. Heat energy can be used directly, such as to heat buildings, or it can be converted to mechanical energy. Imagine a pot of boiling water. The steam rising above the pot is in motion. It is said to have kinetic energy. This energy, when concentrated, can be powerful enough to force movement in machines, such as to turn blades, move pistons, or open valves. In this context, steam is a working fluid. In fact, steam is a popular working fluid because once the desired work has been obtained, the steam can be condensed back to water and reused.

The chemical-to-heat-to-mechanical (C-H-M) energy conversion process powers vehicles, such as cars, trucks, ships, and bulldozers. The C-H-M process is also the main precursor for producing electricity at power plants. In a very simple power plant, coal or some other fuel is burned to produce steam that turns the blades of a turbine. The turbine rotates a magnet that is nestled within or around coiled wire, generating an electric current in the wire. Thus, mechanical energy is converted to electrical energy. This basic technology has been in use since the 19th century. Hydroelectric power also dates from that century. In this process water is the working fluid that helps convert mechanical energy to electrical energy. During the 20th century scientists developed yet another energy conversion process, one based on nuclear energy (the energy held within atomic nuclei). Splitting a uranium atom apart under controlled conditions produces heat that can be used to generate electricity. Wind and solar energy are also increasingly being converted to electrical energy using high-technology devices.

It is important to remember that at each energy conversion stage some of the capacity to do work is lost. For example, some of the heat that is generated by burning fuel escapes to the atmosphere rather than heating the desired target. Conversion losses are inevitable. Therefore, humans strive to find energy sources with large amounts of energy potential and to minimize energy losses at each conversion step.

ENERGY CONTENT

Energy content is the amount of energy that can be obtained from a given amount of energy source. Heat energy is the key factor by which various energy sources are compared. In the United States heat energy is measured using British thermal units (Btu). This term came into use during the 19th century as a benchmark measure: 1 Btu represented the amount of heat required to raise the temperature of 1 pound (0.5 kg) of water by 1 degree Fahrenheit (0.6 degrees Celsius). In modern times, the Btu is precisely defined by controlling the measurement variables, for example, the density of the water that is used in the measurement. In countries that rely on the metric system, the joule is the preferred unit for measuring heat, work, and energy; 1 Btu is equivalent to approximately 1,055 joules.

TABLE 1.1

Btu (British thermal units) content of common energy units

1 barrel (42 gallons) of crude oil	5,800,000 Btu
1 gallon of gasoline	124,262 Btu
1 gallon of diesel fuel	138,690 Btu
1 gallon of heating oil	138,690 Btu
1 barrel of residual fuel oil	6,287,000 Btu
1 cubic foot of natural gas	1,025 Btu
1 gallon of propane	91,333 Btu
1 short ton of coal	19,489,000 Btu
1 kilowatt-hour of electricity	3,412 Btu

Note: The Btu content of each fuel reflects the average energy content for fuels consumed in the United States during 2013.

SOURCE: Adapted from "Btu Content of Common Energy Units," in *Energy Units and Calculators Explained*, U.S. Energy Information Administration, 2014, http://www.eia.gov/energyexplained/index.cfm?page=about_energy_ units (accessed June 27, 2014)

The Btu is a relatively small unit of measure. In "British Thermal Units (Btu)" (April 23, 2012, http://www.eia .gov/EnergyExplained/index.cfm?page=about_btu), the U.S. Energy Information Administration (EIA) within the U.S. Department of Energy (DOE) explains that "one Btu is approximately equal to the energy released in the burning of a wood match."

Table 1.1 compares the Btu content of various fossil fuel energy sources and electricity. One ton (0.9 t) of coal provides 19.5 million Btu, compared with only 5.8 million Btu from a barrel (42 gallons [159 L]) of crude oil.

SUSTAINABILITY

In the United States most energy conversion processes begin with fossil fuels—fuels derived from the below-ground remains of prehistoric organisms that became energy enriched after millions of years of exposure to high temperatures and pressures. Examples include coal, petroleum, and natural gas. Chemically, they are known as hydrocarbons because they are compounds that contain hydrogen and carbon. These fuels and their derivatives have high energy contents because of their enormous carbon contents. Burning fossil fuels produces large amounts of heat, but also liberates large amounts of carbon into the atmosphere, which is an environmental problem.

Fossil fuels are considered to be nonrenewable energy sources. It takes nature millions of years to create them; as such, the amounts available to humans are finite. It is possible to exhaust these supplies because the replenishment time is so long. Uranium is also considered to be nonrenewable. It is found at low concentrations throughout the earth's soils and seawater. In theory, all of this uranium could be exhausted through massive use.

By contrast, other energy sources are said to be renewable because under the right circumstances they can be tapped again and again by humans without eliminating them. Examples include wind, sunlight, flowing water, and the heat stored beneath the earth's crust, which is called geothermal energy. Biomass— biologically based materials other than fossil fuels, such as trees and other vegetation—is also considered a renewable energy source because humans can regrow these materials in a relatively short amount of time. Likewise, combustible wastes produced by humans (e.g., garbage) are constantly being created and, thus, represent a renewable energy source.

ENERGY PRODUCTION AND CONSUMPTION

People have always found ways to harness energy, such as using animals for transportation and work or inventing machines such as windmills and waterwheels to tap the power of wind and water, respectively. Before the 1800s much of the thermal energy used in the United States for heating and cooking was obtained by burning wood. Lighting was provided by wax candles or by lanterns that burned whale oil or some other kind of animal fat.

The EIA indicates in "A Brief History of Coal Use" (2014, http://www.fe.doe.gov/education/energylessons/ coal/coal_history.html) that commercial coal mining in the United States began during the 1740s. Coal has a much higher heat content than wood, and this energy boost fueled the Industrial Revolution (1760–1848), a period of intense industrialization and modernization. One of the most important innovations of the Industrial Revolution was the steam engine—a machine that converted the thermal energy of burning fuel, such as coal, to mechanical energy. Steam engines powered locomotives, ships, and industrial equipment during the 1800s. There were even some steam-powered cars.

The petroleum age began in the United States in 1859, when the first successful modern oil well was drilled. Scientists developed methods to process and refine crude oil into gasoline and other products to power vehicles, ships, and industrial equipment. By the early 20th century petroleum derivatives were in high demand by consumers. Oil also became a vital commodity in regards to national security. The United States' large supply of domestic oil was a crucial component to its success in World War II (1939–1945).

Modern U.S. Energy Production

Table 1.2 shows energy production, by fuel, in the United States between 1950 and 2013. The units are quadrillion Btu, with 1 quadrillion Btu equal to 1,000,000,000,000,000 Btu. In 1950 the primary energy sources were coal (14.1 quadrillion Btu) and crude oil (11.4 quadrillion Btu). Natural gas (6.2 quadrillion Btu) was a distant third. In "The History of Natural Gas" (2014, http://www.fe.doe.gov/education/energylessons/ gas/gas_history.html), the EIA explains that natural gas

TABLE 1.2

Primary energy production, by source, selected years 1950–2013

[Quadrillion Btu]

| | Fossil fuels | | | | | Nuclear electric power | Renewable energy[a] | | | | | | Total |
	Coal	Natural gas (dry)	Crude oil[c]	NGPL[d]	Total		Hydro-electric power[e]	Geothermal	Solar/PV	Wind	Biomass	Total	
1950 Total	14.060	6.233	11.447	0.823	32.563	0.000	1.415	NA	NA	NA	1.562	2.978	35.540
1955 Total	12.370	9.345	14.410	1.240	37.364	0.000	1.360	NA	NA	NA	1.424	2.784	40.148
1960 Total	10.817	12.656	14.935	1.461	39.869	0.006	1.608	(s)	NA	NA	1.320	2.928	42.803
1965 Total	13.055	15.775	16.521	1.883	47.235	0.043	2.059	0.002	NA	NA	1.335	3.396	50.674
1970 Total	14.607	21.666	20.401	2.512	59.186	0.239	2.634	0.006	NA	NA	1.431	4.070	63.495
1975 Total	14.989	19.640	17.729	2.374	54.733	1.900	3.155	0.034	NA	NA	1.499	4.687	61.320
1980 Total	18.598	19.908	18.249	2.254	59.008	2.739	2.900	0.053	NA	NA	2.475	5.428	67.175
1985 Total	19.325	16.980	18.992	2.241	57.539	4.076	2.970	0.097	(s)	NA	3.016	6.084	67.698
1990 Total	22.488	18.326	15.571	2.175	58.560	6.104	3.046	0.171	0.059	0.029	2.735	6.041	70.705
1995 Total	22.130	19.082	13.887	2.442	57.540	7.075	3.205	0.152	0.066	0.033	3.099	6.558	71.174
2000 Total	22.735	19.662	12.358	2.611	57.366	7.862	2.811	0.164	0.066	0.057	3.006	6.104	71.332
2001 Total	23.547	20.166	12.282	2.547	58.541	8.029	2.242	0.164	0.064	0.070	2.624	5.164	71.735
2002 Total	22.732	19.382	12.160	2.559	56.834	8.145	2.689	0.171	0.063	0.105	2.705	5.734	70.713
2003 Total	22.094	19.633	11.960	2.346	56.033	7.960	2.793	0.173	0.062	0.113	2.805	5.947	69.939
2004 Total	22.852	19.074	11.550	2.466	55.942	8.223	2.688	0.178	0.063	0.142	2.998	6.069	70.234
2005 Total	23.185	18.556	10.969	2.334	55.044	8.161	2.703	0.181	0.063	0.178	3.104	6.229	69.434
2006 Total	23.790	19.022	10.771	2.356	55.938	8.215	2.869	0.181	0.068	0.264	3.216	6.599	70.751
2007 Total	23.493	19.786	10.748	2.409	56.436	8.459	2.446	0.186	0.076	0.341	3.480	6.528	71.422
2008 Total	23.851	20.703	10.613	2.419	57.587	8.426	2.511	0.192	0.089	0.546	3.881	7.219	73.233
2009 Total	21.624	21.139	11.333	2.574	56.670	8.355	2.669	0.200	0.098	0.721	3.967	7.655	72.680
2010 Total	22.038	21.806	11.581	2.781	58.207	8.434	2.539	0.208	0.126	0.923	4.332	8.128	74.769
2011 Total	22.221	23.406	11.966	2.970	60.563	8.269	3.103	0.212	0.171	1.168	4.516	9.170	78.002
2012 Total	20.677	24.635	13.767R	3.246	62.325R	8.062	2.629	0.212	0.227	1.340	4.419	8.826	79.213R
2013 Total	19.990	24.889E	15.758R,E	3.465	64.102R	8.268	2.561	0.221	0.307	1.595	4.614	9.298	81.669R

[a]Most data are estimates.

[b]Beginning in 1989, includes waste coal supplied. Beginning in 2001, also includes a small amount of refuse recovery.

[c]Includes lease condensate.

[d]Natural gas plant liquids.

[e]Conventional hydroelectric power.

R = Revised. E = Estimate. NA = Not available. (s) = Less than 0.5 trillion Btu.

Notes: Totals may not equal sum of components due to independent rounding. Geographic coverage is the 50 states and the District of Columbia.

Btu = British thermal units. PV = photovoltaic.

SOURCE: Adapted from "Table 1.2. Primary Energy Production by Source (Quadrillion Btu)," in *Monthly Energy Review: June 2014*, U.S. Energy Information Administration, June 25, 2014, http://www.eia.gov/totalenergy/data/monthly/archive/00351406.pdf (accessed June 27, 2014)

was mostly used during the 1800s as a fuel for street lights. It did not become widely available to individual homes and businesses until after World War II, when extensive pipelines were laid in U.S. cities.

By 1955 crude oil production surpassed that of coal; however, petroleum's reign at the top was short lived. (See Table 1.2.) In 1970 natural gas production surpassed that of crude oil. During the early 1980s these three fossil fuels were roughly equal in terms of domestic production. Over the following decades domestic production fell dramatically for crude oil, but grew stronger for coal and natural gas.

Figure 1.1 shows energy production by source between 1949 and 2013. Note that natural gas plant liquids (NGPL) are hydrocarbons separated from natural gas during processing. Figure 1.1 illustrates that, for decades, the production of fossil fuels (coal, natural gas, crude oil, and NGPL) vastly overshadowed the production of other energy sources. Among the latter, the top competitors were nuclear electric power and renewable energy, specifically biomass and hydroelectric power. (See Table 1.2.)

Figure 1.2 shows energy production, by source, in 2013. At 24.9 quadrillion Btu, natural gas accounted for more energy production in the United States in 2013 than any other energy source. Energy produced from coal was second (20 quadrillion Btu), followed by crude oil (15.8 quadrillion Btu) and nuclear electric power

(8.3 quadrillion Btu). The total energy produced domestically (within the United States) more than doubled, from 35.5 quadrillion Btu in 1950 to 81.7 quadrillion Btu in 2013. (See Table 1.2.)

Modern U.S. Energy Consumption

Between 1950 and 2013 total domestic energy consumption (the amount of energy consumed in the United States) nearly tripled, from 34.6 quadrillion Btu in 1950 to 97.5 quadrillion Btu in 2013. (See Table 1.3.)

One of the reasons that energy consumption has increased in the United States is a growing population. According to the U.S. Census Bureau, in *Measuring America: The Decennial Censuses from 1790 to 2000* (September 2002, http://www.census.gov/prod/2002 pubs/pol02marv.pdf), the U.S. population numbered 151.3 million in 1950. In "U.S. and World Population Clock" (June 27, 2014, http://www.census.gov/pop clock), the Census Bureau estimates the U.S. population was 317.3 million at year-end 2013. Thus, the population doubled between 1950 and 2013. As noted earlier, energy consumption grew even faster, nearly tripling during the same period.

In *Monthly Energy Review: June 2014* (June 2014, http://www.eia.gov/totalenergy/data/monthly/archive/ 00351406.pdf), the EIA divides U.S. energy consumers into five broad sectors: electric power, residential, industrial, commercial, and transportation.

FIGURE 1.1

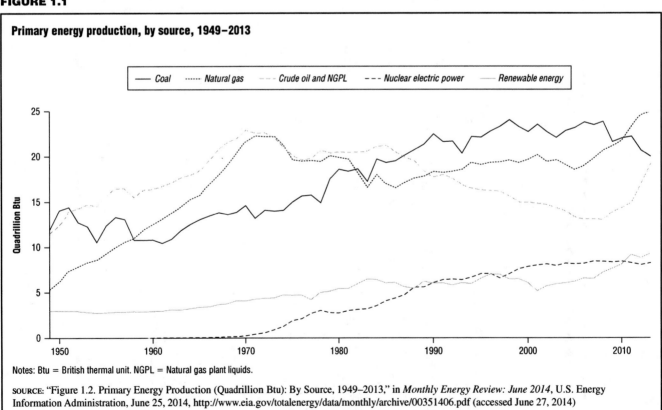

Primary energy production, by source, 1949–2013

Notes: Btu = British thermal unit. NGPL = Natural gas plant liquids.

SOURCE: "Figure 1.2. Primary Energy Production (Quadrillion Btu): By Source, 1949–2013," in *Monthly Energy Review: June 2014*, U.S. Energy Information Administration, June 25, 2014, http://www.eia.gov/totalenergy/data/monthly/archive/00351406.pdf (accessed June 27, 2014)

FIGURE 1.2

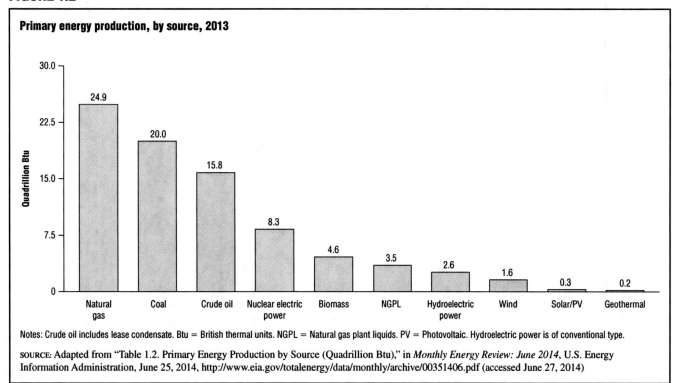

Primary energy production, by source, 2013

Notes: Crude oil includes lease condensate. Btu = British thermal units. NGPL = Natural gas plant liquids. PV = Photovoltaic. Hydroelectric power is of conventional type.

SOURCE: Adapted from "Table 1.2. Primary Energy Production by Source (Quadrillion Btu)," in *Monthly Energy Review: June 2014*, U.S. Energy Information Administration, June 25, 2014, http://www.eia.gov/totalenergy/data/monthly/archive/00351406.pdf (accessed June 27, 2014)

ELECTRIC POWER SECTOR. This sector consumes energy at facilities it operates to sell electricity to the public. Examples include electric utilities and combined heat-and-power plants that sell heat and electricity. It should be noted that this sector does not include power plants that are operated by factories and other industrial enterprises that produce electricity or electricity and heat for their own use. Figure 1.3 shows the primary fuels that were used by the electric power sector between 1949 and 2013. Coal has historically been the main fuel source for electric power generation.

The EIA considers the electric power sector an intermediary in the energy supply chain, not an end user of energy. As is explained in Chapter 8, electricity generation is inherently inefficient; energy content is lost as fuels are converted to electricity and as the electricity travels across transmission lines and distribution systems. Thus, the heat content of the energy sources that enter the electric power sector is far greater than the heat content of the electricity that is delivered to end users.

RESIDENTIAL SECTOR. This end-use sector consumes energy in residential living quarters. Common uses include space heating, water heating, air conditioning, lighting, refrigeration, cooking, and running other appliances. Figure 1.4 shows the major energy sources that were consumed by this sector between 1949 and 2013. Natural gas was historically the most-used source; its dominance, however, was matched by electricity during the first decade of the 21st century. Petroleum, renewable energy, and coal are minor energy sources to this sector.

INDUSTRIAL SECTOR. Energy consumption by this end-use sector powers equipment and facilities that are engaged in producing, processing, or assembling goods. Figure 1.5 shows the major energy sources that were consumed by the industrial sector between 1949 and 2013. During the 1950s petroleum and natural gas replaced coal as the preferred fuel. In 2013 petroleum and natural gas were the top fuels and were used roughly equally. Electricity, renewable energy, and coal played much smaller roles.

COMMERCIAL SECTOR. This end-use sector includes the equipment and facilities that are operated by businesses; federal, state, and local governments; and other private and public organizations, such as religious, social, or fraternal groups. The commercial sector includes institutional living quarters and sewage treatment facilities. Figure 1.6 shows that electricity and natural gas have been the preferred fuels in this sector for decades. In 2013 electricity was the main energy source, followed by natural gas, petroleum, renewable energy, and coal.

TRANSPORTATION SECTOR. Energy consumed by this end-use sector is for vehicles whose primary purpose is transporting people and/or goods from place to place. These vehicles include automobiles; trucks; buses; motorcycles; trains, subways, and other rail vehicles; aircraft; and ships, barges, and other waterborne vehicles. It should be noted that vehicles whose primary purpose is not transportation (e.g., bulldozers, tractors, and forklifts) are classified in the sector of their primary use. Petroleum dominates, by far, the energy consumption in the transportation sector. (See Figure 1.7.) Other energy sources are minor players.

TABLE 1.3

Primary energy consumption, by source, selected years 1950–2013

[Quadrillion Btu]

	Fossil fuels				Nuclear electric power	Renewable energy[a]						Total[f]
	Coal	Natural gas[b]	Petroleum[c]	Total[d]		Hydro-electric power[e]	Geothermal	Solar/PV	Wind	Biomass	Total	
1950 Total	12.347	5.968	13.315	31.632	0.000	1.415	NA	NA	NA	1.562	2.978	34.616
1955 Total	11.167	8.998	17.255	37.410	0.000	1.360	NA	NA	NA	1.424	2.784	40.208
1960 Total	9.838	12.385	19.919	42.137	0.006	1.608	(s)	NA	NA	1.320	2.928	45.086
1965 Total	11.581	15.769	23.246	50.577	0.043	2.059	0.002	NA	NA	1.335	3.396	54.015
1970 Total	12.265	21.795	29.521	63.522	0.239	2.634	0.006	NA	NA	1.431	4.070	67.838
1975 Total	12.663	19.948	32.732	65.357	1.900	3.155	0.034	NA	NA	1.499	4.687	71.965
1980 Total	15.423	20.235	34.205	69.828	2.739	2.900	0.053	NA	NA	2.475	5.428	78.067
1985 Total	17.478	17.703	30.925	66.093	4.076	2.970	0.097	(s)	(s)	3.016	6.084	76.392
1990 Total	19.173	19.603	33.552	72.332	6.104	3.046	0.171	0.059	0.029	2.735	6.041	84.485
1995 Total	20.089	22.671	34.438	77.259	7.075	3.205	0.152	0.069	0.033	3.101	6.560	91.029
2000 Total	22.580	23.824	38.262	84.731	7.862	2.811	0.164	0.066	0.057	3.008	6.106	98.814
2001 Total	21.914	22.773	38.186	82.902	8.029	2.242	0.164	0.064	0.070	2.622	5.163	96.168
2002 Total	21.904	23.510	38.224	83.699	8.145	2.689	0.171	0.063	0.105	2.701	5.729	97.645
2003 Total	22.321	22.831	38.811	84.014	7.960	2.793	0.173	0.062	0.113	2.807	5.948	97.943
2004 Total	22.466	22.923	40.292	85.819	8.223	2.688	0.178	0.063	0.142	3.010	6.081	100.161
2005 Total	22.797	22.565	40.388	85.794	8.161	2.703	0.181	0.063	0.178	3.117	6.242	100.282
2006 Total	22.447	22.239	39.955	84.702	8.215	2.869	0.181	0.068	0.264	3.267	6.649	99.629
2007 Total	22.749	23.663	39.774	86.211	8.459	2.446	0.186	0.076	0.341	3.492	6.541	101.317
2008 Total	22.387	23.843	37.280	83.551	8.426	2.511	0.192	0.089	0.546	3.865	7.202	99.292
2009 Total	19.691	23.416	35.403	78.487	8.355	2.669	0.200	0.098	0.721	3.950	7.638	94.596
2010 Total	20.834	24.575	36.010	81.412	8.434	2.539	0.208	0.126	0.923	4.285	8.081	98.016
2011 Total	19.658	24.955	35.368	79.991	8.269	3.103	0.212	0.171	1.168	4.420	9.074	97.461
2012 Total	17.329	26.083	34.577	77.994	8.062	2.629	0.212	0.227	1.340	4.379	8.786	95.004
2013 Total	18.084	26.630R	35.099	79.796R	8.268	2.561	0.221	0.307	1.595	4.607	9.291	97.534R

[a]Most data are estimates.

[b]Natural gas only; excludes supplemental gaseous fuels.

[c]Petroleum products supplied, including natural gas plant liquids and crude oil burned as fuel. Does not include biofuels that have been blended with petroleum—biofuels are included in "Biomass."

[d]Includes coal coke net imports.

[e]Conventional hydroelectric power.

[f]Includes coal coke net imports and electricity net imports, which are not separately displayed.

R = Revised. NA = Not available. (s) = Less than 0.5 trillion Btu.

Notes: Btu = British thermal units.

Totals may not equal sum of components due to independent rounding. Geographic coverage is the 50 states and the District of Columbia.

SOURCE: "Table 1.3. Primary Energy Consumption by Source (Quadrillion Btu)," in *Monthly Energy Review: June 2014*, U.S. Energy Information Administration, June 25, 2014, http://www.eia.gov/totalenergy/data/monthly/archive/0035l406.pdf (accessed June 27, 2014)

FIGURE 1.3

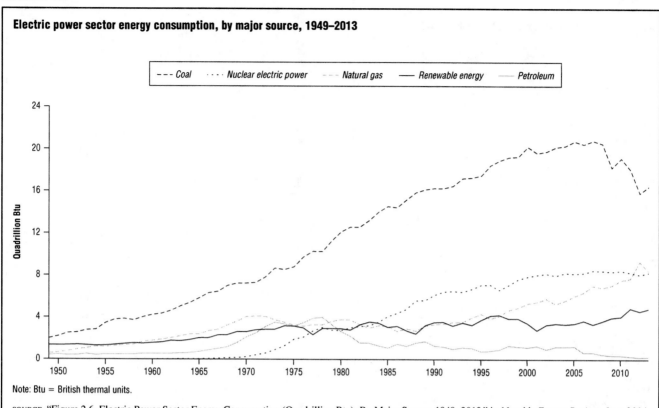

Electric power sector energy consumption, by major source, 1949–2013

Note: Btu = British thermal units.

SOURCE: "Figure 2.6. Electric Power Sector Energy Consumption (Quadrillion Btu): By Major Source, 1949–2013," in *Monthly Energy Review: June 2014*, U.S. Energy Information Administration, June 25, 2014, http://www.eia.gov/totalenergy/data/monthly/archive/00351406.pdf (accessed June 27, 2014)

FIGURE 1.4

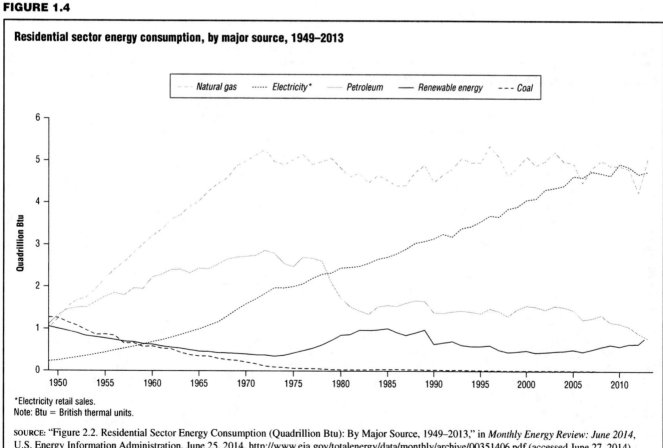

Residential sector energy consumption, by major source, 1949–2013

*Electricity retail sales.
Note: Btu = British thermal units.

SOURCE: "Figure 2.2. Residential Sector Energy Consumption (Quadrillion Btu): By Major Source, 1949–2013," in *Monthly Energy Review: June 2014*, U.S. Energy Information Administration, June 25, 2014, http://www.eia.gov/totalenergy/data/monthly/archive/00351406.pdf (accessed June 27, 2014)

FIGURE 1.5

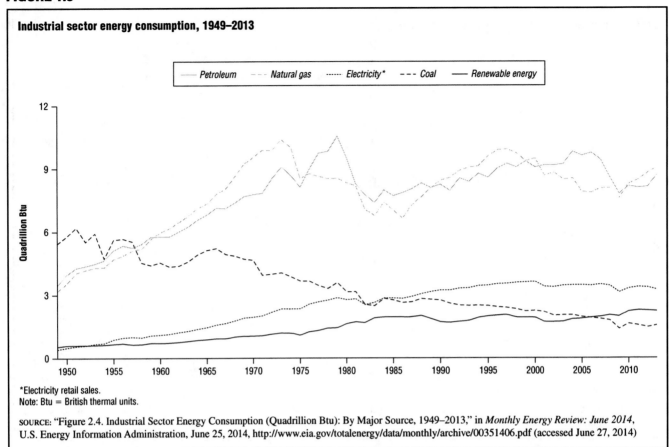

Industrial sector energy consumption, 1949–2013

········ Petroleum   ─·─· Natural gas   ······· Electricity*   ─ ─ ─ Coal   ──── Renewable energy

*Electricity retail sales.
Note: Btu = British thermal units.

SOURCE: "Figure 2.4. Industrial Sector Energy Consumption (Quadrillion Btu): By Major Source, 1949–2013," in *Monthly Energy Review: June 2014*, U.S. Energy Information Administration, June 25, 2014, http://www.eia.gov/totalenergy/data/monthly/archive/00351406.pdf (accessed June 27, 2014)

FIGURE 1.6

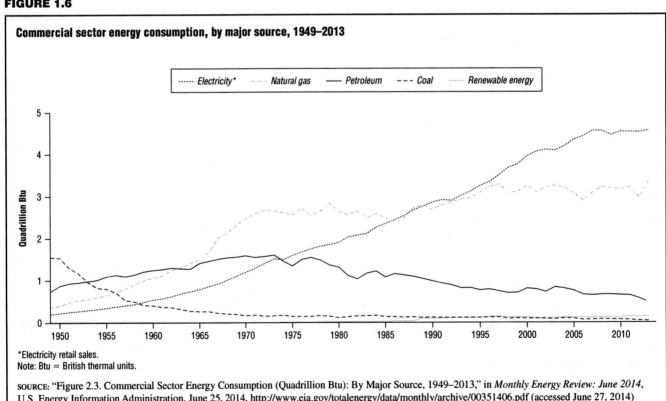

Commercial sector energy consumption, by major source, 1949–2013

······· Electricity*   ─ ─ ─ Natural gas   ──── Petroleum   ─ ─ ─ Coal   ──── Renewable energy

*Electricity retail sales.
Note: Btu = British thermal units.

SOURCE: "Figure 2.3. Commercial Sector Energy Consumption (Quadrillion Btu): By Major Source, 1949–2013," in *Monthly Energy Review: June 2014*, U.S. Energy Information Administration, June 25, 2014, http://www.eia.gov/totalenergy/data/monthly/archive/00351406.pdf (accessed June 27, 2014)

FIGURE 1.7

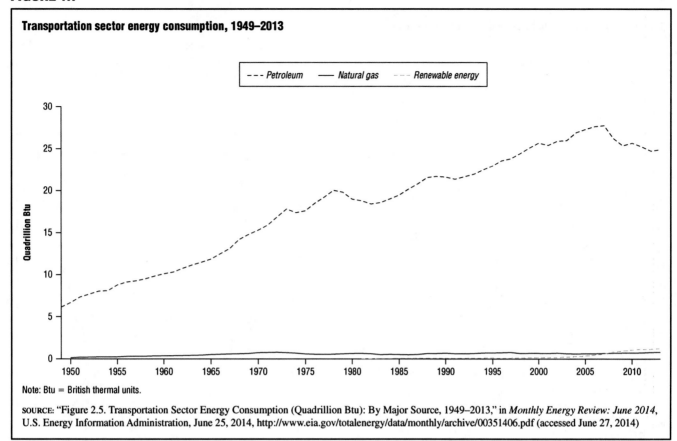

Transportation sector energy consumption, 1949–2013

Note: Btu = British thermal units.

SOURCE: "Figure 2.5. Transportation Sector Energy Consumption (Quadrillion Btu): By Major Source, 1949–2013," in *Monthly Energy Review: June 2014*, U.S. Energy Information Administration, June 25, 2014, http://www.eia.gov/totalenergy/data/monthly/archive/00351406.pdf (accessed June 27, 2014)

SECTORS OVERALL. Historically, industry has been the largest energy consumer of the end-use sectors. (See Figure 1.8.) In 2013 industry used 31.5 quadrillion Btu, compared with 27 quadrillion Btu for the transportation sector, 21.1 quadrillion Btu for the residential sector, and 17.9 quadrillion Btu for the commercial sector.

ENERGY SELF-SUFFICIENCY

Before the 20th century, the United States was largely energy self-sufficient, in that it produced enough energy domestically to satisfy domestic demand. Through the 1950s domestic energy production and consumption were nearly equal. (See Figure 1.9.) During the 1960s consumption slightly outpaced production. During the 1970s the gap widened considerably; it narrowed somewhat during the early 1980s, and thereafter widened year after year. By the beginning of the 21st century the gap between domestic energy production and consumption was quite significant.

Since the 1970s energy imports (particularly of petroleum) have been used to close the gap between domestic energy production and consumption. Petroleum imports have historically accounted for the vast majority of total energy imports. (See Figure 1.10.) The United States' dependence on other countries for oil has created economic and political problems that began in the 1970s.

During that decade the nation experienced an energy crisis because it was hugely dependent on foreign oil, particularly from countries in the Middle East. A political disagreement led some of those countries to temporarily limit the amount of oil they sold to the United States. Lower supply in the face of growing demand sent prices soaring for gasoline and other oil products. The energy embargo had severe repercussions on the overall economy. Energy self-sufficiency became a new national goal, but, as shown in Figure 1.9, this goal has been difficult to achieve.

The United States does export some energy commodities. (See Figure 1.11.) Through the 1990s coal was the predominant export. Since that time petroleum exports have surged dramatically, totaling 7.2 quadrillion Btu in 2013. According to the EIA, in *Monthly Energy Review: June 2014*, U.S. petroleum exports are almost all petroleum products. The United States exports very little crude oil due to regulatory restrictions that are described in Chapter 2.

Figure 1.12 shows domestic energy production, import, export, and consumption flows in 2013. Overall, domestic production was 81.7 quadrillion Btu. Imports added another 25.5 quadrillion Btu, mostly from crude oil and petroleum products. Thus, the total U.S. energy supply was 109.3 quadrillion Btu, of which 75% was domestically produced and 25% was imported. Approximately 11.8 quadrillion

FIGURE 1.8

Total energy consumption, by end-use sector, 1949–2013

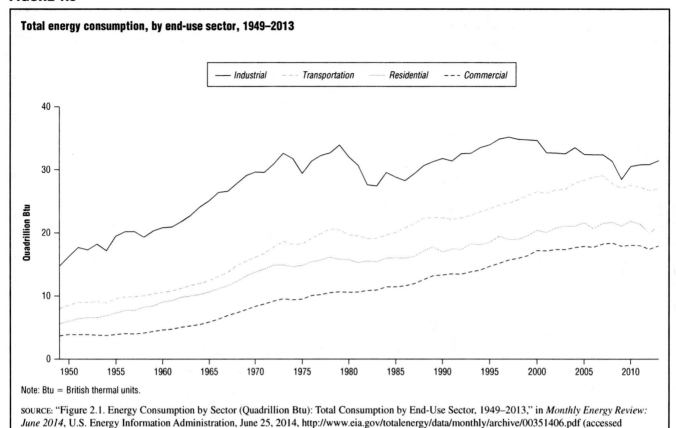

Note: Btu = British thermal units.

SOURCE: "Figure 2.1. Energy Consumption by Sector (Quadrillion Btu): Total Consumption by End-Use Sector, 1949–2013," in *Monthly Energy Review: June 2014*, U.S. Energy Information Administration, June 25, 2014, http://www.eia.gov/totalenergy/data/monthly/archive/00351406.pdf (accessed June 27, 2014)

FIGURE 1.9

Primary energy consumption, production, and trade, 1949–2013

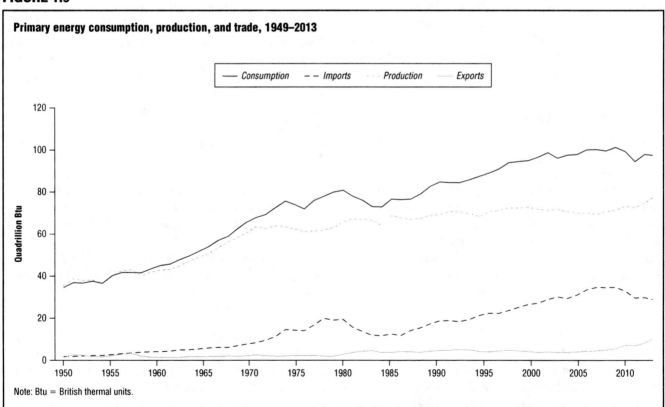

Note: Btu = British thermal units.

SOURCE: "Figure 1.1. Primary Energy Overview (Quadrillion Btu): Overview, 1949–2013," in *Monthly Energy Review: June 2014*, U.S. Energy Information Administration, June 25, 2014, http://www.eia.gov/totalenergy/data/monthly/archive/00351406.pdf (accessed June 27, 2014)

FIGURE 1.10

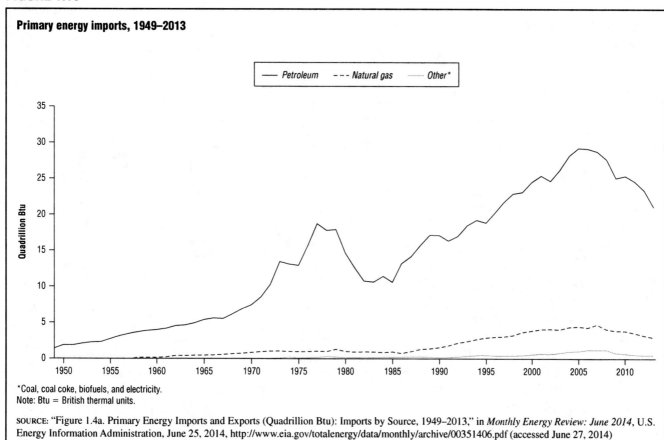

Primary energy imports, 1949–2013

*Coal, coal coke, biofuels, and electricity.
Note: Btu = British thermal units.

SOURCE: "Figure 1.4a. Primary Energy Imports and Exports (Quadrillion Btu): Imports by Source, 1949–2013," in *Monthly Energy Review: June 2014*, U.S. Energy Information Administration, June 25, 2014, http://www.eia.gov/totalenergy/data/monthly/archive/00351406.pdf (accessed June 27, 2014)

FIGURE 1.11

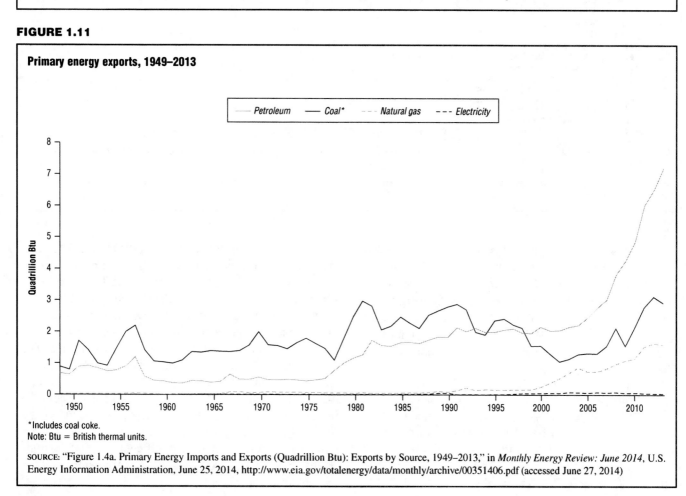

Primary energy exports, 1949–2013

*Includes coal coke.
Note: Btu = British thermal units.

SOURCE: "Figure 1.4a. Primary Energy Imports and Exports (Quadrillion Btu): Exports by Source, 1949–2013," in *Monthly Energy Review: June 2014*, U.S. Energy Information Administration, June 25, 2014, http://www.eia.gov/totalenergy/data/monthly/archive/00351406.pdf (accessed June 27, 2014)

FIGURE 1.12

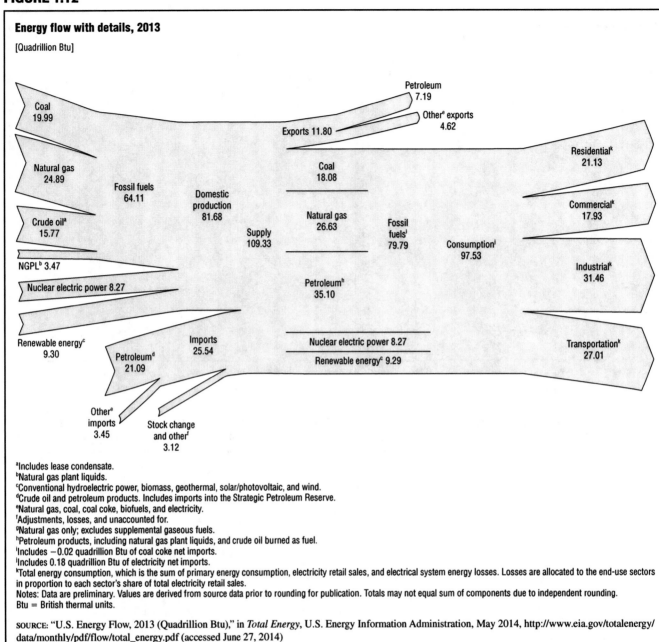

Energy flow with details, 2013

[Quadrillion Btu]

Petroleum 7.19

Other[a] exports 4.62

Exports 11.80

Coal 19.99

Natural gas 24.89

Fossil fuels 64.11

Domestic production 81.68

Coal 18.08

Natural gas 26.63

Crude oil[a] 15.77

Supply 109.33

Fossil fuels[i] 79.79

Consumption[j] 97.53

Residential[k] 21.13

Commercial[k] 17.93

Industrial[k] 31.46

NGPL[b] 3.47

Nuclear electric power 8.27

Petroleum[h] 35.10

Renewable energy[c] 9.30

Imports 25.54

Petroleum[d] 21.09

Nuclear electric power 8.27

Renewable energy[c] 9.29

Transportation[k] 27.01

Other[e] imports 3.45

Stock change and other[f] 3.12

[a]Includes lease condensate.
[b]Natural gas plant liquids.
[c]Conventional hydroelectric power, biomass, geothermal, solar/photovoltaic, and wind.
[d]Crude oil and petroleum products. Includes imports into the Strategic Petroleum Reserve.
[e]Natural gas, coal, coal coke, biofuels, and electricity.
[f]Adjustments, losses, and unaccounted for.
[g]Natural gas only; excludes supplemental gaseous fuels.
[h]Petroleum products, including natural gas plant liquids, and crude oil burned as fuel.
[i]Includes −0.02 quadrillion Btu of coal coke net imports.
[j]Includes 0.18 quadrillion Btu of electricity net imports.
[k]Total energy consumption, which is the sum of primary energy consumption, electricity retail sales, and electrical system energy losses. Losses are allocated to the end-use sectors in proportion to each sector's share of total electricity retail sales.
Notes: Data are preliminary. Values are derived from source data prior to rounding for publication. Totals may not equal sum of components due to independent rounding.
Btu = British thermal units.

SOURCE: "U.S. Energy Flow, 2013 (Quadrillion Btu)," in *Total Energy*, U.S. Energy Information Administration, May 2014, http://www.eia.gov/totalenergy/data/monthly/pdf/flow/total_energy.pdf (accessed June 27, 2014)

Btu (11%) of the U.S. supply was exported. This included 7.2 quadrillion Btu of petroleum products and 4.6 quadrillion Btu of other commodities, such as natural gas, coal, coal coke, biofuels, and electricity. Total U.S. energy consumption in 2013 was 97.5 quadrillion Btu. The majority (81.7 quadrillion Btu, or 75%) of total consumption came from domestic energy products, while 25.5 quadrillion Btu (25%) came from imports.

The United States cannot obtain total energy self-sufficiency without replacing energy imports (almost all of which are petroleum based) with domestic production. Figure 1.13 shows various scenarios for future U.S. oil use as projected by the EIA in *Annual Energy Outlook 2014 with Projections to 2040* (April 2014,

http://www.eia.gov/forecasts/aeo/pdf/0383(2014).pdf). The EIA calculates that net imports (imports minus exports) of oil accounted for around 38% of total U.S. liquid fuels consumption in 2012. Under a scenario in which oil prices are high (thus encouraging production) and domestic oil production increases robustly, the United States could reduce its net oil imports to zero by 2036. The oil company BP (formerly British Petroleum) presents a similarly optimistic prediction in "BP Energy Outlook 2035: US" (January 2014, http://www.bp.com/content/dam/bp/pdf/Energy-economics/Energy-Outlook/Country _insights_US_2035.pdf). BP forecasts that the United States will become energy self-sufficient by 2035, assuming that U.S. energy production grows at a faster rate than does domestic consumption.

FIGURE 1.13

Net imports (imports minus exports) as a share of U.S. liquid fuels consumption, 1990–2012 and projected through 2040

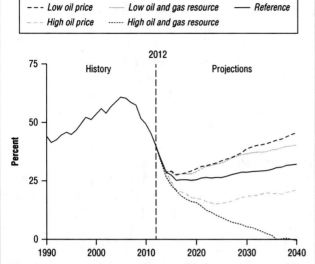

SOURCE: "Figure MT-55. Net Import Share of U.S. Petroleum and Other Liquid Fuels Consumption in Five Cases, 1990–2040 (Percent)," in *Annual Energy Outlook 2014 with Projections to 2040*, U.S. Energy Information Administration, April 2014, http://www.eia.gov/forecasts/aeo/ (accessed June 26, 2014)

TABLE 1.4

Energy price estimates, by type, 2012

[Dollars per million Btu]

Primary energy	
Coal	2.60
Natural gas[a]	5.76
Petroleum	
Distillate fuel oil	27.64
Jet fuel[b]	23.00
LPG[c]	17.65
Motor gasoline[d]	28.77
Residual fuel oil	17.31
Other[e]	22.94
Total	**26.35**
Nuclear fuel	0.70
Biomass: wood and waste[f]	3.58
Total[g, h, i]	**12.78**
Electric power sector	2.40
Retail electricity	28.97
Total energy[g, i]	**21.65**

Btu = British thermal units.
[a]Natural gas as it is consumed; includes supplemental gaseous fuels that are commingled with natural gas.
[b]Includes kerosene-type jet fuel only; naphtha-type jet fuel is included in "Other petroleum."
[c]Liquefied petroleum gases (LPG), includes ethane and olefins.
[d]Motor gasoline as it is consumed; includes fuel ethanol blended into motor gasoline.
[e]Includes asphalt and road oil, aviation gasoline, kerosene, lubricants, and other petroleum products.
[f]Wood, wood-derived fuels, and biomass waste.
[g]There are no direct fuel costs for hydroelectric, geothermal, wind, photovoltaic, or solar thermal energy.
[h]Electricity imports are included in these prices but not shown separately.
[i]The U.S. average includes coal coke net imports, which are not allocated to the states.

SOURCE: Adapted from "Table E1. Primary Energy, Electricity, and Total Energy Price Estimates, 2012 (Dollars per Million Btu)," in *State Energy Data System (SEDS): 1960–2012 (Complete)*, U.S. Energy Information Administration, June 27, 2014, http://www.eia.gov/state/seds/sep_sum/html/pdf/sum_pr_tot.pdf (accessed June 29, 2014)

ENERGY COSTS

Energy costs, like the costs for all commodities, depend on supply and demand factors. These factors are quite complex, and some of the major drivers are discussed in this chapter. In addition, source-specific supply and demand factors are discussed in detail in Chapter 2 for oil, in Chapter 3 for natural gas, in Chapter 4 for coal, in Chapter 5 for nuclear energy, in Chapter 6 for renewable energy, and in Chapter 8 for electricity.

Energy costs can be divided into two broad categories: market costs and external costs.

Market Costs

Market costs are the prices paid in the marketplace for energy products. The EIA tracks various kinds of market costs, including energy production costs, import and export energy costs, and consumer costs for energy. Source-specific costs are discussed in detail in the relevant chapters. Some general information about costing trends, however, is presented here.

In *Annual Energy Review 2011* (September 2012, http://www.eia.gov/totalenergy/data/annual/pdf/aer.pdf), the EIA notes that the nation's overall price tag for total energy purchased by consumers increased from less than $2 per million Btu in 1970 to more than $20 per million Btu in the early 21st century. It should be noted that these are nominal prices, meaning that they do not reflect the effects of inflation over time. As shown in Table 1.4, average U.S. energy prices in 2012 varied considerably from $28.97 per million Btu for retail electricity to $0.70 per million Btu for nuclear fuel. The overall average for all energy types was $21.65 per million Btu.

Overall, consumers spent nearly $1.4 trillion on energy in 2012. (See Table 1.5.) Petroleum had the highest expenditures, at $883.7 billion. Motor gasoline accounted for more than half of the petroleum total. In addition, consumers spent $360.9 billion on retail electricity.

External Costs

External costs are costs other than market costs. In economics, externalities are benefits (positive consequences) and harms (negative consequences) that are not included in marketplace prices. There are positive externalities that are associated with the energy industry. For example, the research and development of energy technologies has produced scientific knowledge that has benefited other industries, and hence the overall economy. However, energy externalities are most often discussed in terms of

TABLE 1.5

U.S. energy expenditure estimates, by type, 2012

[Expenditures in million dollars]

Primary energy	
Coal	
Coking coal	3,915
Steam coal	41,329
Total	**45,244**
Coal coke	
Exports	209
Imports	384
Natural gas[a]	133,115
Petroleum	
Distillate fuel oil	220,408
Jet fuel[b]	66,736
LPG[c]	51,313
Motor gasoline[d]	477,143
Residual fuel oil	14,635
Other[e]	53,451
Total	**883,685**
Nuclear fuel	5,679
Biomass: wood and waste[f]	6,863
Total[g, h]	**1,076,610**
Electric power sector[g, h]	−81,833
Retail electricity	360,900
Total energy[g]	**1,355,677**

[a]Natural gas as it is consumed; includes supplemental gaseous fuels that are commingled with natural gas.
[b]Includes kerosene-type jet fuel only; naphtha-type jet fuel is included in "Other petroleum."
[c]Liquefied petroleum gases (LPG), includes ethane and olefins.
[d]Includes fuel ethanol blended into motor gasoline.
[e]Includes asphalt and road oil, aviation gasoline, kerosene, lubricants, and other petroleum products.
[f]Wood, wood-derived fuels, and biomass waste.
[g]There are no direct fuel costs for hydroelectric, geothermal, wind, photovoltaic, or solar thermal energy.
[h]Electricity imports are included in total primary energy and electric power sector but are not shown separately.

SOURCE: Adapted from "Table ET1. Primary Energy, Electricity, and Total Energy Price and Expenditure Estimates, 1970–2012, United States," in *State Energy Data System (SEDS): 1960–2012 (Complete)*, U.S. Energy Information Administration, June 27, 2014, http://www.eia.gov/state/seds/data.cfm?incfile=/state/seds/sep_prices/total/pr_tot_US.html&sid=US (accessed June 29, 2014)

negative consequences, meaning the external costs that are associated with energy. Although these costs are believed to be substantial, they are difficult to quantify.

The most obvious external cost associated with energy is environmental degradation. Extracting, processing, and burning fossil fuels has environmental consequences, chiefly emissions of contaminants that degrade the air, water, and land and harm ecosystems and ultimately human health. Likewise, the production of nuclear energy and energy from renewable sources has negative environmental impacts to varying degrees.

The energy industry (like all industries) is bound by government regulations to limit its emissions and other environmental impacts through control measures. These measures are inherently imperfect, and the imposition of stricter controls is fraught with political controversy in the United States. Energy—especially domestically produced low-cost energy—is considered to be a vital

commodity for the nation's economic well-being and national security. As a result, the U.S. government supports the energy industry via many measures, which is explained in detail later in this chapter.

Critics complain that the external environmental costs of fossil fuel use have for decades been borne by society at large, rather than by the producers and consumers of the fuels. The criticism grew especially loud during the first decade of the 21st century as energy prices soared and oil and natural gas companies made record profits. At the same time, there was growing concern about global warming and resulting climate change. Scientists believe that large-scale burning of fossil fuels for more than a century has pumped enormous amounts of carbon into the atmosphere. The resulting atmospheric changes have been gradually warming the planet and changing historical climate patterns. These effects are expected to continue well into the future. Although there are other contributing factors to global warming, including deforestation, the combustion of coal, natural gas, and oil and its derivatives (such as gasoline) is believed to be the main culprit. Thus, the negative impacts of global warming, including melting ice caps, coastal flooding, and disruptive climate changes, are considered to be external costs of fossil fuel usage.

Some people believe the federal government should force external environmental costs into the market costs for fossil fuels, such as by taxing carbon emissions from fossil fuel combustion. Advocates of this approach argue that it would show consumers the "true" costs of fossil fuels. Of course, prices would be much higher for coal, natural gas, oil, gasoline, and electricity, which is largely fossil fuel based in the United States. Price shocks do lower demand for expensive commodities. Many consumers would likely switch to alternatives, in this case, to energy that is produced from renewable sources such as wind and solar power. A carbon tax or similar provision would certainly push the nation away from fossil fuels and toward renewables, which is a highly desirable outcome in some opinions. However, severe price shocks, especially for a widely used and vital commodity such as energy, would stress the nation's economy, perhaps on a large and calamitous scale. As a result, as of October 2014 the U.S. government had not implemented taxes that were specifically designed to capture the external environmental costs of fossil fuel use.

GOVERNMENT INTERVENTION

Government intervention has long been a factor in energy supply and demand in the United States. Over the decades presidents have set energy policies and proposed federal budgets that reflected their energy priorities. Congress has passed laws and spending bills that sometimes supported presidential priorities and sometimes reflected alternative priorities. Politics has always been a major consideration in the nation's energy decisions. At the heart of the debate is how large a role the government should play in a private market. In general, it is agreed that energy is so precious a commodity that the government should play some role, chiefly by promoting domestic production and conservation, which are both elements of the overall goal of energy self-sufficiency. This puts the government in the odd position of both encouraging domestic suppliers to bring more energy to market and at the same time encouraging buyers to use less energy. Also, because most U.S. energy is fossil fuel based, government support of domestic fossil fuel production engenders environmental problems, including global warming. These seemingly contradictory outcomes are just some of the difficulties involved in government manipulation of the energy market.

National Energy Policy

The energy policy of President Barack Obama (1961–) has been laid out in several key documents:

- *Blueprint for a Secure Energy Future* (March 30, 2011, http://www.whitehouse.gov/sites/default/files/blueprint _secure_energy_future.pdf)

- *The President's Climate Action Plan* (June 2013, http://www.whitehouse.gov/sites/default/files/image/ president27sclimateactionplan.pdf)

- *The All-of-the-Above Energy Strategy as a Path to Sustainable Economic Growth* (May 2014, http:// www.whitehouse.gov/sites/default/files/docs/aota _energy_strategy_as_a_path_to_sustainable_economic _growth.pdf)

In the latter document the president notes the unexpected energy boom that the United States began experiencing during the first decade of the 21st century. As is described in Chapters 2 and 3, domestic production of oil and natural gas has skyrocketed thanks to new technologies that allow extraction of previously unrealized sources of these fossil fuels. This ongoing development provides key economic benefits, including job creation, and empowers the United States to become more energy independent in the future; however, continued reliance on fossil fuels has environmental consequences. The Obama administration is particularly worried about carbon emissions from fossil fuel combustion. Subsequent chapters will summarize federal programs and regulations aimed at limiting the energy sector's carbon emissions. These efforts are politically controversial because they are seen in some circles as an unnecessary financial burden on energy companies and hence the nation's economy overall.

In *The All-of-the-Above Energy Strategy as a Path to Sustainable Economic Growth*, President Obama establishes an energy agenda that supports energy sources, such as wind, solar, and nuclear power, with low or zero carbon emissions; reduces energy demand by promoting energy efficiency; and endorses the use of carbon capture, utilization, and storage for coal and natural gas power plants and industrial facilities. A more detailed energy policy is expected to be revealed in early 2015 with publication of the nation's first-ever quadrennial energy review. (The term *quadrennial* means recurring every four years.) In January 2014 President Obama (http://www.whitehouse .gov/the-press-office/2014/01/09/presidential-memorandum-establishing-quadrennial-energy-review) created an interagency task force that is charged with gathering "ideas and advice" from government agencies, academia, businesses, consumers, and other stakeholders across the country for the quadrennial energy review.

Tax Provisions

The government collects taxes as a matter of course on economic activity. Energy products, like other commodities in commerce, are subject to these taxes. In addition, the government uses taxes in some areas of the energy industry to offset some of the external costs that are associated with energy development and consumption.

Taxes are sometimes imposed specifically to discourage certain activities, whereas tax breaks are granted to encourage other activities. For example, in *Fuel Economy Guide: Model Year 2014* (October 28, 2014, http:// www.fueleconomy.gov/feg/pdfs/guides/FEG2014.pdf), the DOE and the U.S. Environmental Protection Agency describe two tax provisions that were active in 2014. A "gas guzzler" tax was imposed on auto manufacturers that sold cars with "exceptionally low fuel economy." By contrast, a federal income tax credit was offered to consumers who bought certain electric or partially electric vehicles (cars using little to no gasoline). Both tax provisions directly support national goals for energy self-sufficiency.

TARGETED TAXES. Government entities at the federal, state, and local levels often use taxes that target particular energy sectors, such as coal mining. One purpose of these targeted taxes is to offset some of the external costs that are associated with energy production and consumption, such as health, social, and environmental consequences. The collected monies may be put into trust funds that are administered by government agencies. The trust funds provide monies to cover external costs that are ongoing or may occur in the future. One example is the Oil Spill Liability Trust Fund, which was created by Congress in 1986. Its purpose is to cover certain damages that are associated with oil spills.

Government entities also commonly impose excise taxes (taxes that target specific goods) on gasoline. These taxes are often used for building and maintaining transportation infrastructure, such as roads and bridges.

FIGURE 1.14

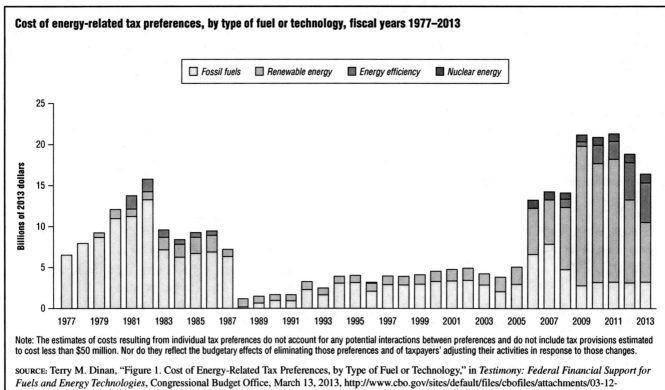

Cost of energy-related tax preferences, by type of fuel or technology, fiscal years 1977–2013

Note: The estimates of costs resulting from individual tax preferences do not account for any potential interactions between preferences and do not include tax provisions estimated to cost less than $50 million. Nor do they reflect the budgetary effects of eliminating those preferences and of taxpayers' adjusting their activities in response to those changes.

SOURCE: Terry M. Dinan, "Figure 1. Cost of Energy-Related Tax Preferences, by Type of Fuel or Technology," in *Testimony: Federal Financial Support for Fuels and Energy Technologies*, Congressional Budget Office, March 13, 2013, http://www.cbo.gov/sites/default/files/cbofiles/attachments/03-12-EnergyTechnologies.pdf (accessed June 29, 2014)

A severance tax (a tax that targets the removal of nonrenewable resources) is another type of tax. Many states levy severance taxes on companies that extract subsurface resources, such as oil, natural gas, and coal, within their boundaries. Cassarah Brown of the National Council of State Legislators provides in *State Revenues and the Natural Gas Boom: An Assessment of State Oil and Gas Production Taxes* (June 2013, http://www.ncsl.org/documents/energy/pdf_version_final.pdf) a table that details how states typically spend the severance taxes they collect from oil and gas extraction. Some states allocate the money to their general funds, whereas others earmark it for specific programs or funds.

Whatever their purpose, taxes on energy products elevate the prices that consumers ultimately pay for those products.

Federal Financial Support

The federal government's financial support to the energy industry amounts to billions of dollars annually. In *Federal Financial Support for the Development and Production of Fuels and Energy Technologies* (March 2012, http://www.cbo.gov/sites/default/files/cbofiles/attachments/03-06-FuelsandEnergy_Brief.pdf), Terry Dinan and Philip Webre of the Congressional Budget Office discuss historical energy tax preferences and financial incentives through 2012. In March 2013 Dinan testified before the U.S. House of Representatives' Committee on Science, Space, and Technology, Subcommittee on

Energy, and presented data that were updated through 2013. His testimony was published in *Testimony: Federal Financial Support for Fuels and Energy Technologies* (March 13, 2013, http://www.cbo.gov/sites/default/files/cbofiles/attachments/03-12-EnergyTechnologies.pdf). Dinan notes that the federal government financially supports the energy industry using two tools: tax preferences (special tax law provisions that reduce tax liabilities) and spending programs that are administered by the DOE.

FEDERAL TAX PREFERENCES. The United States has a long history of using tax preferences to encourage domestic energy development. Molly F. Sherlock of the Congressional Research Service notes in *Energy Tax Policy: Historical Perspectives on and Current Status of Energy Tax Expenditures* (May 2, 2011, http://www.leahy.senate.gov/imo/media/doc/R41227EnergyLegReport.pdf) that the first federal energy tax breaks were implemented in 1916. Sherlock indicates that from 1916 through 1970 tax policy "focused almost exclusively" on increasing domestic reserves and production of oil and natural gas. During the 1970s the United States suffered an energy crisis due to high reliance on foreign oil. At the same time, awareness was arising about the environmental consequences of fossil fuels.

The federal government's fiscal year (FY) begins in October and ends in September; thus, FY 2015 covers October 1, 2014, to September 30, 2015. Figure 1.14 shows the estimated costs for energy-related federal tax preferences between FYs 1977 and 2013. Preferences for the fossil fuel industry accounted for the majority of the yearly costs through 2007. Preferences for the renewable energy industry increased dramatically after that time.

It should be noted that government intervention does not always achieve the desired results. For example, tax preferences that were favorable to renewable energy sources had little effect during the late 1990s because oil prices were historically low. Consumers responded to the low oil prices by buying large sport-utility vehicles and other vehicles that had relatively poor fuel economy.

Energy economics changed as energy prices began rising. Congress responded with new laws, such as the Energy Policy Act of 2005. In *Energy Tax Policy: Issues in the 113th Congress* (December 19, 2013, http://fas.org/ sgp/crs/misc/R43206.pdf), Sherlock notes the law "included an estimated $9 billion, over five years, in tax incentives distributed among renewable energy, conservation, and traditional energy sources." The United States suffered from a severe economic downturn dubbed the Great Recession from late 2007 to mid-2009. In 2008 Congress passed the Emergency Economic Stabilization Act, which extended many previous energy tax breaks, mostly to the renewable energy industries. It also raised taxes on the oil and natural gas industries to help offset the lost revenues to the government from the tax breaks that were extended to the renewable energy industries. Provisions in the American Recovery and Reinvestment Act of 2009 (ARRA) also greatly affected the energy industry. Sherlock states, "Collectively, ARRA's energy tax provisions lowered the cost of selected renewable energy [sources] relative to energy from other sources, such as oil and gas."

During the early years of the 21st century several bills were passed that expanded and extended energy tax breaks devoted to renewable energy sources, energy efficiency, and alternative fuel vehicles. Some of the measures expired at year-end 2013. As of October 2014, Congress was still debating whether to reinstate the measures.

Table 1.6 provides a breakdown of the $16.4 billion in total energy-related tax preferences for FY 2013. As shown in Figure 1.15, renewable energy had the largest share (45%), followed by energy efficiency (29%), fossil fuels (20%), and nuclear energy (7%). Nonetheless, in *Testimony: Federal Financial Support for Fuels and Energy Technologies*, Dinan notes that most of the provisions for energy efficiency and renewable energy are temporary, whereas those for fossil fuels and nuclear energy are mostly permanent. This difference is emblematic of a long political struggle over what types of energy sources the government should and should not promote.

President Obama has repeatedly asked Congress to end many of the financial incentives that are given to the fossil fuel industry. In *Budget of the U.S. Government, Fiscal Year 2015* (February 2014, http://www.white house.gov/sites/default/files/omb/budget/fy2015/assets/ budget.pdf), the president proposes that Congress eliminate $4 billion in annual subsidies provided to the fossil fuel industry. The Environmental and Energy Study Institute notes in "Issue Brief: Obama FY2015 Budget Proposal: Sustainable Energy, Buildings, Transportation and Climate" (March 6, 2014, http://www.eesi.org/papers/ view/obama-fy-2015-budget-proposal-sustainable-energy- buildings-transportation-a) that President Obama proposes making permanent some temporary tax credits for renewable energy production. As of October 2014, the FY 2015 budget had not been finalized by Congress.

DOE SPENDING PROGRAMS. Although federal tax laws are written and passed by Congress, the administrative branch (the president and the offices under his control) directly impacts the energy industry through spending programs administered by the DOE. According to Dinan, in *Testimony: Federal Financial Support for Fuels and Energy Technologies*, the DOE's support for energy technologies and energy efficiency takes two forms: direct investments (primarily for research and development purposes) and loans or loan guarantees. Figure 1.16 shows the total amounts of financial support by the DOE between FYs 1980 and 2013. Table 1.7 provides a breakdown of the $3.4 billion that was spent in FY 2013. Dinan notes that $42 million was devoted to credit programs (loans and loan guarantees) in FY 2013. This area of support has proven to be especially controversial.

In "The DOE Loan Guarantee Program: A Primer" (September 1, 2010, https://financere.nrel.gov/finance/ content/doe-loan-guarantee-program-primer), the DOE indicates that its loan guarantee program was created by the Energy Policy Act of 2005 and modified by the ARRA. The program supports "innovative energy efficiency, renewable energy, and advanced transmission and distribution projects." The government does not provide the loans; they are obtained from private lenders, such as banks. Neverthless, the government guarantees the lenders that the loans will be repaid. The DOE states, "For each loan guarantee award, the federal government sets aside a sum (the credit subsidy) in the project's name, which acts as insurance in the case of project failure."

According to the DOE, the first loan guarantee was made in 2009 to Solyndra, Inc., for the manufacture of cylindrical solar photovoltaic panels. The loan amount was $535 million. Solyndra, however, declared bankruptcy in 2011 and defaulted on (failed to pay) the loan. This raised a firestorm of criticism about the loan program; nevertheless, it has continued to operate. As of October 2014, the DOE (http://energy.gov/lpo/projects) had provided $32.4 billion in loan guarantees to private companies in the energy sector.

TABLE 1.6

Cost of energy-related tax preferences, by type of fuel or technology, fiscal year 2013

Primary target of support	Tax preference	Total cost in 2013 [Billions of dollars]	Expiration date
		Energy-related tax preferences affecting income taxes	
Energy efficiency	Credit for energy-efficiency improvements to existing homes	3.0	12/31/2013
	Residential efficiency property credit	0.9	12/31/2016
	Credit for plug-in electric vehicles	0.4	Expires for each manufacturer when the number of vehicles it sells reaches the limit set by the government
	Credit for the production of energy-efficient appliances	0.2	12/31/2013
	Deduction for expenditures on energy-efficient commercial building property	0.2	12/31/2013
	Ten-year depreciation for smart meters or other devices for monitoring and managing electrical distribution	0.1	None
Renewable energy	Credits for the production of electricity from renewable resources[a]	1.7	12/31/2013
	Credit for investment in advanced-energy property, including property used in producing energy from wind, the sun, or geothermal sources	0.3	Fixed dollar amount of credits; available until used
	Credit for investments in solar and geothermal equipment, fuel cells, and microturbines	0.5	12/31/2016
	Five-year depreciation for certain renewable energy equipment	0.3	None
Fossil fuels	Option to expense depletion costs on the basis of gross income rather than actual costs	1.1	None
	Expensing of exploration and development costs for oil and natural gas	0.9	None
	Amortization of air pollution control facilities	0.4	None
	Option to expense 50 percent of qualified property used to refine liquid fuels	0.4	12/31/2013
	Credit for investment in clean-coal facilities	0.2	Fixed dollar amount of credits; available until used
	Fifteen-year depreciation for natural gas pipelines	0.1	12/31/2010[b]
	Amortization of certain expenditures associated with oil and gas exploration	0.1	None
Nuclear energy	Special tax rate for nuclear decommissioning reserve funds	1.1	None
	Subtotal, tax preferences affecting income taxes	11.9	n.a.
		Energy-related tax preferences affecting excise taxes[c]	
Renewable energy	Excise tax credit for biodiesel	1.9	12/31/2013
		Grants in lieu of tax credits[d]	
Renewable energy	Section 1603 grants	2.6[e]	12/31/2011
		All energy-related tax preferences	
Total		**16.4**	**n.a.**

n.a. = not applicable.

[a]The production tax credit is generally available for 10 years beginning on the date that a facility is put in service. The American Taxpayer Relief Act of 2012 defined eligible facilities as those whose construction began before January 1, 2014.

[b]Effects of depreciation extend beyond the expiration date.

[c]The Joint Committee on Taxation and the Administration generally do not estimate tax expenditures in the excise tax system. They do, however, provide information on revenue reductions from excise tax credits for alcohol and biodiesel.

[d]Companies that began constructing a facility and applied for the grant before December 31, 2011, are eligible; because grants are paid when facilities are placed in service, they are still being disbursed.

[e]The Office of Management and Budget has determined that the Section 1603 grants are subject to sequestration. CBO applied the sequestration percentages published by OMB for nondefense mandatory programs (5.1 percent) to the estimated 2013 spending on those grants.

OMB = The Office of Management and Budget.

CBO = Congressional Budget Office.

Notes: The estimates of costs resulting from individual tax preferences do not account for any potential interactions between preferences and do not include tax provisions estimated to cost less than $50 million. Nor do they reflect the budgetary effects of eliminating those preferences and of taxpayers' adjusting their activities in response to those changes.

SOURCE: Terry M. Dinan, "Table 1. Energy-Related Tax Preferences in Fiscal Year 2013," in *Testimony: Federal Financial Support for Fuels and Energy Technologies*, Congressional Budget Office, March 13, 2013, http://www.cbo.gov/sites/default/files/cbofiles/attachments/03-12-EnergyTechnologies.pdf (accessed June 29, 2014)

Resource Leases

Another way in which the government influences energy markets is through resource leases. U.S. law provides that underground resources, such as minerals or natural gas, belong to the property owner. Thus, individuals and companies that own land can sell their underground resources to others. The federal and state governments own huge swaths of land across the United States, both onshore and offshore (i.e., off the coastlines beneath ocean waters). Government entities can sell the resources beneath the land within their jurisdictions so long as those sales do not violate existing law. As is explained in later chapters, some

FIGURE 1.15

Breakdown of the cost of energy-related tax preferences, by type of fuel or technology, fiscal year 2013

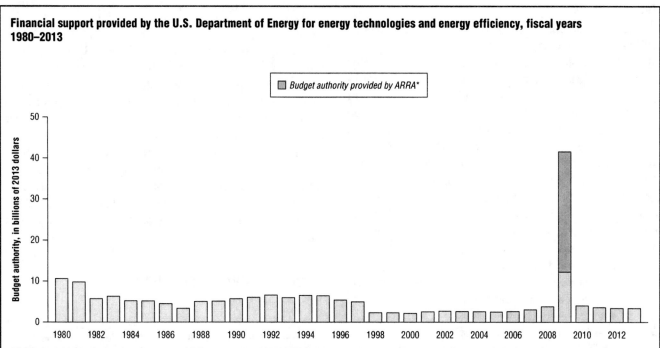

Nuclear energy 7%

Fossil fuels 20%

Renewable energy 45%

Energy efficiency 29%

SOURCE: Terry M. Dinan, "Figure 2. Allocation of Energy-Related Tax Preferences in Fiscal Year 2013, by Type of Fuel or Technology," in *Testimony: Federal Financial Support for Fuels and Energy Technologies*, Congressional Budget Office, March 13, 2013, http://www.cbo.gov/sites/default/files/cbofiles/attachments/03-12-Energy Technologies.pdf (accessed June 29, 2014)

government lands have been deemed off limits for resource exploration and extraction.

Resource sales by the government are carried out through legal contracts called leases. Leases cover particular tracts of land and are typically sold through auctions to the highest bidder. In addition, the leases require developers to pay the government royalties (a specific percentage of the value of any resources that are extracted). The government's control of resource leases on public lands is fraught with controversy. Policy makers, the energy industry, environmentalists, and other parties can have strong disagreements about where the leases should be offered and how much they should cost.

The Office of Natural Resources Revenue (ONRR) within the U.S. Department of the Interior manages the revenues that are raised through the private use of public natural resources (e.g., fossil fuels, minerals, and other commodities) on the outer continental shelf and onshore federal and Native American lands. According to the ONRR (2014, http://statistics.onrr.gov/ReportTool.aspx), it collected nearly $14.4 billion during FY 2013 from royalties, rents, and other revenues. More than half ($7.6 billion) of the total was from oil royalties alone.

FIGURE 1.16

Financial support provided by the U.S. Department of Energy for energy technologies and energy efficiency, fiscal years 1980–2013

☐ Budget authority provided by ARRA*

*Funding provided by the American Recovery and Reinvestment Act of 2009 (ARRA) reflects transfers and rescissions of budget authority for Section 1705 loan guarantees made after ARRA was enacted.

Notes: As of the date of this testimony (March 13, 2013), no full-year regular appropriation bills have been enacted for fiscal year 2013. Instead, all agencies are operating under a continuing resolution that expires on March 27, 2013. The estimate of budget authority reflects the assumption that accounts are funded at the annualized level provided by the continuing resolution, as reduced by the across-the-board cuts mandated by the Budget Control Act of 2011.

SOURCE: Terry M. Dinan, "Figure 3. DOE's Financial Support for Energy Technologies and Energy Efficiency," in *Testimony: Federal Financial Support for Fuels and Energy Technologies*, Congressional Budget Office, March 13, 2013, http://www.cbo.gov/sites/default/files/cbofiles/attachments/03-12-EnergyTechnologies.pdf (accessed June 29, 2014)

TABLE 1.7

Financial support provided by the U.S. Department of Energy for energy technologies and energy efficiency, fiscal year 2013

	Budget authority (billions of dollars)
Direct investments	
Energy efficiency and renewable energy	1.7
Nuclear energy	0.7
Fossil-energy research and development	0.5
Advanced research projects agency—energy	0.3
Electricity delivery and energy reliability	0.1
Ultra-deepwater and unconventional natural gas and other petroleum research fund	*
Subtotal	**3.4**
Credit programs	
Advanced technology vehicles manufacturing loan program account	*
Title 17 innovative technology loan guarantee program	*
Total	**3.4**

DOE = Department of Energy; * = between zero and $50 million.
Notes: As of the date of this testimony (March 13, 2013), no full-year regular appropriation bills have been enacted for fiscal year 2013. Instead, all agencies are operating under a continuing resolution that expires on March 27, 2013. The estimates of budget authority reflect the assumption that accounts are funded at the annualized level provided by the continuing resolution, as reduced by the across-the-board cuts mandated by the Budget Control Act of 2011.

SOURCE: Terry M. Dinan, "Table 2. DOE's Financial Support for Energy Technologies and Energy Efficiency in Fiscal Year 2013," in *Testimony: Federal Financial Support for Fuels and Energy Technologies*, Congressional Budget Office, March 13, 2013, http://www.cbo.gov/sites/default/files/cbofiles/attachments/03-12-EnergyTechnologies.pdf (accessed June 29, 2014)

Liability Limits

U.S. law includes provisions that limit the financial liability of certain energy sectors in the event of disasters within the industry. Energy accidents, such as oil spills and radiation leaks, can have enormous costs. The liability limits were set to grant the industries a level of financial protection in their exploration and production endeavors. Most of the limits were originally set decades ago. For example, the Atomic Energy Act of 1954 established liability limits on accidents that were associated with the U.S. nuclear power industry. Lawmakers feared that without the limits, the fledgling industry would not grow because companies would not be able to afford the premiums for insurance policies protecting them against damages. In addition, the limits have served to keep energy prices lower because they represent a cost savings to energy producers. In the 21st century, however, the limits have become quite controversial because they are seen as relatively low in comparison to the massive costs that can arise from an energy-related disaster. Liability limits specific to various energy sectors are described in subsequent chapters.

Regulations and Mandates

The government uses regulations and mandates to exert control over energy production and consumption factors. For example, the energy industry is subject to extensive environmental regulations that limit the types and amounts of emissions that energy producers can release to the air, land, and water. These regulations are designed to minimize the external costs that are associated with energy production, but their imposition does increase the market costs of energy sources.

Mandates are usually directed at supporting a particular type of energy source. Chapter 6 describes federal and state government mandates for use of specified levels of biomass and other renewable energy sources.

THE DOMESTIC OUTLOOK

In *Annual Energy Outlook 2014 with Projections to 2040*, the EIA forecasts energy supply, demand, and prices through 2040 for various scenarios based on expected supply and demand factors. Table 1.8 summarizes key information known for 2011 and 2012 and projected for 2020 through 2040 for a reference case that assumes future energy markets and policies will be similar to those currently in place.

As shown in Table 1.8, total domestic energy production is projected to increase from 79.2 quadrillion Btu in 2012 to 102.1 quadrillion Btu in 2040, or 0.9% annually. Total energy imports are forecast to decrease 0.4% annually, whereas energy exports are forecast to increase 2% annually. Overall, domestic consumption is expected to increase from 95 quadrillion Btu in 2012 to 106.3 quadrillion Btu in 2040, or 0.4% annually.

Energy prices are shown in Table 1.8 for two price types: nominal and real. Nominal prices are not adjusted for inflation; they represent the actual dollar amounts that consumers pay at specific times. Real prices are adjusted for inflation—that is, they assume the dollar has the same value over time, in this case the value it had in 2012. Comparison of real prices between 2012 and 2040 shows effects due solely to market factors. Real prices for all energy commodities are expected to rise by 2040. Natural gas shows the largest annual price increase (3.7%), whereas electricity shows the lowest increase (0.4%).

WORLD ENERGY PRODUCTION AND CONSUMPTION

Table 1.9 shows world energy production for 2011 for the world, by region, and for the top-20 producers. Total world production in 2011 was 518.3 quadrillion Btu. The two largest producing regions were Asia and Oceania (154.2 quadrillion Btu) and North America (105.7 quadrillion Btu). Top producers in 2011 were China, the United States, Russia, Saudi Arabia, and Canada. The U.S. production of 78 quadrillion Btu in 2011 accounted for 15% of the total world production.

TABLE 1.8

Total energy supply, disposition, and price summary, 2011–12 and forecast selected years 2020–40

[Quadrillion Btu per year, unless otherwise noted]

Supply, disposition, and prices	Reference case							Annual growth 2012–2040 (percent)
	2011	2012	2020	2025	2030	2035	2040	
Production								
Crude oil and lease condensate	12.20	13.87	20.36	19.19	17.71	16.81	16.00	0.5%
Natural gas plant liquids	3.11	3.21	3.54	3.84	3.98	4.08	3.99	0.8%
Dry natural gas	23.04	24.59	29.73	32.57	35.19	36.89	38.37	1.6%
Coal[a]	22.22	20.60	21.70	22.36	22.61	22.68	22.61	0.3%
Nuclear/uranium[b]	8.26	8.05	8.15	8.15	8.18	8.23	8.49	0.2%
Hydropower	3.11	2.67	2.81	2.84	2.87	2.89	2.90	0.3%
Biomass[c]	3.90	3.78	4.66	5.08	5.29	5.44	5.61	1.4%
Other renewable energy[d]	1.70	1.97	3.01	3.09	3.23	3.44	3.89	2.5%
Other[e]	0.80	0.41	0.24	0.24	0.24	0.24	0.24	−2.0%
Total	**78.35**	**79.15**	**94.19**	**97.36**	**99.30**	**100.70**	**102.09**	**0.9%**
Imports								
Crude oil	19.52	18.57	13.15	13.70	15.00	16.12	17.43	−0.2%
Petroleum and other liquids[f]	5.21	4.26	4.21	4.20	4.08	4.00	3.93	−0.3%
Natural gas[g]	3.56	3.21	2.39	2.04	2.01	2.06	2.28	−1.2%
Other imports[h]	0.43	0.36	0.17	0.15	0.12	0.11	0.10	−4.5%
Total	**28.71**	**26.40**	**19.92**	**20.09**	**21.22**	**22.29**	**23.73**	**−0.4%**
Exports								
Petroleum and other liquids[i]	5.95	6.29	6.30	6.48	6.91	7.40	7.70	0.7%
Natural gas[j]	1.52	1.63	4.30	5.45	6.96	7.60	8.09	5.9%
Coal	2.75	3.22	3.13	3.31	3.55	3.81	3.79	0.6%
Total	**10.22**	**11.14**	**13.73**	**15.24**	**17.42**	**18.81**	**19.58**	**2.0%**
Discrepancy[k]	**−0.27**	**−0.61**	**−0.35**	**−0.24**	**−0.17**	**−0.11**	**−0.07**	**—**
Consumption								
Petroleum and other liquids[l]	36.56	35.87	36.86	36.28	35.65	35.37	35.35	−0.1%
Natural gas	24.91	26.20	27.65	28.97	30.03	31.10	32.32	0.8%
Coal[m]	19.62	17.34	18.56	19.03	19.01	18.82	18.75	0.3%
Nuclear/uranium[b]	8.26	8.05	8.15	8.15	8.18	8.23	8.49	0.2%
Hydropower	3.11	2.67	2.81	2.84	2.87	2.89	2.90	0.3%
Biomass[n]	2.60	2.53	3.35	3.74	3.95	4.10	4.26	1.9%
Other renewable energy[d]	1.70	1.97	3.01	3.09	3.23	3.44	3.89	2.5%
Other[o]	0.35	0.39	0.34	0.35	0.35	0.33	0.35	−0.4%
Total	**97.11**	**95.02**	**100.73**	**102.45**	**103.27**	**104.28**	**106.31**	**0.4%**
Prices (2012 dollars per unit)								
Crude oil spot prices (dollars per barrel)								
Brent	113.24	111.65	96.57	108.99	118.99	129.77	141.46	0.8%
West Texas Intermediate	96.55	94.12	94.57	106.99	116.99	127.77	139.46	1.4%
Natural gas at Henry Hub (dollars per million Btu)	4.07	2.75	4.38	5.23	6.03	6.92	7.65	3.7%
Coal (dollars per ton) at the minemouth[p]	41.74	39.94	46.52	49.67	53.15	56.37	59.16	1.4%
Coal (dollars per million Btu) at the minemouth[p]	2.07	1.98	2.33	2.49	2.67	2.82	2.96	1.4%
Average end-use[q]	2.61	2.60	2.85	3.02	3.17	3.29	3.43	1.0%
Average electricity (cents per kilowatthour)	10.1	9.8	10.1	10.1	10.4	10.7	11.1	0.4%
Prices (nominal dollars per unit)								
Crude oil spot prices (dollars per barrel)								
Brent	111.26	111.65	109.37	134.25	160.19	193.27	234.53	2.7%
West Texas Intermediate	94.86	94.12	107.11	131.78	157.49	190.30	231.22	3.3%
Natural gas at Henry Hub (dollars per million Btu)	4.00	2.75	4.96	6.45	8.12	10.31	12.69	5.6%
Coal (dollars per ton) at the minemouth[p]	41.01	39.94	52.69	61.18	71.55	83.96	98.08	3.3%
Coal (dollars per million Btu) at the minemouth[p]	2.04	1.98	2.63	3.07	3.59	4.21	4.91	3.3%
Average end-use[q]	2.56	2.60	3.23	3.72	4.27	4.90	5.68	2.8%
Average electricity (cents per kilowatthour)	9.9	9.8	11.5	12.5	14.0	16.0	18.5	2.3%

The total world energy consumption in 2011 was 519.2 quadrillion Btu. (See Table 1.10.) Asia and Oceania (199.8 quadrillion Btu) and North America (118.5 quadrillion Btu) were the leading regions in terms of consumption. On a national basis China, the United States, Russia, India, and Japan were the top-five consumers. The U.S. consumption of 97.5 quadrillion Btu in 2011 accounted for 19% of the total world consumption.

Analysts believe that energy consumption will grow as more people gain access to electricity. The World Bank is an international financial institution affiliated with the United Nations (UN) that specializes in giving financial advice and loans to developing nations. In "Energy Overview" (http://www.worldbank.org/en/topic/energy/overview), the World Bank estimates that as of September 2014 approximately 1.2 billion people around the world

aIncludes waste coal.
bThese values represent the energy obtained from uranium when it is used in light water reactors. The total energy content of uranium is much larger, but alternative processes are required to take advantage of it.
cIncludes grid-connected electricity from wood and wood waste; biomass, such as corn, used for liquid fuels production; and non-electric energy demand from wood.
dIncludes grid-connected electricity from landfill gas; biogenic municipal waste; wind; photovoltaic and solar thermal sources; and non-electric energy from renewable sources, such as active and passive solar systems. Excludes electricity imports using renewable sources and nonmarketed renewable energy.
eIncludes non-biogenic municipal waste, liquid hydrogen, methanol, and some domestic inputs to refineries.
fIncludes imports of finished petroleum products, unfinished oils, alcohols, ethers, blending components, and renewable fuels such as ethanol.
gIncludes imports of liquefied natural gas that are later re-exported.
hIncludes coal, coal coke (net), and electricity (net). Excludes imports of fuel used in nuclear power plants.
iIncludes crude oil, petroleum products, ethanol, and biodiesel.
jIncludes re-exported liquefied natural gas.
kBalancing item. Includes unaccounted for supply, losses, gains, and net storage withdrawals.
lEstimated consumption. Includes petroleum-derived fuels and non-petroleum derived fuels, such as ethanol and biodiesel, and coal-based synthetic liquids. Petroleum coke, which is a solid, is included. Also included are natural gas plant liquids and crude oil consumed as a fuel.
mExcludes coal converted to coal-based synthetic liquids and natural gas.
nIncludes grid-connected electricity from wood and wood waste, non-electric energy from wood, and biofuels heat and coproducts used in the production of liquid fuels, but excludes the energy content of the liquid fuels.
oIncludes non-biogenic municipal waste, liquid hydrogen, and net electricity imports.
pIncludes reported prices for both open market and captive mines. Prices weighted by production, which differs from average minemouth prices published in EIA data reports where it is weighted by reported sales.
qPrices weighted by consumption; weighted average excludes export free-alongside-ship (f.a.s.) prices.
Btu = British thermal units
— = Not applicable.
EIA = Energy Information Administration.
Note: Totals may not equal sum of components due to independent rounding. Data for 2011 and 2012 are model results and may differ from official EIA data reports.

SOURCE: "Table A1. Total Energy Supply, Disposition, and Price Summary," in *Annual Energy Outlook 2014 with Projections to 2040*, U.S. Energy Information Administration, April 2014, http://www.eia.gov/forecasts/aeo/ (accessed June 26, 2014)

lacked access to electricity. At that time the Census Bureau (http://www.census.gov/popclock) estimated the world population at 7.2 billion. Thus, around 17% of the global population lacked access to electricity. The World Bank estimates that approximately 2.8 million people around the world are forced to cook their meals using solid fuels, such as wood, which has devastating consequences on the air quality in and around their homes. The organization's Sustainable Energy for All initiative seeks to achieve "universal access to electricity and clean cooking fuels" by 2030. Two related goals are to double the amount of the world's energy supplied by renewable sources and to double the improvement rate in energy efficiency.

THE WORLD OUTLOOK

Two international organizations—the World Energy Council (WEC) and the International Energy Agency (IEA)—provide projections of future world energy production and consumption. The WEC (2014, http://www.worldenergy.org/about-wec) is a UN-affiliated organization that calls itself a "global energy body." As of 2014, it had more than 3,000 member organizations. The IEA (2014, http://www.iea.org/aboutus) is an independent member organization devoted to energy issues. As of 2014, it had 29 member countries, including the United States and other developed nations.

International organizations often use the unit tonne of oil equivalent (toe) when discussing large energy amounts. One toe is the amount of energy released when 1 tonne (1.1 ton) of oil is burned. Different kinds of oil have varying heat contents, so the exact conversion factors used can vary by organization.

The WEC notes in *World Energy Resources 2013 Survey* (October 2013, http://www.worldenergy.org/wp-content/uploads/2013/09/Complete_WER_2013_Survey.pdf) that it and the IEA equate 1 toe to 41.9 gigajoules. This is equivalent to 39.7 million Btu. The WEC estimates world demand for energy in 2020 will be 17,208 million toe (Mtoe), up from 14,092 Mtoe in 2011. The council projects that fossil fuels will provide around 76% of the world's energy in 2020, down from 82% in 2011. The share of energy provided by renewable sources (excluding large hydroelectric projects) is expected to increase from 11% in 2011 to 16% in 2020. The WEC predicts that the proportion of the world's energy provided by nuclear energy will increase from 5% to 6% over the same period, while hydroelectric power's share will remain flat at 2%.

The IEA provides its own forecast in *World Energy Investment Outlook: Special Report* (May 2014, http://www.iea.org/publications/freepublications/publication/WEIO2014.pdf). The agency predicts worldwide energy demand will rise 1.2% annually between 2012 and 2035, reaching 17,376 Mtoe in 2035. Most of the demand will come from developing nations as they expand and industrialize their economies. The IAE projects that 76% of the worldwide energy demand in 2035 will be met by fossil fuels.

TABLE 1.9

World primary energy production, by region and selected country, 2011

[Quadrillion Btu]

	2011
World	518.3
Regions	
Asia & Oceania	154.2
North America	105.7
Middle East	76.4
Eurasia	72.7
Europe	43.6
Africa	33.9
Central & South America	31.7
Countries	
China	90.6
United States	78.0
Russia	54.6
Saudi Arabia	26.4
Canada	18.8
India	15.9
Iran	14.9
Indonesia	14.4
Australia	12.4
Brazil	9.9
Qatar	9.5
Norway	9.0
Mexico	8.9
United Arab Emirates	8.3
Venezuela	7.2
Algeria	7.0
Nigeria	6.7
Kuwait	6.2
South Africa	6.2
Kazakhstan	6.1

Note: Btu = British thermal units.

SOURCE: Adapted from "Table. Total Primary Energy Production (Quadrillion Btu)," in *International Energy Statistics*, U.S. Energy Information Administration, 2014, http://www.eia.gov/cfapps/ipdbproject/iedindex3.cfm?tid=44&pid=44&aid=1&cid=regions&syid=2011&eyid=2011&unit=QBTU (accessed June 29, 2014)

TABLE 1.10

World primary energy consumption, by region and selected country, 2011

[Quadrillion Btu]

	2011
World	519.2
Regions	
Asia & Oceania	199.8
North America	118.5
Europe	82.1
Eurasia	44.1
Middle East	30.4
Central & South America	27.6
Africa	16.6
Countries	
China	104.3
United States	97.5
Russia	29.8
India	23.6
Japan	21.0
Germany	13.5
Canada	13.3
Brazil	11.6
Korea, South	11.3
France	10.8
Iran	9.4
Saudi Arabia	8.5
United Kingdom	8.4
Mexico	7.7
Italy	7.5
Indonesia	6.3
Australia	6.3
Spain	6.1
South Africa	5.6
Ukraine	5.4

Note: Btu = British thermal units.

SOURCE: Adapted from "Table. Total Primary Energy Consumption (Quadrillion Btu)," in *International Energy Statistics*, U.S. Energy Information Administration, 2014, http://www.eia.gov/cfapps/ipdbproject/iedindex3.cfm?tid=44&pid=44&aid=2&cid=regions&syid=2011&eyid=2011&unit=QBTU (accessed June 29, 2014)

CHAPTER 2
OIL

On August 27, 1859, Edwin Drake (1819–1880) struck oil 69 feet (21 m) below the surface of the earth near Titusville, Pennsylvania. This was the first successful modern oil well and ushered in a new wave of modernization. Not only did oil help meet the growing demand for new and better fuels for heating and lighting but also it proved to be an excellent source of gasoline for the internal combustion engine, which was developed during the late 1800s. Oil has become one of the most valuable commodities on the earth. Its supply is finite, and the United States consumes more oil every year than any other country, primarily because of Americans' love of the automobile. This addiction has its price; the United States has been forced for decades to import oil from countries that are sometimes less than friendly, sometimes downright hostile. Thus, oil self-sufficiency is a major goal for the United States.

UNDERSTANDING OIL

Oil is a generic term for liquid fossil fuels. As explained in Chapter 1, fossil fuels are the below-ground remains of prehistoric organisms that became energy enriched after millions of years of exposure to high temperatures and pressures. Oil and natural gas are often found together because they both originate from microscopic plants and animals that died in ancient water bodies (mostly swamps) and were gradually buried under many layers of sediment. Over several millennia the layers were compressed and baked into rock beds. The original microorganisms were chemically transformed into hydrocarbon chemicals, specifically oil and natural gas.

Oil and natural gas are less dense than their source rock, so once formed, they begin moving through the pores and fractures of surrounding rock formations. They migrate upward toward areas of lower pressure until a completely solid rock layer stops them or they seep from the ground into the open air. Underground oil and natural gas accumulations are called reservoirs, fields, or pools. They are typically found in sandstone or limestone formations that are overlaid with a shield layer of impermeable rock or shale. The oil and natural gas are trapped beneath the shield within the numerous pores and fractures of the reservoir rock. Because gas is lighter than liquid, the natural gas accumulates at the top of the traps above the oil pools. Anticlines (archlike folds in a bed of rock), faults, and salt domes are common trapping formations. (See Figure 2.1.) Oil fields can be found at varying depths below the ground surface.

Oil Properties

Some key properties of oil include density, viscosity (thickness, or resistance to flow), heat content, and the amounts of water, minerals, combustible gases, and sulfur (which is considered an impurity). Oil's viscosity can vary considerably. Oil that flows easily (like water) is said to be "light," while thick dense oil is said to be "heavy." In addition, oil is called "sweet" if it contains only a small amount of sulfur and "sour" if it contains a lot of sulfur. Lighter oils are the easiest to extract from the ground because they flow readily into wells. Refiners prefer sweet light oil because it is easy to pump and does not require extensive treatment for sulfur removal.

Conventional and Unconventional Oils

Raw (unprocessed) oil is known as crude oil and can be sourced from hydrocarbons in liquid, semisolid, and solid forms. Liquid crude oil is called a conventional oil because historically it has been the preferred type due to its ease of extraction. Evolving technologies, however, have allowed the collection of unconventional oils that are much more difficult to extract from the ground.

Unconventional oils can be derived from oily solids or semisolids, such as kerogen and bitumen. Kerogen is a

FIGURE 2.1

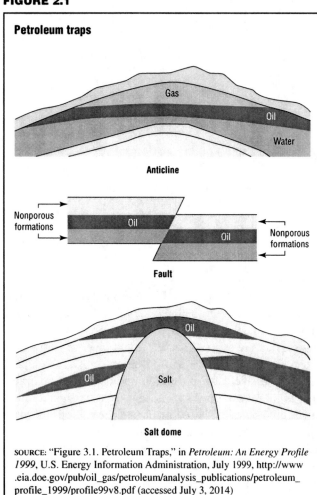

Petroleum traps

Anticline

Nonporous formations

Fault

Salt dome

SOURCE: "Figure 3.1. Petroleum Traps," in *Petroleum: An Energy Profile 1999*, U.S. Energy Information Administration, July 1999, http://www.eia.doe.gov/pub/oil_gas/petroleum/analysis_publications/petroleum_profile_1999/profile99v8.pdf (accessed July 3, 2014)

waxy material found in formations of sedimentary rock known as oil shale. The U.S. Department of the Interior's Bureau of Land Management notes in "Frequently Asked Questions" (2014, http://ostseis.anl.gov/faq/index.cfm) that petroleum-like liquids are released when the rock is heated. Bitumen is a black tarry substance found in underground formations called tar sands, oil sands, or tight sands. It can be diluted with liquid chemicals to flow through pipelines.

Unconventional oils also include liquid deposits that are trapped in very dense rocks, such as shale, sandstone, or carbonate. These formations have very low permeability, meaning that liquids (and gases) do not move easily through them. In the United States the term *tight oil* is used to refer to the oil extracted from such formations. Tight oil obtained from shale formations is known as "shale oil." In the rest of the world the terms *tight oil* and *shale oil* are often used interchangeably.

As will be explained later, the extraction of unconventional oils is far more difficult than that of crude oil. However, technological advances and rising oil prices have made it more economically worthwhile to extract

unconventional oils. They can then be processed and refined along with conventional crude oil.

Petroleum

The generic term *petroleum* is often used as a synonym for oil. The word *petroleum* is derived from the Latin words *petra* (meaning rock) and *oleum* (meaning oil). In *Monthly Energy Review: June 2014* (June 2014, http://www.eia.gov/totalenergy/data/monthly/archive/00351406.pdf), the U.S. Energy Information Administration (EIA) notes that petroleum is "a broadly defined class of liquid hydrocarbon mixtures" that includes crude oil and its derivatives and other liquids, particularly liquids associated with natural gas extraction. The latter include lease condensate and natural gas plant liquids (NGPL). Lease condensate is a liquid recovered from natural gas at the well (the extraction point). It consists primarily of chemical compounds called pentanes and heavier hydrocarbons and is generally blended with crude oil for refining. NGPL, such as butane and propane, are recovered during the refinement of natural gas in processing plants. The EIA also includes in its definition of petroleum the refined products that are obtained from the processing of raw oils.

Oil Deposit Locations

The locations of oil deposits around the world are driven solely by geology. Regions and countries that are known to have large oil fields include the Middle East, Russia, China, northern South America, Mexico, Canada, and the United States.

Many of the earth's oil fields are offshore (i.e., they lie beneath the oceans). The EIA explains in "What Is Offshore?" (August 8, 2013, http://www.eia.gov/energyexplained/index.cfm?page=oil_offshore) that the United States lays claim to an Exclusive Economic Zone (EEZ) that extends outward 200 miles (322 km) from its coastline. This applies to the U.S. mainland, Alaska, Hawaii, and all U.S. territories. (See Figure 2.2.) Figure 2.3 shows the extent of the EEZ and a conceptual side view of a continental shelf. The latter is the "shelf" of underwater land that extends outward from the coastline of each continent. The outward extent of the North American continental shelf ranges from around 12 miles (20 km) to 250 miles (400 km). According to the EIA, the water depth above this continental shelf is typically less than 492 feet (150 m) to 656 feet (200 m) at its deepest point. The continental shelf ends with a sharp drop off to the continental slope, which underlies deep ocean. (See Figure 2.3.) The United States claims exclusive rights to the resources (such as oil) underlying the continental shelf off its coastlines.

In general, the continental shelf is relatively narrow along the Pacific coast, wide along much of the Atlantic coast and the Gulf of Alaska, and widest in the Gulf of

FIGURE 2.2

Map of U.S. Exclusive Economic Zone

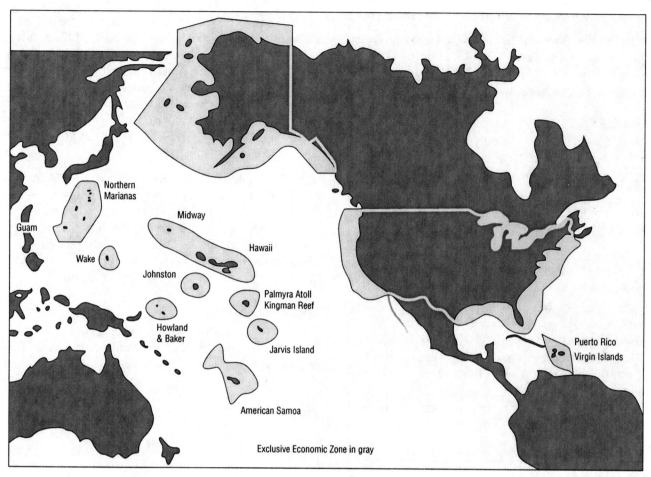

SOURCE: "Map Showing Exclusive Economic Zone around the United States and Territories," in *Oil: Crude and Petroleum Products Explained: Offshore Oil and Gas*, U.S. Energy Information Administration, July 3, 2012, http://www.eia.gov/energyexplained/images/charts/EEZmap.png (accessed July 3, 2014)

FIGURE 2.3

Offshore side view

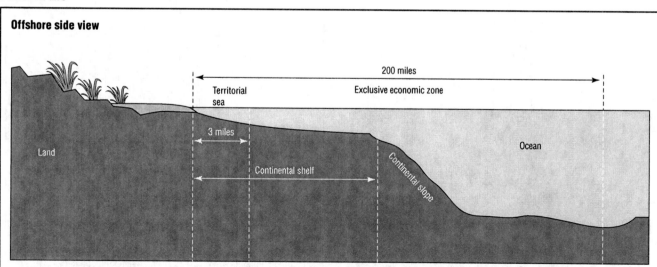

SOURCE: "Diagram of Shore and Ocean Overlaid with Territorial Sea, Exclusive Economic Zone, the Continental Shelf, and Continental Slope," in *Oil: Crude and Petroleum Products Explained: Offshore Oil and Gas*, U.S. Energy Information Administration, July 3, 2012, http://www.eia.gov/energyexplained/images/continentalshelf.gif (accessed July 3, 2014)

Mexico. Most coastal states have resource rights extending outward 3 miles (5 km) from their coastlines. Resources beyond that limit fall under federal government control in an area called the outer continental shelf (OCS). Water above the OCS can be up to 600 feet (183 m) deep.

Estimates of the total amounts of oil deposits around the world and in the United States that have not yet been extracted are provided in Chapter 7, along with information about oil exploration and development activities.

Measuring Oil

Raw oil volumes are typically measured in barrels. A barrel is equivalent to 42 gallons (159 L). Because a barrel is a relatively small unit of measure, oil data are typically expressed in units of thousand barrels or million barrels. A commonly used unit for production and consumption data is million barrels per day (mbpd).

OIL EXTRACTION
Crude Oil

Most crude oil wells are drilled with a rotary drilling system, or rotary rig, as illustrated in Figure 2.4. A rotating bit at the end of a pipe drills a hole into the ground. Drilling mud is pushed down through the pipe and the drill bit, forcing small pieces of drilled rock to the surface. As the well gets deeper, more pipe is added. The oil derrick above the ground supports equipment that can lift the pipe and drill bit from the well when drill bits need to be changed or replaced.

Drilling takes place both onshore and offshore. Figure 2.5 shows a typical offshore rig. The development of offshore oil and gas resources began with the drilling of the Summerland oil field along the coast of California in 1896, where about 400 wells were drilled. Since then, the industry has continually improved drilling technology. In the 21st century deepwater petroleum and natural gas exploration occurs from platforms and drill ships, and shallow-water exploration occurs from gravel islands (artificially made islands of gravel and sand) and mobile units (ship-based drilling units).

After crude oil reservoirs have been tapped for several years or decades, their supply of readily accessible oil becomes depleted. Several techniques can be used to recover additional oil, including the injection of water, chemicals, or steam to force more oil from the rock. These recovery techniques can be expensive and add to the cost of producing each barrel of crude oil.

Unconventional Oils

As noted earlier, some unconventional oils are derived from deposits that are solid or semisolid. They cannot be pumped out of the ground like crude oil. Kerogen and bitumen lying near the surface are typically

FIGURE 2.4

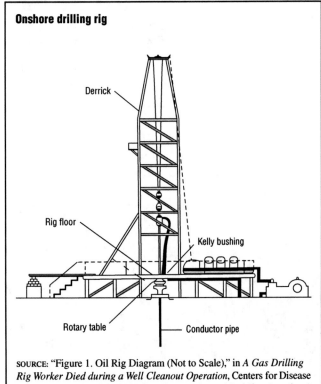

SOURCE: "Figure 1. Oil Rig Diagram (Not to Scale)," in *A Gas Drilling Rig Worker Died during a Well Cleanout Operation*, Centers for Disease Control and Prevention, 2003, http://www.cdc.gov/niosh/face/stateface/ok/03ok034.html (accessed June 30, 2014)

FIGURE 2.5

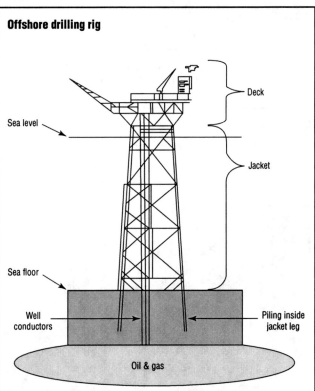

SOURCE: "Schematic of Typical Gulf of Mexico Offshore Oil or Gas Platform," in *Platform Removal Observer Program*, National Oceanic and Atmospheric Administration, 2014, http://www.galvestonlab.sefsc.noaa.gov/platforms/ (accessed June 30, 2014)

FIGURE 2.6

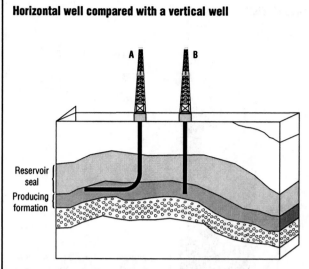

Horizontal well compared with a vertical well

SOURCE: "Figure 1. Greater Length of Producing Formation Exposed to the Wellbore in a Horizontal Well (A) Than in a Vertical Well (B)," in *Drilling Sideways—A Review of Horizontal Well Technology and Its Domestic Application*, U.S. Energy Information Administration, April 1993, http://www.eia.gov/pub/oil_gas/natural_gas/analysis_publications/drilling_sideways_well_technology/pdf/tr0565.pdf (accessed June 30, 2014)

FIGURE 2.7

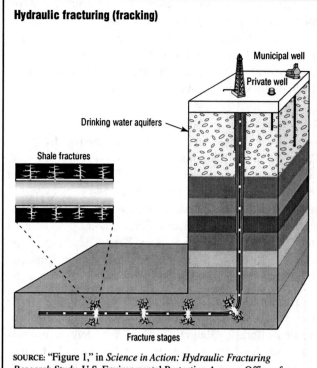

Hydraulic fracturing (fracking)

SOURCE: "Figure 1," in *Science in Action: Hydraulic Fracturing Research Study*, U.S. Environmental Protection Agency, Office of Research and Development, June 2010, http://www.epa.gov/safewater/uic/pdfs/hfresearchstudyfs.pdf (accessed June 27, 2014)

dug out using mining techniques, which can have large land impacts. This makes their extraction extremely controversial from an environmental standpoint. Once mined, the materials are heated (or retorted) to liquefy the oil. Deposits that are deep within the earth can be heated in situ (in place) by injecting steam through drilled wells. The liquefied oil is then pumped to the surface. Other methods are used as well, but all efforts amount to expensive and specialized processes.

Tight oil is typically liberated from dense rock formations using horizontal drilling or hydraulic fracturing. A horizontal well extends vertically down to the formation of interest and then extends horizontally across it. (See well A in Figure 2.6.) This arrangement exposes a greater surface area of the producing formation to extraction than does a completely vertical well. Hydraulic fracturing (fracking) is a specialized well-based technique for extracting oil and natural gas from unconventional geological sources, such as shale.

Figure 2.7 shows a typical fracking operation. A vertical well is drilled down and into the desired geological formation. Then, a horizontal leg extends through the formation. Perforated pipes are inserted into the horizontal leg, and water is forced through the perforations under very high pressure, which causes numerous small fractures in the rock. The water contains sand, tiny ceramic beads, or other solids that serve as propping agents (they prop open the fractures so they do not close when the pressure is released and the water is removed).

Oil and natural gas then escape from the rock fractures into the well and flow to the surface.

Fracking is a relatively new extraction process, in that it has only been used for several decades. It is controversial because large amounts of water are required and there is a danger that oil and natural gas could be accidentally introduced into aquifers (underground freshwater pools).

Because unconventional oil is typically blended into crude oil, many analysts refer to all "raw" oil as crude oil. This naming convention will be followed in this book when referring to oil past the extraction stage.

CRUDE OIL TRANSPORT

According to the EIA, in "Petroleum and Other Liquids: Imports by Area of Entry" (September 29, 2014, http://www.eia.gov/dnav/pet/pet_move_imp_dc_NUS-Z00_mbbl_a.htm), 2.8 billion barrels of crude oil and 66.3 million barrels of NGPL and liquefied refinery gases were imported into the United States in 2013. Much of this oil traveled by sea in enormous oil tankers. In addition, there are more than a dozen oil pipelines connecting the United States and Canada. Two of the largest Canadian companies involved in piping crude oil to the United States are Enbridge Inc. (2014, http://www.enbridge.com/DeliveringEnergy/OurPipelines/LiquidsPipelines.aspx) and TransCanada Corporation (2014, http://www.transcanada.com/oil-pipelines.html).

The United States features a massive, mostly interconnected network of pipelines for moving crude oil around the country. (For a map of the pipelines, see the American Petroleum Institute's "U.S. Refineries, Crude Oil, and Refined Products Pipelines" [2014, http://www.api.org/~/media/Files/Oil-and-Natural-Gas/pipeline/US-Pipeline-Map-API-Website3.pdf].)

The Keystone XL Project

In 2010 TransCanada sought permission from the U.S. government to construct a new crude oil pipeline from Canada into the United States. The project is named Keystone XL (http://keystone-xl.com) and is proposed to run from Alberta, Canada, across the U.S. border into Montana and down to Steele City, Nebraska. There, it would connect with an existing TransCanada pipeline called the Keystone pipeline. The latter ends in Cushing, Oklahoma, which is a key hub for U.S. oil resources.

The Keystone XL project has encountered stiff resistance from environmentalists and the administration of President Barack Obama (1961–). Presidential permission is required for a pipeline to cross the U.S. border. The president's critics have been dismayed by his reluctance to approve the project, which they believe would benefit the U.S. economy and reduce reliance on oil imported from overseas. In 2011 TransCanada submitted a comprehensive report, called an Environmental Impact Statement (EIS), for the project. At that time the pipeline was designed to traverse the Sand Hills region of Nebraska, an environmentally sensitive area. Obama declined to approve the permit. TransCanada developed an alternative route that avoids the Sand Hills region and submitted a revised EIS. The final version of the document (http://keystonepipeline-xl.state.gov/finalseis/index.htm) was published in January 2014. As of October 2014, Obama had not approved the permit for the project.

OIL REFINING

Crude oil has little practical use in its raw state. It is a mixture of different liquid hydrocarbons that are separable by distillation. (See Figure 2.8.) The liquid components (or fractions) vaporize at different boiling points. Light fractions, such as butane, boil off at relatively low temperatures. Heavy components with high boiling points, such as residual fuel oil, must be heated to high temperatures to boil off. All the separated vapors are then cooled to condense them back to liquids. The heavier fractions are often subjected to additional refining processes called cracking and reforming to break up heavy petroleum products into lighter ones.

Refining produces numerous petroleum products, all of which have different physical and chemical properties. These products include gasoline, diesel fuel, jet fuel, and lubricants for transportation; heating oil, residual oil, and

FIGURE 2.8

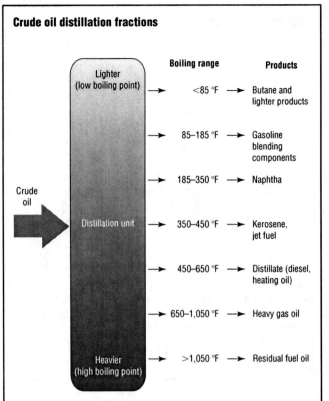

Crude oil distillation fractions

SOURCE: "Crude Oil Distillation Unit and Products," in *Today in Energy: Crude Oil Distillation and the Definition of Refinery Capacity*, U.S. Energy Information Administration, July 5, 2012, http://www.eia.gov/todayinenergy/detail.cfm?id=6970# (accessed June 30, 2014)

kerosene for heat; butane, ethane, and propane; and heavy residuals for paving and roofing. Petroleum by-products are also vital to the chemical industry, ending up in many different foams, plastics, synthetic fabrics, paints, dyes, inks, and even pharmaceutical drugs. Because of their dependence on petroleum, many chemical plants are directly connected by pipelines to nearby refineries.

REFINERY NUMBERS AND CAPACITY

According to the EIA, in "Petroleum and Other Liquids: Number and Capacity of Petroleum Refineries" (June 25, 2014, http://www.eia.gov/dnav/pet/pet_pnp_cap1_dcu_nus_a.htm), as of January 1, 2014, there were 142 operable refineries in the United States, down from 150 in 2009. Refinery capacity in 2014 was about 17.9 mbpd. The number of refineries has dropped for a variety of reasons, including retirement of older inefficient plants and consolidation within the oil industry. In addition, some countries that export oil to the United States have begun refining their own oil and selling the petroleum products directly.

In "When Was the Last Refinery Built in the United States?" (2014, http://www.eia.gov/tools/faqs/faq.cfm?id=29&t=6), the EIA notes that as of 2014, the last large U.S. refinery to begin operating was built during the late

1970s in Louisiana. A small refinery began operating in 2008 in Wyoming. Another small refinery under construction in North Dakota was expected to be operational by December 2014.

In 2010 Hyperion Energy, a Texas-based company, obtained an air permit for a proposed $10 billion refinery in South Dakota. Environmental groups, including the Sierra Club, challenged the project in court. In early 2013 the South Dakota Supreme Court ruled in favor of Hyperion; however, the company's air permit expired later that year. As of October 2014, Hyperion Energy had not reapplied for a permit for the proposed refinery.

DOMESTIC CRUDE OIL PRODUCTION

Figure 2.9 shows domestic production of crude oil (including lease condensate) and NGPL between 1949 and 2013. Production peaked in 1970 and then slowly declined into the first decade of the 21st century. Production then rose sharply, reaching nearly 8 mbpd in 2013. Table 2.1 provides a breakdown of production by oil type and jurisdiction. Chiefly, it distinguishes Alaskan oil from that produced in the 48 contiguous states. During the 1990s Alaskan production accounted for over 22% of total domestic production; however, its share has since fallen. As explained in Chapter 7, certain pristine areas of northern Alaska are off limits to drilling.

The sharp uptick in domestic oil production that began during the latter half of the first decade of the 21st century is due almost entirely to tight oil. Figure 2.10 shows a map of the six regions that accounted for 95% of domestic oil production growth between 2011 and 2013. The Permian, Eagle Ford, and Bakken basins have been particularly productive. The EIA indicates in "Tight Oil Production Pushes U.S. Crude Supply to over 10% of World Total" (March 26, 2014, http://www.eia.gov/todayinenergy/detail.cfm?id=15571) that U.S. tight oil production in 2005 was around 0.3 mbpd. By February 2014 it had soared to nearly 3.5 mbpd, making the United States the world's leading tight oil supplier. Canada was in second place with around 0.3 mbpd.

U.S. oil production is affected by crude oil availability and legislative, legal, and cost issues related to drilling and extraction. For example, U.S. producers spend more money than do Middle Eastern producers to drill and extract crude oil because oil is available in enormous, easily accessible reservoirs in the Middle East. U.S. oil is not as easily recovered. When the cost of oil recovery severely reduces the profit margin on a barrel of oil, U.S. producers may shut down their most expensive wells, especially in times when oil prices are low. When oil prices are high, even the most expensive extraction methods can become cost effective.

FIGURE 2.9

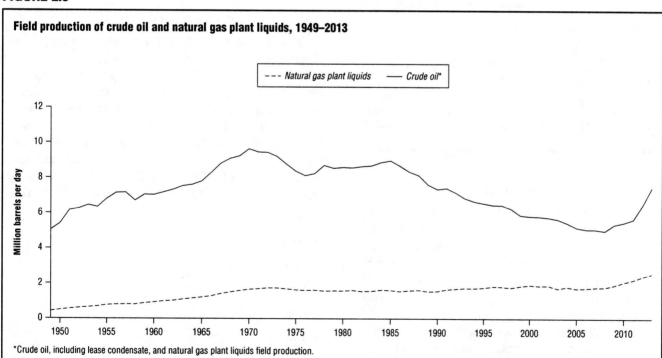

Field production of crude oil and natural gas plant liquids, 1949–2013

*Crude oil, including lease condensate, and natural gas plant liquids field production.

SOURCE: "Figure 3.1. Petroleum Overview (Million Barrels per Day): Crude Oil and Natural Gas Plant Liquids Field Production, 1949–2013," in *Monthly Energy Review: June 2014*, U.S. Energy Information Administration, June 25, 2014, http://www.eia.gov/totalenergy/data/monthly/archive/00351406.pdf (accessed June 27, 2014)

TABLE 2.1

Field production of crude oil and natural gas plant liquids, by location, selected years 1950–2013

[Thousand barrels per day]

	Field production[a]				
	Crude oil[b, c]				
	48 States[d]	Alaska	Total	NGPL[e]	Total[c]
1950 average	5,407	0	5,407	499	5,906
1955 average	6,807	0	6,807	771	7,578
1960 average	7,034	2	7,035	929	7,965
1965 average	7,774	30	7,804	1,210	9,014
1970 average	9,408	229	9,637	1,660	11,297
1975 average	8,183	191	8,375	1,633	10,007
1980 average	6,980	1,617	8,597	1,573	10,170
1985 average	7,146	1,825	8,971	1,609	10,581
1990 average	5,582	1,773	7,355	1,559	8,914
1995 average	5,076	1,484	6,560	1,762	8,322
2000 average	4,851	970	5,822	1,911	7,733
2001 average	4,839	963	5,801	1,868	7,670
2002 average	4,759	985	5,744	1,880	7,624
2003 average	4,675	974	5,649	1,719	7,369
2004 average	4,533	908	5,441	1,809	7,250
2005 average	4,317	864	5,181	1,717	6,898
2006 average	4,347	741	5,088	1,739	6,827
2007 average	4,355	722	5,077	1,783	6,860
2008 average	4,317	683	5,000	1,784	6,783
2009 average	4,708	645	5,353	1,910	7,263
2010 average	4,871	600	5,471	2,074	7,545
2011 average	5,091	561	5,652	2,216	7,869
2012 average	5,960[R]	526	6,486[R]	2,408	8,893[R]
2013 average	6,929[R, E]	515[E]	7,443[R, E]	2,556	10,000[R, E]

[a]Crude oil production on leases, and natural gas liquids (liquefied petroleum gases, pentanes plus, and a small amount of finished petroleum products) production at natural gas processing plants. Excludes what was previously classified as "Field Production" of finished motor gasoline, motor gasoline blending components, and other hydrocarbons and oxygenates.
[b]Includes lease condensate.
[c]Once a month, data for crude oil production, total field production, and adjustments are revised going back as far as the data year of the U.S. Energy Information Administration's (EIA) last published *Petroleum Supply Annual (PSA)*—these revisions are released at the same time as EIA's *Petroleum Supply Monthly*. Once a year, data for these series are revised going back as far as 10 years—these revisions are released at the same time as the PSA.
[d]United States excluding Alaska and Hawaii.
[e]Natural gas plant liquids.
R = Revised. E = Estimate. NA = Not available.
NGPL = natural gas plant liquids.
Notes: Totals may not equal sum of components due to independent rounding.
Geographic coverage is the 50 states and the District of Columbia.

SOURCE: Adapted from "Table 3.1. Petroleum Overview (Thousand Barrels per Day)," in *Monthly Energy Review: June 2014*, U.S. Energy Information Administration, June 25, 2014, http://www.eia.gov/totalenergy/data/monthly/archive/00351406.pdf (accessed June 27, 2014)

The Domestic Production Outlook

The EIA publishes annual projections of future U.S. and world production of crude oil and petroleum products. In *Annual Energy Outlook 2014 with Projections to 2040* (April 2014, http://www.eia.gov/forecasts/aeo/pdf/0383(2014).pdf), the EIA indicates that it considers five future scenarios: a reference case, low and high economic growth cases, and low and high oil price cases. All of the projections are based on the assumption that existing energy-related laws and regulations will remain in effect.

Figure 2.11 shows EIA projections for U.S. crude oil production through 2040 for the reference case by extraction location. Alaskan production is predicted to continue

to fall over the coming decades. Offshore production for the lower 48 states is forecast to increase slightly through the second decade of the 21st century and then become relatively flat. The biggest expected difference is in onshore production in the lower 48 states. It is projected to rise dramatically through the second decade of the 21st century and remain high for around a decade. According to the EIA, this growth "is primarily a result of continued development of tight oil resources in the Bakken, Eagle Ford, and Permian Basin formations." By the mid-2020s the productivity of these basins is expected to begin falling as the most readily accessible oil is depleted. The EIA warns, however, "there is considerable uncertainty about the expected peak level of tight oil production" and notes that additional U.S. tight oil resources could be found and exploited.

DOMESTIC CRUDE OIL TRADE

The United States has been importing crude oil since World War II (1939–1945). Initially, the imported amounts were very small. Figure 2.12 shows historical imports of crude oil and petroleum products between 1949 and 2013. At first, imported oil was cheap and readily available, suiting the demands of a growing American population and economy. Furthermore, relatively low world crude oil prices often dampened domestic oil production: when the world price was lower than the cost of producing oil from some U.S. wells, domestic oil became unprofitable and was not produced. Consequently, more oil was imported.

Concern about Foreign Oil Dependency

The Organization of the Petroleum Exporting Countries (OPEC) is a cartel (a group of countries that agree to control production and marketing to avoid competing with one another). It was formed in 1960 by five major oil-producing countries: Iran, Iraq, Kuwait, Saudi Arabia, and Venezuela. Since 1973 OPEC has tried to influence the worldwide oil supply to achieve higher prices. Over the decades various countries have joined and quit the cartel. As of 2014, OPEC (http://www.opec.org/opec_web/en/about_us/25.htm) had 12 member countries:

- Algeria
- Angola
- Ecuador
- Iran
- Iraq
- Kuwait
- Libya
- Nigeria
- Qatar

FIGURE 2.10

Key basins for tight oil and shale gas production

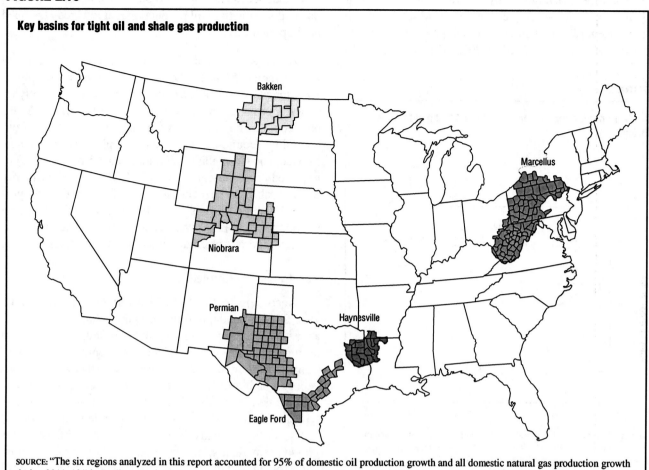

SOURCE: "The six regions analyzed in this report accounted for 95% of domestic oil production growth and all domestic natural gas production growth during 2011–13," in *Drilling Productivity Report for Key Tight Oil and Shale Gas Regions*, U.S. Energy Information Administration, June 2014, http://www.eia.gov/petroleum/drilling/pdf/dpr-full.pdf (accessed June 30, 2014)

- Saudi Arabia
- United Arab Emirates
- Venezuela

The United States was hugely dependent on OPEC oil during the 1970s and early 1980s. (See Figure 2.13.) In 1973 some Arab countries, including those in OPEC, cut their oil exports to the United States in retaliation for U.S. aid to Israel during the Yom Kippur War, which was fought between Israel and neighboring Arab countries. The embargo lasted only six months, but the price of oil rose dramatically during that period. Americans experienced sudden price hikes for products that were produced from oil, such as gasoline and home heating oil, and faced temporary shortages. The energy problem quickly became an energy crisis, which led to occasional blackouts in cities and industries, temporary shutdowns of factories and schools, and frequent lines at gasoline service stations. The sudden increase in energy prices during the early 1970s is widely considered to have been a major cause of the economic recession of 1974 and 1975. Nevertheless, the United States obtained nearly three-fourths of its imported oil from OPEC by 1977. (See Figure 2.13.)

U.S. leaders became concerned that so much of the country's economic structure, based heavily on imported oil, was dependent on decisions in OPEC countries. Oil resources became an issue of national security, and OPEC countries, especially the Arab members, were often portrayed as potentially strangling the U.S. economy. Efforts were made to reduce imports by raising public awareness and by encouraging industry to create more energy-efficient products, such as automobiles with better gas mileage. These measures are described in detail in Chapter 9. Nonetheless, total petroleum imports rose through the end of the 1970s. (See Figure 2.12 and Figure 2.13.) Imports declined and then rebounded over the following decades as conservation efforts waned in the face of low oil prices. In fact, fuel efficiency gains in automobiles during the 1990s were offset by the public's growing preference for large vehicles, such as sport-utility vehicles. As a result, total oil imports grew steadily. Nevertheless, as shown in Figure 2.13, by this time the United States was obtaining more than half of its imported oil from non-OPEC countries, such as Canada and Mexico.

Concern about continued U.S. reliance on OPEC oil grew after the terrorist attacks of September 11, 2001.

The concern was heightened by the war on terror, the war with Iraq, and the subsequent unrest in Middle Eastern nations. Regardless, demand for the product persisted, and total oil imports peaked in 2005. (See Figure 2.13.)

FIGURE 2.11

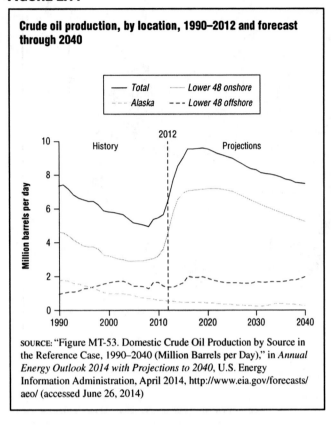

Crude oil production, by location, 1990–2012 and forecast through 2040

SOURCE: "Figure MT-53. Domestic Crude Oil Production by Source in the Reference Case, 1990–2040 (Million Barrels per Day)," in *Annual Energy Outlook 2014 with Projections to 2040*, U.S. Energy Information Administration, April 2014, http://www.eia.gov/forecasts/aeo/ (accessed June 26, 2014)

Later that decade the United States experienced a dramatic rise in domestic tight oil production that lowered U.S. need for imported oil.

As shown in Figure 2.14, in 2013 imports accounted for 7.7 mbpd (51%) of the total U.S. crude oil supply of 15.2 mbpd. A breakdown of the imports by supplying entity is provided in Table 2.2. In 2013 the United States obtained 4.2 mbpd (55%) of its imported crude oil from non-OPEC countries. The major suppliers were Canada, Mexico, and Colombia. The remaining 3.5 mbpd (45%) of imported crude oil came from OPEC countries, primarily Saudi Arabia, Venezuela, and Iraq. Overall, Canada provided 2.6 mbpd (33% of U.S. imports), while Saudi Arabia provided 1.3 mbpd (17%). These two countries were the leading importers of crude oil to the United States in 2013.

The Canadian Connection

According to the EIA, in *Monthly Energy Review: June 2014*, Canada, unlike the United States, almost balanced its domestic oil supply and petroleum consumption during the latter decades of the 20th century. Portions of Canada, particularly the province of Alberta, have vast deposits of bitumen. As described earlier, crude oil can be obtained from this black tarry substance, which is typically found in rock formations called tar sands, oil sands, or tight sands. Canada's bitumen industry has grown dramatically, allowing the nation to produce more crude oil than it needs. The EIA indicates that in 2013 Canada's crude oil production averaged 3.3 mbpd, while its petroleum consumption was only 2.3 mbpd.

FIGURE 2.12

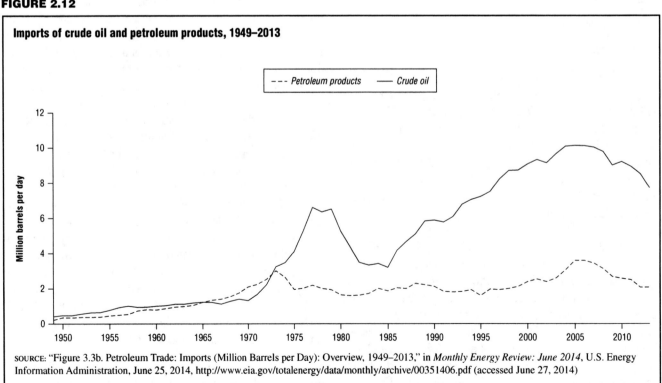

Imports of crude oil and petroleum products, 1949–2013

SOURCE: "Figure 3.3b. Petroleum Trade: Imports (Million Barrels per Day): Overview, 1949–2013," in *Monthly Energy Review: June 2014*, U.S. Energy Information Administration, June 25, 2014, http://www.eia.gov/totalenergy/data/monthly/archive/00351406.pdf (accessed June 27, 2014)

FIGURE 2.13

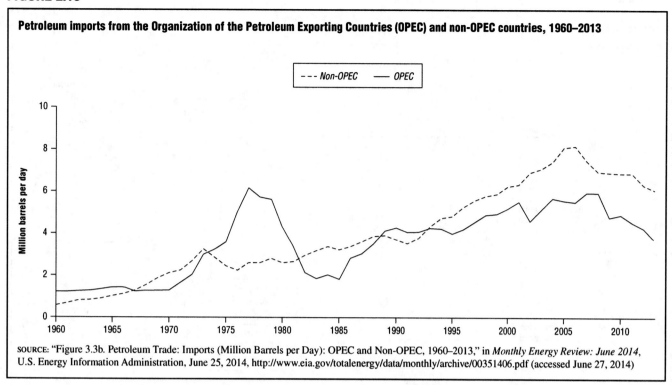

Petroleum imports from the Organization of the Petroleum Exporting Countries (OPEC) and non-OPEC countries, 1960–2013

SOURCE: "Figure 3.3b. Petroleum Trade: Imports (Million Barrels per Day): OPEC and Non-OPEC, 1960–2013," in *Monthly Energy Review: June 2014*, U.S. Energy Information Administration, June 25, 2014, http://www.eia.gov/totalenergy/data/monthly/archive/00351406.pdf (accessed June 27, 2014)

Canada's close proximity to the United States and the existing pipelines and transportation systems between the two countries have facilitated cross-border trade of Canadian crude oil. As shown in Figure 2.15, U.S. imports of the oil soared from around 0.2 mbpd in 1980 to over 2.5 mbpd in 2013.

U.S. Strategic Petroleum Reserve

In 1975, in response to growing concern over U.S. dependence on imported oil, Congress created the Strategic Petroleum Reserve (SPR). Crude oil is stored in deep salt caverns in Louisiana and Texas. (The caverns are used because oil does not dissolve salt the way water does.) If the United States suddenly finds its crude oil imports cut, the reserves can be accessed via existing pipelines.

At the end of 2013 the SPR contained 700 million barrels of crude oil. (See Figure 2.16.) As shown in Figure 2.14, crude oil imports in 2013 averaged 7.7 mbpd. At that usage rate the SPR would last the United States a maximum of 90 days (i.e., assuming no crude oil imports at all). The non-SPR crude oil stocks shown in Figure 2.16 are amounts in the hands of the U.S. oil industry, including Alaskan crude oil in transit to the 48 contiguous states.

Although the SPR was created to compensate against drastic import disruptions, it has been tapped under other circumstances. In "SPR Quick Facts and FAQs" (2014, http://energy.gov/fe/services/petroleum-reserves/strategic-petroleum-reserve/spr-quick-facts-and-faqs#Q1), the

U.S. Department of Energy (DOE) describes some of the historical events that have triggered sales or loans of SPR crude oil. SPR loans to oil companies have to be paid back with interest—that is, including an extra amount above the borrowed amount. In 2012 the Marathon Oil Company borrowed 1 million barrels after Hurricane Isaac disrupted oil production in the U.S. Gulf Coast. Major sales of SPR oil took place in 1990 due to the Persian Gulf War and in 2011 following a revolution in Libya. The latter sale occurred at the direction of the International Energy Agency (IEA), which is an independent organization devoted to energy issues. As of 2014, the United States and 28 other developed countries were IEA members.

Management of the SPR is a highly politicized topic in the United States. During times of high oil and gasoline prices some politicians clamor for a release of SPR oil to dampen prices and ease the financial burden on consumers. The U.S. government, however, has historically maintained that releases should take place only due to special events that lower (or threaten to lower) crude oil supply availability to the United States. The United States is also bound by IAE requirements regarding crude oil reserves. According to the DOE, the IAE requires each member nation to maintain at least a 90-day reserve including both private and government supplies.

Domestic Crude Oil Exports

As shown in Table 2.3, the United States has historically exported very little crude oil. Annual exports have ranged from a low of 3,000 barrels per day (bpd) in 1965

FIGURE 2.14

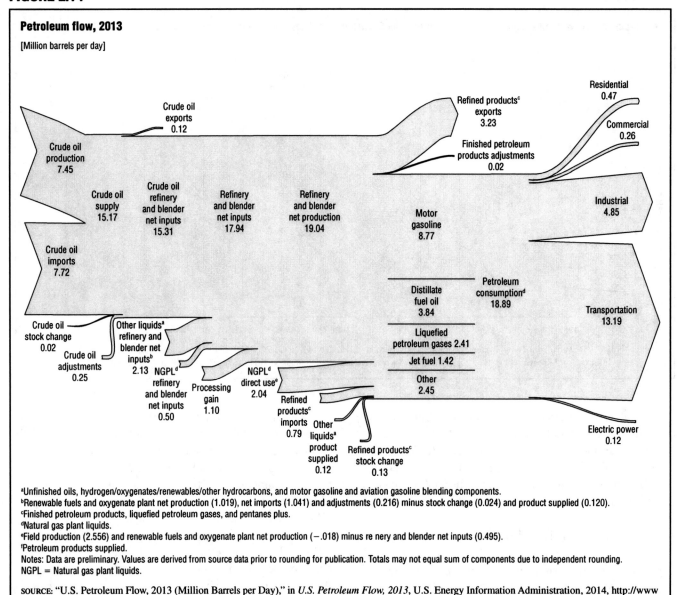

Petroleum flow, 2013

[Million barrels per day]

[a]Unfinished oils, hydrogen/oxygenates/renewables/other hydrocarbons, and motor gasoline and aviation gasoline blending components.
[b]Renewable fuels and oxygenate plant net production (1.019), net imports (1.041) and adjustments (0.216) minus stock change (0.024) and product supplied (0.120).
[c]Finished petroleum products, liquefied petroleum gases, and pentanes plus.
[d]Natural gas plant liquids.
[e]Field production (2.556) and renewable fuels and oxygenate plant net production (−.018) minus re nery and blender net inputs (0.495).
[f]Petroleum products supplied.
Notes: Data are preliminary. Values are derived from source data prior to rounding for publication. Totals may not equal sum of components due to independent rounding.
NGPL = Natural gas plant liquids.

SOURCE: "U.S. Petroleum Flow, 2013 (Million Barrels per Day)," in *U.S. Petroleum Flow, 2013*, U.S. Energy Information Administration, 2014, http://www .eia.gov/totalenergy/data/monthly/pdf/flow/petroleum.pdf (accessed July 1, 2014)

to a high of 287,000 bpd in 1980. The average for 2013 was 120,000 bpd, up dramatically from earlier years in the 21st century. During the 1970s the U.S. government imposed strict export requirements on crude oil to keep as much of it as possible in the domestic supply and hold prices down. Christian Berthelsen and Lynn Cook explain in "U.S. Ruling Loosens Four-Decade Ban on Oil Exports" (WSJ.com, June 24, 2014) that U.S. companies are free to export refined oil (petroleum products), such as gasoline; however, crude oil exports are allowed only "in limited circumstances that require a special license." The major exception is for crude oil exports to Canada, which are allowed "with a special permit."

The U.S. tight oil boom has encouraged domestic producers to seek permission to export some minimally processed crude oil that qualifies for foreign sales.

According to Berthelsen and Cook, the U.S. Department of Commerce decided in 2014 to allow two U.S. companies to sell condensate (a type of ultralight oil) that had been stabilized and distilled. These steps are considered "far short of refining," but prepare the product for transport. U.S. producers of ultralight tight oil argue that they can fetch higher prices from foreign buyers than from domestic refiners. Berthelsen and Cook note that the decision is politically controversial because some lawmakers oppose loosening the export ban for fear of pushing up petroleum prices in the United States.

PETROLEUM PRODUCT CONSUMPTION

Crude oil is a raw material that is refined and processed into multiple petroleum products. In "Oil: Crude and Petroleum Products Explained" (June 19, 2014,

TABLE 2.2

Crude oil imports, by supplying nation or group, 2013

[Thousand barrels per day]

All countries	**7,719**
Non-OPEC countries	4,229
OPEC countries	3,490
Persian Gulf countries	1,994
By country:	
Canada	2,569
Saudi Arabia	1,325
Mexico	850
Venezuela	755
Colombia	367
Iraq	341
Kuwait	326
Nigeria	239
Ecuador	228
Angola	202
Brazil	109
Chad	66
Russia	45
Libya	43
Algeria	29
Azerbaijan	29
Gabon	24
United Kingdom	21
Congo (Brazzaville)	18
Indonesia	18
Equatorial Guinea	17
Norway	17
Argentina	13
Vietnam	13
Peru	11
Thailand	9
Trinidad and Tobago	8
Guatemala	7
Egypt	4
Ghana	3
Mauritania	3
Oman	3
United Arab Emirates	2
Belize	2
Netherlands	2
Australia	1
Bolivia	1
China	1

OPEC = Organization of the Petroleum Exporting Countries.

SOURCE: "U.S. Imports by Country of Origin," in *Petroleum & Other Liquids: Data: Crude Oil*, U.S. Energy Information Administration, June 27, 2014, http://www.eia.gov/dnav/pet/pet_move_impcus_a2_nus_epc0_im0_mbblpd_a.htm (accessed July 2, 2014)

http://www.eia.gov/energyexplained/index.cfm?page=oil_home), the EIA states that in 2013 a barrel (42 gallons [159 L]) of crude oil provided approximately 45 gallons' (170 L) worth of petroleum products. The agency notes that "this gain from processing the crude oil is similar to what happens to popcorn, which gets bigger after it is popped."

The United States makes petroleum products from domestically produced and imported crude oil. In addition, petroleum products are imported directly from foreign nations. As shown in Figure 2.14, average domestic consumption of petroleum products in 2013 was 18.9 mbpd.

Figure 2.17 shows petroleum product consumption by energy-using sector between 1949 and 2013. (Note that the sectors are defined in detail in Chapter 1.) The transportation sector has historically been the largest consumer of petroleum. Average consumption by sector in 2013 was:

- Transportation—13.2 mbpd, or 70% of total
- Industrial sector—4.9 mbpd, or 26% of total
- Residential sector—0.5 mbpd, or 3% of total
- Commercial sector—0.3 mbpd, or 1% of total
- Electric power sector—0.1 mbpd, or 1% of total

Most petroleum used in the transportation sector is for motor gasoline. According to the EIA, motor gasoline has historically accounted for nearly half of total petroleum products supplied. (See Figure 2.18.) Other major products are shown in Figure 2.19. They include distillate fuel oils (such as diesel oil), jet fuel, propane, and residual fuel oil. In *Monthly Energy Review: June 2014*, the EIA explains that residual fuel oil is a heavy oil used to power U.S. Navy ships and in industrial and commercial heating and electric power generation.

WORLD OIL PRODUCTION AND CONSUMPTION

Table 2.4 shows total oil production for 2012 for the world, by region, and for the top-20 producers. The values include crude oil, lease condensate, NGPL, other liquids, and refinery processing gains, which are due to chemicals added during refining. A majority of the leading oil-producing nations in 2012 were OPEC members, including the top supplier Saudi Arabia.

Total world oil production was 89.8 mbpd in 2012. The Middle East was the largest producing region, accounting for 27.7 mbpd (31% of the world total). North America was second with 17.9 mbpd (20%). Saudi Arabia led all countries with 11.7 mbpd (13% of the world total). The United States was second with 11.1 mbpd (12%), followed by Russia, China, and Canada. According to the EIA (2014, http://www.eia.gov/cfapps/ipdbproject/iedindex3.cfm?tid=5&pid=53&aid=1&cid=regions&syid=2013&eyid=2013&unit=TBPD), preliminary data for 2013 show the United States as the world's leading oil producer with output of 12.4 mbpd, or nearly 14% of the world total of 90.1 mbpd.

The total world petroleum consumption was 89.4 mbpd in 2012. (See Table 2.5.) The United States was the leading petroleum consumer, at 18.5 mbpd (21% of the world total). Other top consumers in 2012 included China, Japan, India, and Russia.

World Outlook

As noted earlier, the EIA prepares forecasts in which it considers scenarios including a reference case and high and low oil price cases. As shown in Figure 2.20, the agency predicts world petroleum consumption will rise to

FIGURE 2.15

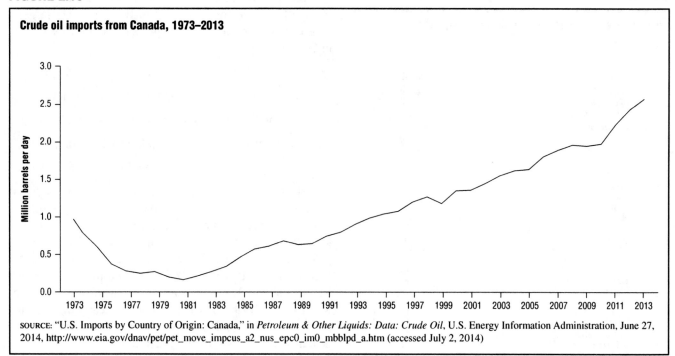

Crude oil imports from Canada, 1973–2013

SOURCE: "U.S. Imports by Country of Origin: Canada," in *Petroleum & Other Liquids: Data: Crude Oil*, U.S. Energy Information Administration, June 27, 2014, http://www.eia.gov/dnav/pet/pet_move_impcus_a2_nus_epc0_im0_mbblpd_a.htm (accessed July 2, 2014)

FIGURE 2.16

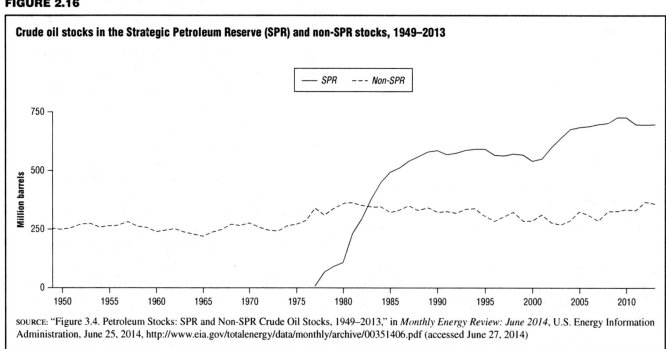

Crude oil stocks in the Strategic Petroleum Reserve (SPR) and non-SPR stocks, 1949–2013

SOURCE: "Figure 3.4. Petroleum Stocks: SPR and Non-SPR Crude Oil Stocks, 1949–2013," in *Monthly Energy Review: June 2014*, U.S. Energy Information Administration, June 25, 2014, http://www.eia.gov/totalenergy/data/monthly/archive/00351406.pdf (accessed June 27, 2014)

around 120 mbpd by 2040. The EIA categorizes nations by whether they are members of the Organisation for Economic Co-operation and Development (OECD). The OECD is a collection of dozens of mostly Western nations (including the United States) that are devoted to global economic development. Developed nations concentrate on energy conservation measures and alternative fuel sources to reduce their reliance on oil. The EIA expects OECD petroleum consumption to grow only slightly between 2012 and 2040. By contrast, consumption among non-OECD members (such as China, India, and Russia) is projected to soar from around 43 mbpd in 2012 to around 70 mbpd in 2040.

Many non-OECD members are considered developing nations that are undergoing rapid industrialization and heavy use of resources, much as the United States and western Europe did during the mid-20th century. At

TABLE 2.3

Crude oil and petroleum product exports, selected years 1950–2013

[Thousand barrels per day]

		Exports	
	Crude oil*	Petroleum products	Total
1950 average	95	210	305
1955 average	32	336	368
1960 average	8	193	202
1965 average	3	184	187
1970 average	14	245	259
1975 average	6	204	209
1980 average	287	258	544
1985 average	204	577	781
1990 average	109	748	857
1995 average	95	855	949
2000 average	50	990	1,040
2001 average	20	951	971
2002 average	9	975	984
2003 average	12	1,014	1,027
2004 average	27	1,021	1,048
2005 average	32	1,133	1,165
2006 average	25	1,292	1,317
2007 average	27	1,405	1,433
2008 average	29	1,773	1,802
2009 average	44	1,980	2,024
2010 average	42	2,311	2,353
2011 average	47	2,939	2,986
2012 average	67	3,137	3,205
2013 average	120	3,474	3,594

*Includes lease condensate.

SOURCE: Adapted from "Table 3.3b. Petroleum Trade: Imports and Exports by Type (Thousand Barrels per Day)," in *Monthly Energy Review: June 2014*, U.S. Energy Information Administration, June 25, 2014, http://www.eia.gov/totalenergy/data/monthly/archive/00351406.pdf (accessed June 27, 2014)

that time the world oil industry was dominated by Western companies, most of which were based in the United States. The article "Supermajordämmerung" (Economist.com, August 3, 2013) notes that during the 1950s the industry leaders were the so-called seven sisters: BP (formerly British Petroleum), Esso, Gulf Oil, Mobil, Royal Dutch Shell, Southern Oil Company of California, and Texaco. All were based in the United States except BP, which was based in the United Kingdom, and Royal Dutch Shell, which was based in the United Kingdom and the Netherlands. These companies held enormous economic power and wielded great control over the world's oil resources. Over time, they and their successors were dubbed "Big Oil." (It is important to note that most large oil companies also trade in natural gas because the two fuels are often found together.)

The oil industry encompasses a range of tasks, such as finding and extracting oil, refining it into multiple petroleum products, and distributing the products. The Big Oil companies grew to domination by practicing vertical integration, meaning that they performed (or purchased smaller companies that performed) all of these tasks. This gave them broad economic power, for example, from the oil well to the gas pump. Over the decades the big companies have undergone ownership transitions, such as mergers and acquisitions, and have changed names in some cases. However, the industry has sustained only a handful of Big Oil companies. As of 2014, they were generally considered to include BP,

FIGURE 2.17

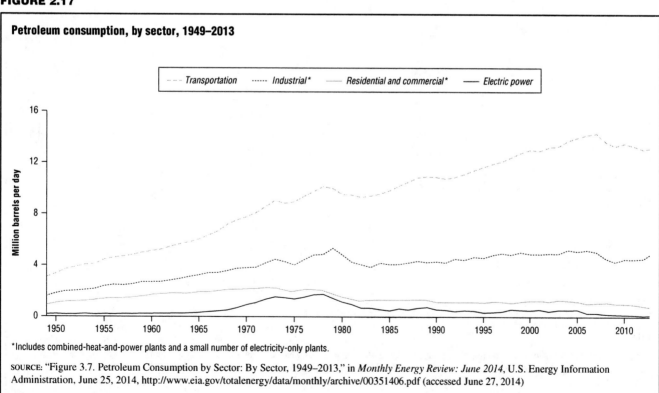

Petroleum consumption, by sector, 1949–2013

······ Transportation   ------ Industrial*   ········· Residential and commercial*   —— Electric power

*Includes combined-heat-and-power plants and a small number of electricity-only plants.

SOURCE: "Figure 3.7. Petroleum Consumption by Sector: By Sector, 1949–2013," in *Monthly Energy Review: June 2014*, U.S. Energy Information Administration, June 25, 2014, http://www.eia.gov/totalenergy/data/monthly/archive/00351406.pdf (accessed June 27, 2014)

FIGURE 2.18

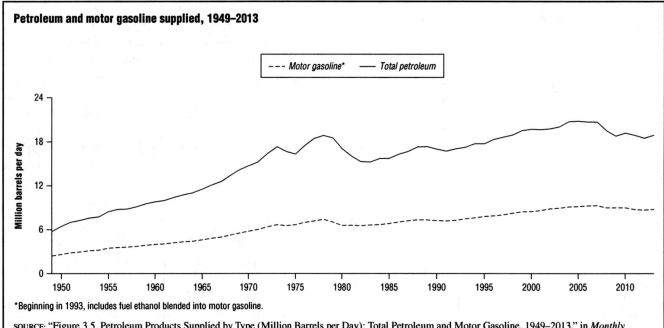

Petroleum and motor gasoline supplied, 1949–2013

--- Motor gasoline*   —— Total petroleum

*Beginning in 1993, includes fuel ethanol blended into motor gasoline.

SOURCE: "Figure 3.5. Petroleum Products Supplied by Type (Million Barrels per Day): Total Petroleum and Motor Gasoline, 1949–2013," in *Monthly Energy Review: June 2014*, U.S. Energy Information Administration, June 25, 2014, http://www.eia.gov/totalenergy/data/monthly/archive/00351406.pdf (accessed June 27, 2014)

FIGURE 2.19

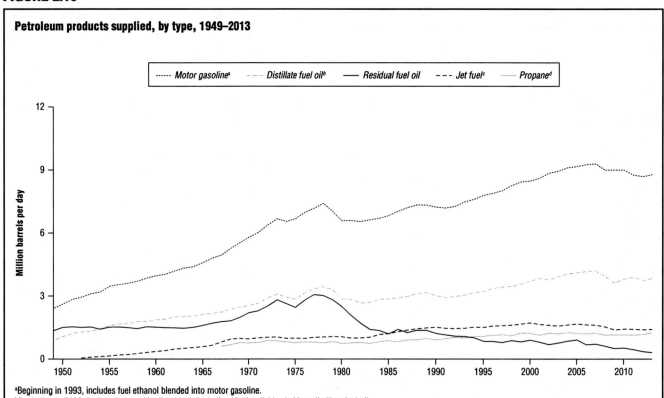

Petroleum products supplied, by type, 1949–2013

······ Motor gasolineª   ····· Distillate fuel oilᵇ   —— Residual fuel oil   --- Jet fuelᶜ   ······· Propaneᵈ

ªBeginning in 1993, includes fuel ethanol blended into motor gasoline.
ᵇBeginning in 2009, includes renewable diesel fuel (including biodiesel) blended into distillate fuel oil.
ᶜBeginning in 2005, includes kerosene-type jet fuel only.
ᵈIncludes propylene.

SOURCE: "Figure 3.5. Petroleum Products Supplied by Type (Million Barrels per Day): Selected Products, 1949–2013," in *Monthly Energy Review: June 2014*, U.S. Energy Information Administration, June 25, 2014, http://www.eia.gov/totalenergy/data/monthly/archive/00351406.pdf (accessed June 27, 2014)

TABLE 2.4

World production of crude oil, including lease condensate and other petroleum liquids, by region and selected country, 2012

[Million barrels per day]

	2012
World	89.8
Regions	
Middle East	27.7
North America	17.9
Eurasia	13.4
Africa	10.0
Asia & Oceania	9.0
Central & South America	7.8
Europe	4.0
Countries	
Saudi Arabia	11.7
United States	11.1
Russia	10.4
China	4.4
Canada	3.9
Iran	3.6
United Arab Emirates	3.2
Iraq	3.0
Mexico	2.9
Kuwait	2.8
Brazil	2.7
Nigeria	2.5
Venezuela	2.5
Qatar	2.0
Norway	1.9
Algeria	1.9
Angola	1.8
Kazakhstan	1.6
Libya	1.5
India	1.0

SOURCE: Adapted from "Table. Total Oil Supply (Thousand Barrels per Day)," in *International Energy Statistics*, U.S. Energy Information Administration, 2014, http://www.eia.gov/cfapps/ipdbproject/iedindex3.cfm?tid=5&pid=53&aid=1&cid=regions&syid=2012&eyid=2012&unit=TBPD (accessed July 1, 2014)

TABLE 2.5

World petroleum consumption, by region and selected country, 2012

[Million barrels per day]

	2012
World	89.4
Regions	
Asia & Oceania	29.8
North America	22.9
Europe	14.5
Middle East	7.6
Central & South America	6.8
Eurasia	4.5
Africa	3.4
Countries	
United States	18.5
China	10.3
Japan	4.7
India	3.6
Russia	3.2
Saudi Arabia	2.9
Brazil	2.8
Germany	2.4
Korea, South	2.3
Canada	2.3
Mexico	2.1
France	1.7
Iran	1.7
Indonesia	1.6
United Kingdom	1.5
Singapore	1.4
Italy	1.4
Spain	1.3
Australia	1.1
Taiwan	1.1

SOURCE: Adapted from "Table. Total Petroleum Consumption (Thousand Barrels per Day)," in *International Energy Statistics*, U.S. Energy Information Administration, 2014, http://www.eia.gov/cfapps/ipdbproject/iedindex3.cfm?tid=5&pid=5&aid=2&cid=regions&syid=2012&eyid=2012&unit=TBPD (accessed July 1, 2014)

Chevron (U.S. based), ExxonMobil (U.S. based), Royal Dutch Shell, and Total (France based).

As developing nations began to mature during the 20th century, many of them created national oil companies (NOCs) that eventually grew to rival the commercial firms. The United States and other countries that embrace capitalism and free enterprise allow private companies to develop and sell natural resources, such as oil. This is not the case in nations where oil is viewed as a commodity best managed by the national government. NOCs are companies that are wholly or majority-owned by the national government. The article "Supermajordämmerung" explains that many of the NOCs were initially very dependent on the Big Oil firms to develop and process their oil resources. Over time, however, the NOCs grew into powerful industry forces that operate much more independently. As of 2014, some of the most notable NOCs were:

- Abu Dhabi National Oil Corporation (United Arab Emirates)
- CNOOC (China)
- Gazprom (Russia)
- Iraqi Oil Ministry (Iraq)
- Kuwait Petroleum Corporation (Kuwait)
- National Iranian Oil Company (Iran)
- Nigerian National Petroleum (Nigeria)
- PDVSA (Venezuela)
- Pemex (Mexico)
- Petrobras (Brazil)
- PetroChina (China)
- Petronas (Malaysia)
- Qatar Petroleum (Qatar)
- Rosneft (Russia)
- Saudi Aramco (Saudi Arabia)
- Sinopec (China)
- Statoil (Norway)

In addition, as of 2014, the Italian government owned about one-third of the shares in Eni, a company based in Italy. This ownership does not technically constitute

FIGURE 2.20

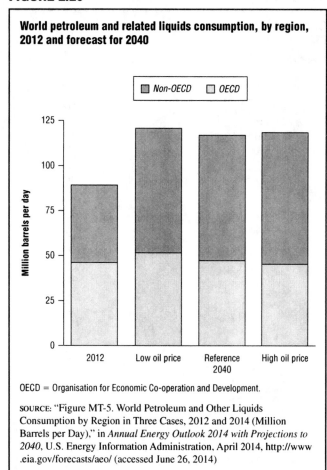

World petroleum and related liquids consumption, by region, 2012 and forecast for 2040

OECD = Organisation for Economic Co-operation and Development.

SOURCE: "Figure MT-5. World Petroleum and Other Liquids Consumption by Region in Three Cases, 2012 and 2014 (Million Barrels per Day)," in *Annual Energy Outlook 2014 with Projections to 2040*, U.S. Energy Information Administration, April 2014, http://www.eia.gov/forecasts/aeo/ (accessed June 26, 2014)

majority control of the company; however, the government's shares are "golden shares," meaning it has special powers over how the company is managed.

OIL PRICES

When discussing oil prices, it is important to understand that there is no single price for a barrel of oil in the marketplace. Instead, analysts and investors monitor several benchmark prices. Table 2.6 shows various prices for crude oil and for liquid fuels produced from crude oil between the first quarter of 2013 and the first quarter of 2014. The West Texas intermediate spot average for crude oil was around $98 per barrel as of the first quarter 2014. West Texas intermediate oil is a light sweet grade, and its price serves as a reference point for other U.S. oil prices. Another benchmark price of note is the Brent spot average. It represents a light sweet crude oil sourced from the North Sea in northern Europe. As of the first quarter of 2014, the Brent spot price for crude oil was around $108 per barrel. The two other crude oil prices shown in Table 2.6 are the imported average (the average price of a barrel of crude oil imported to the United States) and the refiner average acquisition cost (the average price paid by U.S. refiners for a barrel of crude oil).

Table 2.7 shows crude oil refiner acquisition costs between 1965 and 2013. According to the EIA, in *Monthly Energy Review: June 2014*, the costs include the price of the oil purchased plus transportation costs and fees. The costs are expressed in nominal dollars

TABLE 2.6

Prices for crude oil and petroleum products, first quarter 2013–first quarter 2014

	2013				2014
	1st	2nd	3rd	4th	1st
Crude oil (dollars per barrel)					
West Texas intermediate spot average	94.34	94.10	105.84	97.34	98.75
Brent spot average	112.49	102.58	110.27	109.21	108.17
Imported average	98.71	97.39	103.07	92.95	94.01
Refiner average acquisition cost	101.14	99.45	105.24	95.98	96.77
Liquid fuels (cents per gallon)					
Refiner prices for resale					
Gasoline	289	290	288	259	272
Diesel fuel	312	295	306	299	303
Heating oil	308	276	295	296	303
Refiner prices to end users					
Jet fuel	316	287	298	294	297
No. 6 residual fuel oil[a]	252	243	247	250	249
Retail prices including taxes					
Gasoline regular grade[b]	357	360	357	329	340
Gasoline all grades[b]	363	367	364	337	348
On-highway diesel fuel	403	388	391	387	396
Heating oil	389	365	366	373	397

Prices are not adjusted for inflation.
[a]Average for all sulfur contents.
[b]Average self-service cash price.
Notes: Prices exclude taxes unless otherwise noted.

SOURCE: Adapted from "Table 2. U.S. Energy Prices," in *Short-Term Energy Outlook, June 2014*, U.S. Energy Information Administration, June 10, 2014, http://www.eia.gov/forecasts/steo/archives/jun14.pdf (accessed July 1, 2014)

TABLE 2.7

Crude oil refiner acquisition costs, selected years 1965–2013

[Dollars per barrel]

| | Refiner acquisition cost | | |
	Domestic	Imported	Composite
1950 average	NA	NA	NA
1955 average	NA	NA	NA
1960 average	NA	NA	NA
1965 average	NA	NA	NA
1970 average	3.46^E	2.96^E	3.40^E
1975 average	8.39	13.93	10.38
1980 average	24.23	33.89	28.07
1985 average	26.66	26.99	26.75
1990 average	22.59	21.76	22.22
1995 average	17.33	17.14	17.23
2000 average	29.11	27.70	28.26
2001 average	24.33	22.00	22.95
2002 average	24.65	23.71	24.10
2003 average	29.82	27.71	28.53
2004 average	38.97	35.90	36.98
2005 average	52.94	48.86	50.24
2006 average	62.62	59.02	60.24
2007 average	69.65	67.04	67.94
2008 average	98.47	92.77	94.74
2009 average	59.49	59.17	59.29
2010 average	78.01	75.86	76.69
2011 average	100.71	102.63	101.87
2012 average	100.72	101.09	100.93
2013 average	102.91	98.11	100.49

NA = Not available. E = Estimate.

Notes: Prices are in nominal dollars; they are not adjusted for inflation. Annual averages are the averages of the monthly prices, weighted by volume. Geographic coverage is the 50 states, the District of Columbia, Puerto Rico, the Virgin Islands, and all U.S. Territories and Possessions.

SOURCE: Adapted from "Table 9.1. Crude Oil Price Summary (Dollars per Barrel)," in *Monthly Energy Review: June 2014*, U.S. Energy Information Administration, June 25, 2014, http://www.eia.gov/totalenergy/data/monthly/archive/00351406.pdf (accessed June 27, 2014)

(current to that year), which do not take into account the effects of inflation over time. Refiner acquisition costs grew steadily through 2008. As noted in Chapter 1, the United States suffered a severe economic downturn called the Great Recession, which lasted from December 2007 to June 2009. Consumer demand dropped severely during that period. Correspondingly, refiner acquisition costs plummeted to less than $60 per barrel in 2009, but then rebounded to around $100 per barrel over subsequent years.

Gasoline Prices

As noted earlier, motor gasoline has historically accounted for nearly half of total petroleum products supplied each year. Thus, the price of gasoline is very dependent on crude oil prices. In "Gasoline and Diesel Fuel Update" (October 27, 2014, http://www.eia.gov/petroleum/gasdiesel), the EIA provides the following average breakdown of costs for each gallon of regular gasoline that was sold to consumers in September 2014:

- Crude oil—64% of total
- Refining—14% of total
- Taxes—13% of total
- Distribution and marketing—10% of total

A similar breakdown is provided by the EIA for diesel fuel in September 2014:

- Crude oil—58% of total
- Distribution and marketing—17% of total
- Taxes—13% of total
- Refining—12% of total

It should be noted that the individual amounts sum to more than 100% due to rounding.

Table 2.8 shows average annual gasoline and diesel prices for selected years between 1950 and 2013 and monthly prices for January to May 2014. Different gasoline grades and formulations are represented. The prices are in nominal dollars, meaning they are not adjusted for inflation. Gasoline and diesel prices have more than doubled since 2000.

Oil Pricing Factors

As is true for all commodities, oil pricing is dependent on supply and demand factors. In general, when demand outpaces supply, prices go up. Likewise, when supply outpaces demand, prices go down. Higher prices encourage oil producers to produce more. They may start new wells that are more expensive to operate due to higher developmental and operational expenses, for example, wells in off-shore and remote areas. Higher prices, however, tend to spur consumers to cut back on their petroleum consumption. This demand drop can then push prices lower. Energy markets are quite complex, and this is particularly true for oil because so much of it is imported into the United States. In addition, the U.S. government takes actions that affect the oil markets and hence oil pricing.

WEATHER CONDITIONS. The demand for petroleum products varies. Heating oil demand rises during the winter. A cold spell, which leads to a sharp rise in demand, may result in a corresponding price increase. A warm winter may be reflected in lower prices as suppliers try to clear out their inventory. Gasoline demand rises during the summer—people drive more for recreation—so gas prices rise as a consequence.

Weather disasters, such as Hurricane Katrina along the Gulf Coast during the summer of 2005, can disrupt production and refining capabilities and temporarily raise oil and petroleum product prices.

FOREIGN UNREST. Wars and other types of political unrest in oil-producing nations add volatility to petroleum prices, which fluctuate—sometimes dramatically—depending on the situation at the time. In *IEA Response System for Oil Supply Emergencies* (June 2012, http://www.iea.org/publications/freepublications/publication/EPPD_Brochure_English_2012_02.pdf), the IEA describes events that have occurred since the last half of the 20th century that have caused major disruptions in the world's

TABLE 2.8

Retail motor gasoline and highway diesel fuel prices, selected years 1950–2013 and January–May 2014

[Dollars[a] per gallon, including taxes]

| | Platt's/Bureau of Labor Statistics data | | | | U.S. Energy Information Administration data | | | |
| | Motor gasoline by grade | | | | Regular motor gasoline by area type | | | |
	Leaded regular	Unleaded regular	Unleaded premium[b]	All grades[c]	Conventional gasoline areas[d]	Reformulated gasoline areas[e]	All areas	On-highway diesel fuel
1950 average	0.268	NA	NA	NA	—	—	—	—
1955 average	0.291	NA	NA	NA	—	—	—	—
1960 average	0.311	NA	NA	NA	—	—	—	—
1965 average	0.312	NA	NA	NA	—	—	—	—
1970 average	0.357	NA	NA	NA	—	—	—	—
1975 average	0.567	NA	NA	NA	—	—	—	—
1980 average	1.191	1.245	NA	1.221	—	—	—	—
1985 average	1.115	1.202	1.340	1.196	—	—	—	—
1990 average	1.149	1.164	1.349	1.217	NA	NA	NA	NA
1995 average	—	1.147	1.336	1.205	1.103	1.163	1.111	1.109
2000 average	—	1.510	1.693	1.563	1.462	1.543	1.484	1.491
2001 average	—	1.461	1.657	1.531	1.384	1.498	1.420	1.401
2002 average	—	1.358	1.556	1.441	1.313	1.408	1.345	1.319
2003 average	—	1.591	1.777	1.638	1.516	1.655	1.561	1.509
2004 average	—	1.880	2.068	1.923	1.812	1.937	1.852	1.810
2005 average	—	2.295	2.491	2.338	2.240	2.335	2.270	2.402
2006 average	—	2.589	2.805	2.635	2.533	2.654	2.572	2.705
2007 average	—	2.801	3.033	2.849	2.767	2.857	2.796	2.885
2008 average	—	3.266	3.519	3.317	3.213	3.314	3.246	3.803
2009 average	—	2.350	2.607	2.401	2.315	2.433	2.353	2.467
2010 average	—	2.788	3.047	2.836	2.742	2.864	2.782	2.992
2011 average	—	3.527	3.792	3.577	3.476	3.616	3.521	3.840
2012 average	—	3.644	3.922	3.695	3.552	3.757	3.618	3.968
2013 average	—	3.526	3.843	3.584	3.443	3.635	3.505	3.922
2014								
January	—	3.320	3.651	3.378	3.252	3.438	3.313	3.893
February	—	3.364	3.694	3.422	3.305	3.464	3.356	3.984
March	—	3.532	3.858	3.590	3.474	3.658	3.533	4.001
April	—	3.659	3.986	3.717	3.590	3.809	3.661	3.964
May	—	3.691	4.020	3.745	3.601	3.824	3.673	3.943

[a]Prices are not adjusted for inflation.
[b]The 1981 average is based on September through December data only.
[c]Also includes grades of motor gasoline not shown separately.
[d]Any area that does not require the sale of reformulated gasoline.
[e]"Reformulated Gasoline Areas" are ozone nonattainment areas designated by the U.S. Environmental Protection Agency that require the use of reformulated gasoline (RFG). Areas are reclassified each time a shift in or out of an RFG program occurs due to federal or state regulations.
NA = Not available.
— = Not applicable.
Notes: Geographic coverage: for columns 1–4, current coverage is 85 urban areas; for columns 5–7, coverage is the 50 states and the District of Columbia; for column 8, coverage is the 48 contiguous states and the District of Columbia.

SOURCE: Adapted from "Table 9.4. Retail Motor Gasoline and On-Highway Diesel Fuel Prices (Dollars per Gallon, Including Taxes)," in *Monthly Energy Review: June 2014*, U.S. Energy Information Administration, http://www.eia.gov/totalenergy/data/monthly/archive/00351406.pdf (accessed June 27, 2014)

oil supply. Most of the events were wars or other violent upheavals in the Middle East, including the war in Iraq in 2003 and a revolution in Libya in 2011.

FOREIGN PRICE MANIPULATION. Some top oil-producing countries have used their market power to manipulate oil prices upward for their own economic and political benefit. They do this by limiting the amount of oil they produce and/or export. Diminished supply (unless accompanied by diminished demand) increases the prices that buyers must pay. As described earlier, OPEC members and other oil-producing countries used their collective clout during the oil embargo of the 1970s.

At other times, OPEC has used production quotas to put upward pressure on prices. This approach, however, sometimes backfires. For example, high oil prices during

the late 1970s to the mid-1980s encouraged conservation, which reduced demand for oil and led to a sharp decline in oil prices. As a result of the decreased demand for oil and lower prices, OPEC lost some of its ability to control its members and, consequently, prices. In addition, OPEC has faced increased competition since the 1970s from nonmember nations, such as Canada, Mexico, and Russia, that have expanded their oil production activities. Nevertheless, OPEC actions can still influence the worldwide petroleum market and the U.S. market. According to the EIA, in *Monthly Energy Review: June 2014*, the United States obtained 37.8% of its imported oil from OPEC in 2013.

GOVERNMENT INTERVENTION. U.S. government actions also affect oil pricing. Taxes push oil prices upward. For example, as noted earlier taxes accounted on average for 13% of the cost of each gallon of gasoline sold in September 2014. Other government actions push oil prices downward, mainly financial incentives, such as tax breaks and subsidies, which encourage domestic oil (and natural gas) production. As shown in Figure 1.14 in Chapter 1, the fossil fuel industry as a whole has long enjoyed these kinds of incentives, which totaled around $3 billion in fiscal year 2013. (See Table 1.6 in Chapter 1.)

The oil industry also benefits from liability limits on oil spills. Quinn Bowman explains in "Oil Spill Liability a Complicated Legal Web" (PBS.org, June 7, 2010) that the Oil Pollution Act, as amended in 1990, limits to $75 million the damages that a responsible party must pay to "make up for lost economic activity, lost tax revenue and damage to natural resources as a result of an oil spill" from an offshore facility. (Note that the costs of "cleaning up and containing" spilled oil are separate costs and have no limit.) Bowman, however, indicates that the $75 million damages limit does not apply if the responsible party is found to have committed "gross negligence, willful misconduct or a failure to comply with operating or safety regulations."

In addition, federal law limits liability amounts for tankers that spill oil in U.S. waters. In "Limits of Liability" (October 22, 2013, http://www.uscg.mil/npfc/Response/RPs/limits_of_liability.asp), the U.S. Coast Guard notes that the limits vary based on the type and tonnage of the vessels involved.

Critics suggest that all the oil spill liability limits are too low given the enormous economic and ecological consequences that a large oil spill can cause. Other provisions, however, are in place to help pay for damages from an oil spill. One is the Oil Spill Liability Trust Fund, which was created by Congress in 1986. According to the U.S. Coast Guard, in "The Oil Spill Liability Trust Fund" (October 22, 2013, http://www.uscg.mil/npfc/About_NPFC/osltf.asp), the fund contained more than $1 billion in October 2013. Over the decades oil industry companies have sometimes been required to pay (depending on changing federal laws) into the fund via taxes on oil products. As of 2014, the tax was $0.08 per barrel of oil produced domestically or imported into the United States. The rate is scheduled to stay at this level until 2017, when it will increase to $0.09 per barrel.

ENVIRONMENTAL ISSUES

Environmental concerns related to the oil industry primarily involve the extraction, transport, refining, and combustion stages. Extraction impacts the environment via invasive drilling and mining to find and remove oil deposits. Crude oil is transported daily across the world's oceans and through a near-global network of pipelines. Although large spills during drilling and transport are relatively rare, when they do occur they have devastating environmental and economic effects. Oil refining and the combustion of petroleum products have air quality impacts due to the release of contaminants such as carbon monoxide, nitrogen dioxide, sulfur dioxide, volatile organic compounds, and particulate matter. In addition, the combustion of oil, a carbon-rich fossil fuel, contributes to global warming and related climate change.

Oil Spills

In recent decades, the modern oil industry has experienced some environmental failures with serious consequences. Two of the most well-known events are the *Exxon Valdez* spill of 1989 and the BP spill in the Gulf of Mexico in 2010.

On March 24, 1989, the oil tanker *Exxon Valdez* hit a reef in Alaska and spilled 11 million gallons (41.6 million L) of crude oil into the waters of Prince William Sound. The spill was an environmental disaster for a formerly pristine area. Exxon was originally levied a $5 billion fine for damages, but that amount was later reduced by the U.S. Supreme Court to about $500 million.

The BP spill happened after an offshore oil platform located 40 miles (64 km) from the Louisiana coast exploded on April 20, 2010, and killed 11 workers. Engineers were unable to quickly cap the well on the ocean floor, which was about 1 mile (1.6 km) under the water's surface. Over a period of nearly three months millions of barrels of crude oil gushed into the Gulf, damaging the aquatic ecosystem and harming the area's fisheries and tourism industries. In November 2012 the U.S. government imposed a $4 billion fine on BP for damages. In addition, two BP oil rig supervisors were charged with manslaughter. The company and its business partners in the oil rig venture still faced private court cases and potentially billions of dollars more in damages. As of October 2014, the spill was considered to be the worst oil spill in U.S. history.

CHAPTER 3
NATURAL GAS

In 1821 William A. Hart, a gunsmith, drilled a well down 27 feet (8 m) and found a reservoir of natural gas in Fredonia, New York. This was the first successful modern natural gas well and resulted in the formation of the first U.S. natural gas company. Natural gas soon became popular as a fuel source for city street lighting, but by the start of the 20th century it had been largely supplanted in this capacity by electricity. Following World War II (1939–1945), the United States constructed a massive pipeline network to carry natural gas to individual homes and businesses. The fuel is available in large amounts domestically at low prices and is widely used in industrial applications and for producing electricity.

UNDERSTANDING NATURAL GAS

The term *natural gas* refers to a gaseous mixture of hydrocarbon compounds, mainly methane. This mixture is found naturally in certain geological formations and can be manufactured in relatively small quantities.

Naturally derived natural gas falls into two categories, depending on its means of formation. Thermogenic natural gas results from the actions of pressure and heat over millions of years on prehistoric aquatic microorganisms. Thus, it is a fossil fuel. Biogenic natural gas results from the decomposition of organic (carbon-containing) matter by bacteria. This process can happen relatively quickly and is not limited to underground spaces; in fact, biogenic natural gas forms in landfills that contain organic garbage. When it is found underground, biogenic natural gas is typically at much shallower depths than thermogenic natural gas.

Thermogenic Natural Gas

Thermogenic natural gas can be further categorized based on its geological source as conventional gas, coalbed methane, shale gas, or tight sand gas. (See Figure 3.1.)

CONVENTIONAL NATURAL GAS. Conventional natural gas, like crude oil, formed from prehistoric microscopic organisms that were converted to hydrocarbons deep underground by millennia of intense pressures and high temperatures. The gas was baked and squeezed more intensely than the crude oil. Thus, the hydrocarbons in natural gas are smaller and lighter than those found in crude oil and are in a gaseous state. Methane, ethane, and propane are the primary constituents of natural gas, with methane making up the vast majority of the total. Once formed, crude oil and natural gas migrated away from their source rocks and toward the surface until they were either trapped beneath a nonporous rock formation (the seal shown in Figure 3.1) or seeped out into the open air. Conventional natural gas trapped above oil pools is called associated gas, while conventional natural gas found by itself is called nonassociated gas.

COALBED METHANE. Coalbed methane is methane gas that naturally occurs as coal is formed. Coal is a dense solid fossil fuel that contains heavy hydrocarbons. In "Natural Gas: Definitions, Sources and Explanatory Notes" (2014, http://www.eia.gov/dnav/ng/TblDefs/ng_prod_coalbed_tbldef2.asp), the U.S. Energy Information Administration (EIA) within the U.S. Department of Energy notes that coalbed methane is trapped within the coal microstructure, but can be liberated and brought to the surface.

SHALE GAS. Shale is a dark dense type of sedimentary rock that is made up of fine tightly packed grains. Shale that contains high concentrations of organic matter is sometimes called black shale. Some shale formations contain significant accumulations of natural gas. The natural gas originally formed within the shale and became trapped in its pores. The gas is typically liberated by a process called hydraulic fracturing (fracking), which is described in Chapter 2.

FIGURE 3.1

Schematic geology of natural gas resources

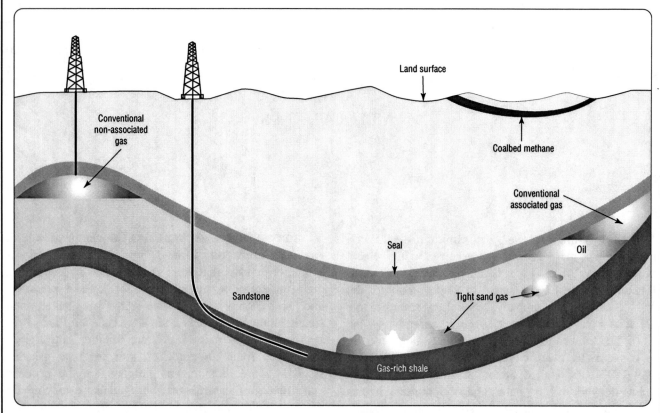

SOURCE: "Schematic Geology of Natural Gas Resources," in *Natural Gas Explained: Where Our Natural Gas Comes From*, U.S. Energy Information Administration, June 26, 2012, http://www.eia.gov/energyexplained/images/charts/NatGasSchematic-large.jpg (accessed July 19, 2014)

TIGHT SAND GAS. In *Annual Energy Review 2011* (September 2012, http://www.eia.gov/totalenergy/data/annual/pdf/aer.pdf), the EIA defines tight sand gas as "natural gas produced from a non-shale formation with extremely low permeability." Tight sand gas is found in sandstone, a type of sedimentary rock that is made up of sand-sized particles. (See Figure 3.1.) Sandstone is more porous than shale, but still typically requires fracking to release the natural gas that is trapped within it. Tight sand gas, or tight gas, is believed to have originated from the same thermogenic processes that produced conventional gas.

Natural Gas Deposits

Like crude oil deposits, natural gas deposits are found only in certain geological formations. Regions and countries that are known to have large natural gas deposits include North America, Russia, the Middle East, and northwestern Europe. Many of the earth's deposits are offshore (i.e., they lie beneath the oceans). Figure 2.2 and Figure 2.3 in Chapter 2 show the extent of offshore underground lands to which the United States claims exclusive rights to extract resources, such as crude oil

and natural gas. Many U.S. natural gas deposits lie in the nation's outer continental shelf, the outermost reaches of the continental shelf that are under federal control.

Estimates of the amounts of natural gas deposits that have not yet been extracted are provided in Chapter 7, along with information about natural gas exploration and development activities.

Measuring Natural Gas

In the United States natural gas volumes are measured in cubic feet. Because a cubic foot is a relatively small unit of measure, natural gas data are often presented in units of billion cubic feet (bcf) or trillion cubic feet (tcf). In countries that rely on the metric system, the cubic meter is the preferred unit for measuring natural gas volumes. Thus, natural gas data are typically expressed in units of billion cubic meters (bcm) or trillion cubic meters (tcm).

NATURAL GAS EXTRACTION

In many cases natural gas is extracted like crude oil, that is, via deeply drilled wells. The EIA notes in *Monthly*

FIGURE 3.2

The natural gas industry

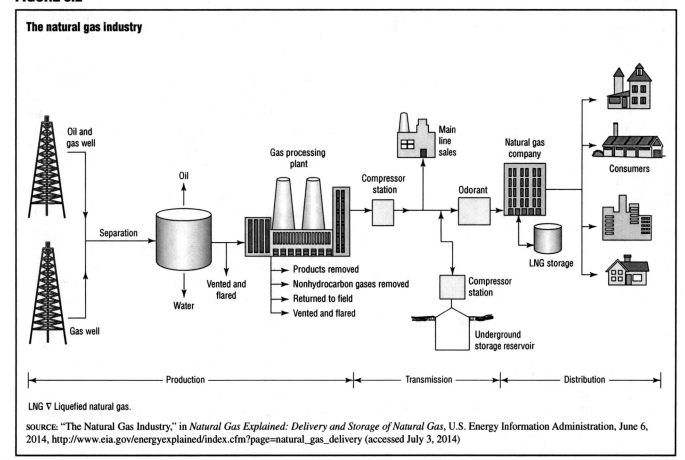

LNG ∇ Liquefied natural gas.

SOURCE: "The Natural Gas Industry," in *Natural Gas Explained: Delivery and Storage of Natural Gas*, U.S. Energy Information Administration, June 6, 2014, http://www.eia.gov/energyexplained/index.cfm?page=natural_gas_delivery (accessed July 3, 2014)

Energy Review: June 2014 (June 2014, http://www.eia .gov/totalenergy/data/monthly/archive/00351406.pdf) that an average of 383 rotary wells were in operation in 2013 solely for natural gas production. In addition, the agency indicates that some oil wells "productively encounter both crude oil and natural gas." (See Figure 3.2.) The number of total wells in operation fluctuates from year to year because new wells are opened and old wells are closed. Weather and economic conditions also affect well operations.

Natural gas is also extracted via fracking, as shown in Figure 2.7 in Chapter 2. This technology has only been used for a few decades and is highly controversial because it requires large amounts of water and could allow natural gas to seep into and contaminate aquifers (underground freshwater pools).

PROCESSING AND TRANSPORTING NATURAL GAS

Most natural gas that is extracted from deep underground is considered "wet" because it contains water vapor and hydrocarbons that easily liquefy at the cooler temperatures found above ground. The hydrocarbon liquids include lease condensate and natural gas plant liquids (NGPL). Lease condensate is a liquid mix of

heavy hydrocarbons that are recovered during natural gas processing at a lease, or field separation, facility. NGPL are a mixture of compounds such as propane and butane that are recovered as liquids at facilities later in the processing stage.

Consumer-grade natural gas is "dry," which means that it has been processed to remove water vapor, nonhydrocarbon gases (such as helium and nitrogen), and lease condensate and NGPL. (See Figure 3.2.) The dry gas flows into a compressor station. In *Natural Gas Compressor Stations on the Interstate Pipeline Network: Developments since 1996* (November 2007, http://www.eia.gov/ pub/oil_gas/natural_gas/analysis_publications/ngcompressor/ ngcompressor.pdf), the EIA states "the purpose of a compressor station is to boost the pressure in a natural gas pipeline and move the natural gas further downstream." There are more than a thousand compressor stations located along the nation's massive natural gas pipeline network. In addition, the network includes multiple underground storage reservoirs.

Underground Storage

Because of seasonal, daily, and even hourly changes in demand, substantial natural gas storage facilities have been created. Many are depleted natural gas reservoirs that are located near transmission lines and marketing

TABLE 3.1

Natural gas in underground storage, selected years 1955–2013

[Volumes in billion cubic feet]

| | Natural gas in underground storage, end of period | | |
	Base gas	Working gas	Total
1955 Total	863	505	1,368
1960 Total	NA	NA	2,184
1965 Total	1,848	1,242	3,090
1970 Total	2,326	1,678	4,004
1975 Total	3,162	2,212	5,374
1980 Total	3,642	2,655	6,297
1985 Total	3,842	2,607	6,448
1990 Total	3,868	3,068	6,936
1995 Total	4,349	2,153	6,503
2000 Total	4,352	1,719	6,071
2001 Total	4,301	2,904	7,204
2002 Total	4,340	2,375	6,715
2003 Total	4,303	2,563	6,866
2004 Total	4,201	2,696	6,897
2005 Total	4,200	2,635	6,835
2006 Total	4,211	3,070	7,281
2007 Total	4,234	2,879	7,113
2008 Total	4,232	2,840	7,073
2009 Total	4,277	3,130	7,407
2010 Total	4,301	3,111	7,412
2011 Total	4,302	3,462	7,764
2012 Total	4,372	3,413	7,785
2013 Total	4,365	2,890	7,255

NA = Not available.

Notes: Through 1964, all volumes are shown on a pressure base of 14.65 psia (pounds per square inch absolute) at 60° Fahrenheit; beginning in 1965, the pressure base is 14.73 psia at 60° Fahrenheit. Totals may not equal sum of components due to independent rounding. Geographic coverage is the 50 states and the District of Columbia (except Alaska, which is excluded through 2012).

SOURCE: Adapted from "Table 4.4. Natural Gas in Underground Storage (Volumes in Billion Cubic Feet)," in *Monthly Energy Review: June 2014*, U.S. Energy Information Administration, June 25, 2014, http://www.eia.gov/totalenergy/data/monthly/archive/00351406.pdf (accessed June 27, 2014)

areas. Gas is injected into storage when the produced supply exceeds demand, and withdrawn from storage when it is needed. Table 3.1 shows the amount of natural gas that was in underground storage between 1955 and 2013. It consisted of base gas (permanently stored gas needed to maintain the proper pressure in the storage area) and working gas (gas that can be released from storage and used). At year-end 2013, nearly 7.3 tcf (205.4 bcm) was in storage, including 4.4 tcf (123.6 bcm) of base gas and 2.9 tcf (81.8 bcm) of working gas.

According to the EIA, in "Underground Natural Gas Storage Capacity" (September 30, 2014, http://www.eia .gov/dnav/ng/ng_stor_cap_dcu_NUS_m.htm), there were 418 storage fields in the U.S. natural gas pipeline network as of July 2014, with a total capacity of 9.2 tcf (260.6 bcm).

Facilitating Natural Gas Transport and Usage

The physical state of natural gas is sometimes changed to facilitate its transport and usage. For example, a volume of natural gas can be compressed under high pressure so that it takes up less space. The EIA (2014, http://www.eia.gov/tools/glossary/index.cfm?id=C) indicates that natural gas can be compressed to a pressure

at or above 2,900 to 3,600 pounds per square inch and stored in "high-pressure containers." Compressed natural gas (CNG) is used as a fuel for vehicles that burn natural gas.

Natural gas can also be liquefied by cooling it to a very cold temperature. In "What Is LNG" (April 29, 2014, http://www.eia.gov/energyexplained/index.cfm? page=natural_gas_lng), the EIA explains that a liquefied volume of natural gas takes up far less space than the same volume of natural gas in a gaseous state. Liquefied natural gas (LNG) can be moved long distances, such as across the oceans, for importation and exportation. Liquefaction is an energy-intensive process in that a lot of energy is required to cool the natural gas to the liquefaction temperature, which is around −260 degrees Fahrenheit (−162 degrees Celsius). LNG can be transported or stored in tanks and returned to a gaseous state, as needed, by heating it above the liquefaction temperature.

Another storage alternative for natural gas involves the use of porous carbon materials. The gas can be tightly packed into the numerous tiny pores because the gas molecules adsorb (adhere in thin compressed layers) to the pore walls. As of 2014, adsorbed natural gas (ANG) containers were still mostly in the research and development stage. For example, the Department of Energy's Advanced Research Projects Agency (2014, http://www.arpa-e.energy.gov/?q=slick-sheet-project/ low-pressure-material-based-natural-gas-fuel-system) indicates that in 2012 the Ford Motor Company was given a $5 million government grant for a three-year project devoted to developing an ANG tank for vehicles.

Transmission and Distribution

A vast network of natural gas pipelines crisscrosses the mainland United States. In "About U.S. Natural Gas Pipelines" (2014, http://www.eia.gov/pub/oil_gas/natural _gas/analysis_publications/ngpipeline/index.html), the EIA provides a map of this network. The agency also notes that the natural gas in this 305,000-mile (491,000-km) system generally flows northeastward, primarily from Texas and Louisiana, the two major gas-producing states, and from Oklahoma and New Mexico. It also flows west to California.

In its original state, natural gas is odorless. As such, an odorant is added to it before it is sold to consumers. (See Figure 3.2.) This odorant, which smells like rotten eggs, helps people notice when natural gas is leaking around their homes or businesses so they can take action quickly by cutting off the gas flow. This safety precaution is necessary because natural gas is highly flammable and can cause tremendous explosions when ignited.

TABLE 3.2

Natural gas withdrawals, production, trade, and consumption, selected years 1950–2013

[Billion cubic feet]

	Gross withdrawals[a]	Marketed production (wet)[b]	NGPL production[c]	Dry gas production[d]	Supplemental gaseous fuels	Trade			Net storage withdrawals[e]	Balancing item[f]	Consumption
						Imports	Exports	Net imports			
1950 Total	8,480	6,282[g]	260	6,022[g]	NA	0	26	−26	−54	−175	5,767
1955 Total	11,720	9,405[g]	377	9,029[g]	NA	11	31	−20	−68	−247	8,694
1960 Total	15,088	12,771[g]	543	12,228[g]	NA	156	11	144	−132	−274	11,967
1965 Total	17,963	16,040[g]	753	15,286[g]	NA	456	26	430	−118	−319	15,280
1970 Total	23,786	21,921[g]	906	21,014[g]	NA	821	70	751	−398	−228	21,139
1975 Total	21,104	20,109[g]	872	19,236[g]	NA	953	73	880	−344	−235	19,538
1980 Total	21,870	20,180	777	19,403	155	985	49	936	23	−640	19,877
1985 Total	19,607	17,270	816	16,454	126	950	55	894	235	−428	17,281
1990 Total	21,523	18,594	784	17,810	123	1,532	86	1,447	−513	307	19,174
1995 Total	23,744	19,506	908	18,599	110	2,841	154	2,687	415	396	22,207
2000 Total	24,174	20,198	1,016	19,182	90	3,782	244	3,538	829	−306	23,333
2001 Total	24,501	20,570	954	19,616	86	3,977	373	3,604	−1,166	99	22,239
2002 Total	23,941	19,885	957	18,928	68	4,015	516	3,499	467	65	23,027
2003 Total	24,119	19,974	876	19,099	68	3,944	680	3,264	−197	44	22,277
2004 Total	23,970	19,517	927	18,591	60	4,259	854	3,404	−114	461	22,403
2005 Total	23,457	18,927	876	18,051	64	4,341	729	3,612	52	236	22,014
2006 Total	23,535	19,410	906	18,504	66	4,186	724	3,462	−436	103	21,699
2007 Total	24,664	20,196	930	19,266	63	4,608	822	3,785	192	−203	23,104
2008 Total	25,636	21,112	953	20,159	61	3,984	963	3,021	34	2	23,277
2009 Total	26,057	21,648	1,024	20,624	65	3,751	1,072	2,679	−355	−103	22,910
2010 Total	26,816	22,382	1,066	21,316	65	3,741	1,137	2,604	−13	115	24,087
2011 Total	28,479	24,036	1,134	22,902	60	3,469	1,506	1,963	−354	−94	24,477
2012 Total	29,542	25,308	1,250	24,058	61	3,138	1,619	1,519	−9	−96	25,533
2013 Total	30,171	25,616[E]	1,335	24,282[E]	57	2,883	1,572	1,311	549	−161[R]	26,037[R]

[a]Gases withdrawn from natural gas, crude oil, coalbed, and shale gas wells. Includes natural gas, natural gas plant liquids, and nonhydrocarbon gases; but excludes lease condensate.
[b]Gross withdrawals minus repressuring, nonhydrocarbon gases removed, and vented and flared.
[c]Natural gas plant liquids (NGPL) production, gaseous equivalent. This data series was previously called "Extraction Loss."
[d]Marketed production (wet) minus NGPL production.
[e]Net withdrawals from underground storage. For 1980–2012, also includes net withdrawals of liquefied natural gas in above-ground tanks.
[f]Beginning in 1980, excludes transit shipments that cross the U.S.-Canada border (i.e., natural gas delivered to its destination via the other country).
[g]Through 1979, may include unknown quantities of nonhydrocarbon gases.
R = Revised. E = Estimate. (s) = Less than 0.5 billion cubic feet and greater than −0.5 billion cubic feet. NA = Not available.
Notes: Through 1964, all volumes are shown on a pressure base of 14.65 psia (pounds per square inch absolute) at 60° Fahrenheit; beginning in 1965, the pressure base is 14.73 psia at 60° Fahrenheit. Totals may not equal sum of components due to independent rounding. Geographic coverage is the 50 states and the District of Columbia (except Alaska, for which underground storage is excluded from "Net Storage Withdrawals" through 2012).

SOURCE: Adapted from "Table 4.1. Natural Gas Overview (Billion Cubic Feet)," in *Monthly Energy Review: June 2014*, U.S. Energy Information Administration, June 25, 2014, http://www.eia.gov/totalenergy/data/monthly/archive/00351406.pdf (accessed June 27, 2014)

DOMESTIC WITHDRAWALS AND PRODUCTION

Table 3.2 shows natural gas gross withdrawals and production data between 1950 and 2013. The withdrawals include gas from natural gas, crude oil, coalbed, and shale gas wells. They totaled 30.2 tcf (854.3 bcm) in 2013 and provided 24.3 tcf (687.6 bcm) of dry gas for consumers. In addition, 1.3 tcf (37.8 bcm) of NGPL was produced during natural gas processing.

Overall, dry gas production climbed dramatically from 1949 through the early 1970s and then fell through the mid-1980s. (See Figure 3.3.) It then rose at a moderate rate through the beginning of the 21st century before sharply increasing. The uptick is due almost entirely to shale gas, which is being extracted from the same basins that provide the tight oil, as described in Chapter 2. Figure 2.10 in Chapter 2 shows a map of the six basins that accounted for 100% of domestic natural gas production growth between 2011 and 2013. The Marcellus, Haynesville, and Eagle Ford basins have been particularly productive. As shown in Figure 3.4, natural gas production from the Marcellus basin soared from less than 1 bcf/day (0.03 bcm/day) in 2007 to more than 14 bcf/day (0.4 bcm/day) in 2014.

Figure 3.5 provides a breakdown of domestic production by source dating back to 1990. Through the 1990s onshore conventional gas wells in the lower 48 states were the largest source of U.S. natural gas. Offshore wells in the lower 48 states and tight gas plays were also major contributors. Very small amounts of natural gas were obtained from Alaskan wells, coalbeds, and shale. The situation changed dramatically after the turn of the century, when shale gas production rose significantly. In *Annual Energy Outlook 2014 with Projections to 2040* (April 2014, http://www.eia.gov/forecasts/aeo/pdf/0383(2014).pdf), the EIA indicates that in 2012 shale gas accounted for 9.7 tcf (274.7 bcm), or 40% of total U.S. natural gas production.

IMPORTS AND EXPORTS

As shown in Table 3.2, domestic dry gas production met or nearly met U.S. consumption through the mid-1980s;

FIGURE 3.3

Natural gas market overview, 1949–2013

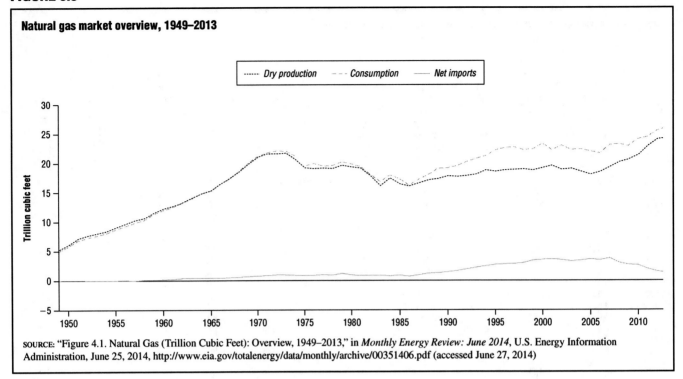

------- Dry production   — — Consumption   ········· Net imports

SOURCE: "Figure 4.1. Natural Gas (Trillion Cubic Feet): Overview, 1949–2013," in *Monthly Energy Review: June 2014*, U.S. Energy Information Administration, June 25, 2014, http://www.eia.gov/totalenergy/data/monthly/archive/00351406.pdf (accessed June 27, 2014)

FIGURE 3.4

Natural gas production from Marcellus basin, 2007–14

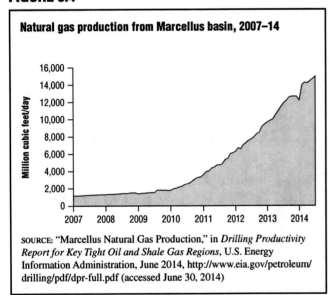

SOURCE: "Marcellus Natural Gas Production," in *Drilling Productivity Report for Key Tight Oil and Shale Gas Regions*, U.S. Energy Information Administration, June 2014, http://www.eia.gov/petroleum/drilling/pdf/dpr-full.pdf (accessed June 30, 2014)

FIGURE 3.5

Natural gas production, by source, 1990–2012 and forecast through 2040

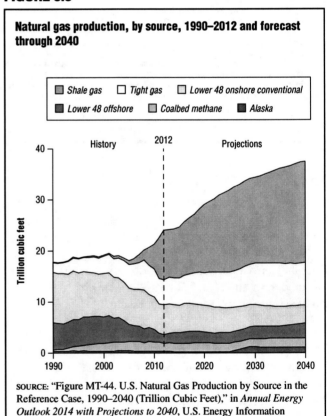

SOURCE: "Figure MT-44. U.S. Natural Gas Production by Source in the Reference Case, 1990–2040 (Trillion Cubic Feet)," in *Annual Energy Outlook 2014 with Projections to 2040*, U.S. Energy Information Administration, April 2014, http://www.eia.gov/forecasts/aeo/ (accessed June 26, 2014)

thus, little natural gas was imported. Thereafter, consumption began to outpace production, and the volume of imported natural gas increased as well. Natural gas imports peaked at 4.6 tcf (130.5 bcm) in 2007 before falling as the U.S. shale gas boom unfolded. In 2013 the United States imported nearly 2.9 tcf (81.6 bcm) of natural gas and exported almost 1.6 tcf (44.5 bcm). Figure 3.3 shows dry production, consumption, and net imports (imports minus exports) between 1949 and 2013. During the first decade of the 21st century the United States dramatically narrowed the gap between its production and consumption of natural gas.

According to the EIA, in *Monthly Energy Review: June 2014*, Canada supplied 2.8 tcf (78.9 bcm), or 97% of the natural gas imported to the United States in 2013.

TABLE 3.3

Natural gas consumption, by sector, selected years 1950–2013

[Billion cubic fee]

			End-use sectors									
				Industrial				Transportation				
			Lease and	Other industrial				Pipelines^d and	Vehicle		Electric power	
	Residential	Commercial^a	plant fuel	CHP^b	Non-CHP^c	Total	Total	distribution^e	fuel	Total	sector^f, g	Total
1950 Total	1,198	388	928	h	2,498	2,498	3,426	126	NA	126	629	5,767
1955 Total	2,124	629	1,131	h	3,411	3,411	4,542	245	NA	245	1,153	8,694
1960 Total	3,103	1,020	1,237	h	4,535	4,535	5,771	347	NA	347	1,725	11,967
1965 Total	3,903	1,444	1,156	h	5,955	5,955	7,112	501	NA	501	2,321	15,280
1970 Total	4,837	2,399	1,399	h	7,851	7,851	9,249	722	NA	722	3,932	21,139
1975 Total	4,924	2,508	1,396	h	6,968	6,968	8,365	583	NA	583	3,158	19,538
1980 Total	4,752	2,611	1,026	h	7,172	7,172	8,198	635	NA	635	3,682	19,877
1985 Total	4,433	2,432	966	h	5,901	5,901	6,867	504	NA	504	3,044	17,281
1990 Total	4,391	2,623	1,236	1,055	5,963^i	7,018^i	8,255	660	(s)	660	3,245^i	19,174^i
1995 Total	4,850	3,031	1,220	1,258	6,906	8,164	9,384	700	5	705	4,237	22,207
2000 Total	4,996	3,182	1,151	1,386	6,757	8,142	9,293	642	13	655	5,206	23,333
2001 Total	4,771	3,023	1,119	1,310	6,035	7,344	8,463	625	15	640	5,342	22,239
2002 Total	4,889	3,144	1,113	1,240	6,287	7,527	8,640	667	15	682	5,672	23,027
2003 Total	5,079	3,179	1,122	1,144	6,007	7,150	8,273	591	18	610	5,135	22,277
2004 Total	4,869	3,129	1,098	1,191	6,066	7,256	8,354	566	21	587	5,464	22,403
2005 Total	4,827	2,999	1,112	1,084	5,518	6,601	7,713	584	23	607	5,869	22,014
2006 Total	4,368	2,832	1,142	1,115	5,412	6,527	7,669	584	24	608	6,222	21,699
2007 Total	4,722	3,013	1,226	1,050	5,604	6,655	7,881	621	25	646	6,841	23,104
2008 Total	4,892	3,153	1,220	955	5,715	6,670	7,890	648	26	674	6,668	23,277
2009 Total	4,779	3,119	1,275	990	5,178	6,167	7,443	670	27	697	6,873	22,910
2010 Total	4,782	3,103	1,286	1,029	5,797	6,826	8,112	674	29	703	7,387	24,087
2011 Total	4,714	3,155	1,323	1,063	5,931	6,994	8,317	688	30	718	7,574	24,477
2012 Total	4,149	2,895	1,396	1,149	6,075	7,224	8,620	728	30	758	9,111	25,533
2013 Total	4,941^R	3,291^R	1,413^E	1,147	6,316	7,463	8,876	743^R, E	33^E	775^E	8,153	26,037^R

^aAll commercial sector fuel use, including that at commercial combined-heat-and-power (CHP) and commercial electricity-only plants.
^bIndustrial combined-heat-and-power (CHP) and a small number of industrial electricity-only plants.
^cAll industrial sector fuel use other than that in "Lease and Plant Fuel" and "CHP."
^dNatural gas consumed in the operation of pipelines, primarily in compressors. Beginning in 2009, includes line loss, which is known volumes of natural gas that are the result of leaks, damage, accidents, migration, and/or blow down.
^eNatural gas used as fuel in the delivery of natural gas to consumers. Beginning in 2009, includes line loss, which is known volumes of natural gas that are the result of leaks, damage, accidents, migration, and/or blow down.
^fThe electric power sector comprises electricity-only and combined-heat-and-power (CHP) plants within the NAICS 22 category whose primary business is to sell electricity, or electricity and heat, to the public.
^gThrough 1988, data are for electric utilities only. Beginning in 1989, data are for electric utilities and independent power producers.
^hIncluded in "Non-CHP."
^iFor 1989–1992, a small amount of consumption at independent power producers may be counted in both "Other Industrial" and "Electric Power Sector."
R = Revised. E = Estimate. NA = Not available. (s) = Less than 500 million cubic feet.
Notes: Data are for natural gas, plus a small amount of supplemental gaseous fuels. Through 1964, all volumes are shown on a pressure base of 14.65 psia (pounds per square inch absolute) at 60° Fahrenheit; beginning in 1965, the pressure base is 14.73 psia at 60° Fahrenheit. Totals may not equal sum of components due to independent rounding. Geographic coverage is the 50 states and the District of Columbia.

SOURCE: Adapted from "Table 4.3. Natural Gas Consumption by Sector (Billion Cubic Feet)," in *Monthly Energy Review: June 2014*, U.S. Energy Information Administration, June 25, 2014, http://www.eia.gov/totalenergy/data/monthly/archve/00351406.pdf (accessed June 27, 2014)

Canada was the largest market for U.S. exports in 2013, receiving 911 bcf (25.8 bcm), or 58% of the total. The remaining exports—661 bcf (18.7 bcm), or 42% of the total—went to Mexico. The EIA notes that most natural gas travels to and from the United States by pipelines; small amounts are exported as LNG or CNG.

DOMESTIC CONSUMPTION

Natural gas fulfills an important part of the country's energy needs. It is an attractive fuel not only because its price is relatively low but also because it burns relatively cleanly and efficiently, which helps the country meet its environmental goals.

Natural gas consumption rose between 1949 and 1972 and then generally declined through 1986. (See Table 3.2 and Figure 3.3.) Since 1986 natural gas consumption has been rising. As shown in Table 3.2, it hit an all-time high of 26 tcf (737.3 bcm) in 2013.

Table 3.3 shows natural gas consumption by energy-using sector between 1950 and 2013. The industrial sector has historically been the largest consumer; however, its dominance is being challenged by the electric power sector. (See Figure 3.6.)

The EIA notes in "Use of Natural Gas" (April 26, 2013, http://www.eia.gov/energyexplained/index.cfm?page=natural_gas_use) that the industrial sector uses natural gas to produce products that require large amounts of heat for manufacture. Examples include steel, glass, and paper. Natural gas hydrocarbons are used as raw materials to make products such as paints,

FIGURE 3.6

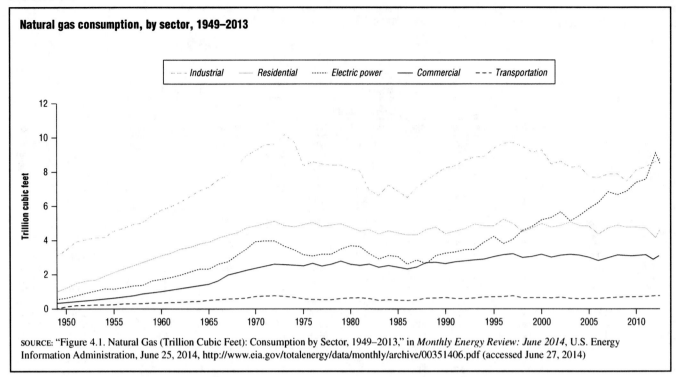

Natural gas consumption, by sector, 1949–2013

······· Industrial   ········· Residential   ······ Electric power   ——— Commercial   – – – Transportation

SOURCE: "Figure 4.1. Natural Gas (Trillion Cubic Feet): Consumption by Sector, 1949–2013," in *Monthly Energy Review: June 2014*, U.S. Energy Information Administration, June 25, 2014, http://www.eia.gov/totalenergy/data/monthly/archive/00351406.pdf (accessed June 27, 2014)

plastics, and medicines. The industrial sector also uses natural gas in its own power plants to generate electricity and in combined heat and power plants that generate heat and electricity. In addition, natural gas is used by the oil and gas industry in its extraction and processing activities. These are designated in Table 3.3 as "lease and plant fuel." According to the EIA, in "Natural Gas: Definitions, Sources and Explanatory Notes" (2014, http://www.eia.gov/dnav/ng/tbldefs/ng_cons_sum_tbldef2.asp), lease fuel is natural gas used in well, field, and lease operations, such as drilling. Plant fuel is natural gas used as fuel in plants that process natural gas.

Consumption in the industrial sector was 8.9 tcf (251.3 bcm) in 2013. (See Table 3.3 and Figure 3.6.) The electric power sector was the second-largest consumer of natural gas, with 8.2 tcf (230.9 bcm). As is explained in Chapter 8, the share of fossil fuel–fired electric power generation held by natural gas grew tremendously between the 1980s and 2013 for a variety of reasons.

The residential and commercial sectors ranked third and fourth, respectively, in natural gas consumption in 2013. (See Table 3.3 and Figure 3.6.) The residential sector used 4.9 tcf (139.9 bcm) and the commercial sector used 3.3 tcf (93.2 bcm). Usage by both sectors has been relatively flat since the 1970s. In "Use of Natural Gas," the EIA notes that slightly more than half of U.S. homes used natural gas as their primary heating fuel in 2012. Other residential uses include cooking, water heating, and clothes drying. Natural gas consumption for heating

homes and commercial buildings depends heavily on weather conditions, in that colder winters result in increased demand. Residential consumption is also affected by conservation practices and the efficiency of gas appliances such as water heaters, stoves, and clothes dryers.

The transportation sector consumed only 775 bcf (22 bcm) of natural gas in 2013. (See Table 3.3 and Figure 3.6.) The gas is used within the natural gas industry (e.g., during piping and distribution) and as a vehicle fuel.

WORLD NATURAL GAS PRODUCTION AND CONSUMPTION

Table 3.4 shows total natural gas production for 2012 for the world, by region, and for the top-20 producers. Total production was 118.9 tcf (3.4 tcm). North America was the largest producing region, accounting for 30.8 tcf (872.5 bcm), or 26% of world production. Eurasia was second with 28.1 tcf (796.4 bcm), or 24% of the total. The United States led all countries with 24.1 tcf (681.2 bcm), or 20% of world production. Russia was second with 21.7 tcf (614.1 bcm), or 18% of the total, followed by Iran, Qatar, and Canada.

The total world natural gas consumption in 2012 was 120 tcf (3.4 tcm). (See Table 3.5.) The United States was the leading consumer at 25.5 tcf (723 bcm), accounting for 21% of the world total. Other top consumers in 2012 included Russia, Iran, China, and Japan.

TABLE 3.4

TABLE 3.5

World production of dry natural gas, by region and selected country, 2012

[Billion cubic feet]

	2012
World	118,865.9
Regions	
North America	30,812.0
Eurasia	28,124.6
Middle East	19,291.6
Asia & Oceania	17,226.8
Europe	10,183.1
Africa	7,489.5
Central & South America	5,738.2
Countries	
United States	24,058.0
Russia	21,685.3
Iran	5,649.1
Qatar	5,523.2
Canada	5,069.6
Norway	4,155.3
China	3,810.6
Saudi Arabia	3,584.9
Algeria	3,053.1
Netherlands	2,840.3
Indonesia	2,559.4
Turkmenistan	2,492.4
Uzbekistan	2,221.5
Malaysia	2,176.2
Egypt	2,141.0
Australia	1,901.7
United Arab Emirates	1,853.9
Mexico	1,684.4
Pakistan	1,462.3
India	1,459.5

SOURCE: Adapted from "Dry Natural Gas Production (Billion Cubic Feet)," in *International Energy Statistics*, U.S. Energy Information Administration, 2014, http://www.eia.gov/cfapps/ipdbproject/iedindex3.cfm?tid=3&pid=26&aid=1&cid=regions&syid=2012&eyid=2012&unit=BCF (accessed July 4, 2014)

World consumption of dry natural gas, by region and selected country, 2012

[Billion cubic feet]

	2012
World	120,016.5
Regions	
North America	31,014.6
Asia & Oceania	23,625.3
Eurasia	22,013.7
Europe	18,684.4
Middle East	14,826.1
Central & South America	5,577.2
Africa	4,275.2
Countries	
United States	25,533.0
Russia	15,436.7
Iran	5,511.0
China	5,180.9
Japan	4,617.0
Saudi Arabia	3,584.9
Germany	3,079.5
Canada	3,057.5
Italy	2,645.6
United Kingdom	2,640.5
Mexico	2,424.1
United Arab Emirates	2,235.2
India	2,056.3
Egypt	1,881.7
Uzbekistan	1,861.3
Ukraine	1,855.9
Thailand	1,796.3
Korea, South	1,764.2
Australia	1,718.5
Argentina	1,641.4

SOURCE: Adapted from "Dry Natural Gas Consumption (Billion Cubic Feet)," in *International Energy Statistics*, U.S. Energy Information Administration, 2014, http://www.eia.gov/cfapps/ipdbproject/iedindex3.cfm?tid=3&pid=26&aid=2&cid=regions&syid=2012&eyid=2012&unit=BCF (accessed July 4, 2014)

NATURAL GAS PRICES

Analysts typically track three types of natural gas prices: wellhead prices, citygate prices, and consumer prices.

In *Monthly Energy Review: June 2014*, the EIA explains that the wellhead is the point at which natural gas exits the ground. The wellhead price includes all production costs, such as gathering and compressing the gas, and state charges. The citygate price is "a point or measuring station at which a distribution gas utility receives gas from a natural gas pipeline company or transmission system." Consumer prices are the prices paid by consumers to their local gas utilities. Natural gas prices vary across the nation because federal and state rate structures differ. Location also plays a role. For example, consumer prices are lower in major natural gas–producing areas where transmission costs are lower.

Table 3.6 lists wellhead, citygate, and consumer prices, by sector, between 1950 and 2013 on an average annual basis. These are nominal prices, meaning that they reflect the prices at the time of purchase and have not been adjusted for inflation. Overall, residential customers

paid the highest price ($10.33 per thousand cubic feet) for natural gas in 2013, followed by commercial customers ($8.13 per thousand cubic feet), industrial customers ($4.66 per thousand cubic feet), and electric power customers ($4.49 per thousand cubic feet).

Natural Gas Pricing Factors

Some of the factors described in Chapter 2 as affecting oil pricing, such as supply and demand and weather, also affect natural gas pricing. Nonetheless, because the United States produces nearly all the natural gas it consumes and obtains almost all of its imports from Canada, natural gas pricing in the United States is not as dependent on foreign events and manipulation as is oil pricing. Chapter 2 also explains various government interventions that are designed to benefit the oil and natural gas industry.

The biggest impact on natural gas pricing within the United States in the 20th century was the deregulation of the natural gas industry, which began during the 1970s. Deregulation meant an end to government-protected monopolies and opened the industry to competition. These events and the subsequent restructuring of companies

TABLE 3.6

Natural gas prices, by pricing location and consuming sector, selected years 1950–2013

[Dollars[a] per thousand cubic feet]

			Consuming sectors								
			Residential		Commercial[b]		Industrial[c]		Transportation	Electric power[d]	
	Wellhead price	Citygate price	Price[e]	Percentage of sector	Price[e]	Percentage of sector	Price[e]	Percentage of sector	Vehicle fuel[f] price[e]	Price[e]	Percentage of sector[g]
1950 average	0.07	NA	NA	NA	NA	NA	NA	NA	NA	NA	NA
1955 average	0.10	NA	NA	NA	NA	NA	NA	NA	NA	NA	NA
1960 average	0.14	NA	NA	NA	NA	NA	NA	NA	NA	NA	NA
1965 average	0.16	NA	NA	NA	NA	NA	NA	NA	NA	NA	NA
1970 average	0.17	NA	1.09	NA	0.77	NA	0.37	NA	NA	0.29	NA
1975 average	0.44	NA	1.71	NA	1.35	NA	0.96	NA	NA	0.77	96.1
1980 average	1.59	NA	3.68	NA	3.39	NA	2.56	NA	NA	2.27	96.9
1985 average	2.51	3.75	6.12	NA	5.50	NA	3.95	68.8	NA	3.55	94.0
1990 average	1.71	3.03	5.80	99.2	4.83	86.6	2.93	35.2	3.39	2.38	76.8
1995 average	1.55	2.78	6.06	99.0	5.05	76.7	2.71	24.5	3.98	2.02	71.4
2000 average	3.68	4.62	7.76	92.6	6.59	63.9	4.45	19.8	5.54	4.38	50.5
2001 average	4.00	5.72	9.63	92.4	8.43	66.0	5.24	20.8	6.60	4.61	40.2
2002 average	2.95	4.12	7.89	97.9	6.63	77.4	4.02	22.7	5.10	3.68[d]	83.9
2003 average	4.88	5.85	9.63	97.5	8.40	78.2	5.89	22.1	6.19	5.57	91.2
2004 average	5.46	6.65	10.75	97.7	9.43	78.0	6.53	23.6	7.16	6.11	89.8
2005 average	7.33	8.67	12.70	98.1	11.34	82.1	8.56	24.0	9.14	8.47	91.3
2006 average	6.39	8.61	13.73	98.1	12.00	80.8	7.87	23.4	8.72	7.11	93.4
2007 average	6.25	8.16	13.08	98.0	11.34	80.4	7.68	22.2	8.50	7.31	92.2
2008 average	7.97	9.18	13.89	97.5	12.23	79.7	9.65	20.4	11.75	9.26	101.1
2009 average	3.67	6.48	12.14	97.4	10.06	77.8	5.33	18.8	8.13	4.93	101.1
2010 average	4.48	6.18	11.39	97.4	9.47	77.5	5.49	18.0	6.25	5.27	100.8
2011 average	3.95	5.63	11.03	96.3	8.91	67.3	5.13	16.3	7.48	4.89	101.2
2012 average	2.66[E]	4.73	10.71	95.3	8.10	65.2	3.89	16.2	8.04	3.54	95.5
2013 average	NA	4.88	10.33	95.5	8.13	66.4	4.66	16.8	NA	4.49	94.9

[a]Prices are not adjusted for inflation.
[b]Commercial sector, including commercial combined-heat-and-power (CHP) and commercial electricity-only plants.
[c]Industrial sector, including industrial combined-heat-and-power (CHP) and industrial electricity-only plants.
[d]The electric power sector comprises electricity-only and combined-heat-and-power (CHP) plants within the NAICS 22 category whose primary business is to sell electricity, or electricity and heat, to the public. Through 2001, data are for electric utilities only; beginning in 2002, data also include independent power producers.
[e]Includes taxes.
[f]Much of the natural gas delivered for vehicle fuel represents deliveries to fueling stations that are used primarily or exclusively by fleet vehicles. Thus, the prices are often those associated with the cost of gas in the operation of fleet vehicles.
[g]Percentages exceed 100 percent when reported natural gas receipts are greater than reported natural gas consumption—this can occur when combined-heat-and-power plants report fuel receipts related to non-electric generating activities.
NA = Not available. E = Estimate.
Notes: Prices are for natural gas, plus a small amount of supplemental gaseous fuels. Prices are intended to include all taxes. Wellhead annual and year-to-date prices are simple averages of the monthly prices; all other annual and year-to-date prices are volume-weighted averages of the monthly prices. Geographic coverage is the 50 states and the District of Columbia.

SOURCE: Adapted from "Table 9.10. Natural Gas Prices (Dollars per Thousand Cubic Feet)," in *Monthly Energy Review: June 2014*, U.S. Energy Information Administration, June 25, 2014, http://www.eia.gov/totalenergy/data/monthly/archive/00351406.pdf (accessed June 27, 2014)

within the industry brought about a period of sharply rising prices. However, once the industry adjusted to deregulation, prices dropped.

Natural gas prices began to climb at the turn of the century and by 2008 the citygate price reached a record high of $9.18 per thousand cubic feet. (See Table 3.6.) This period coincides with the skyrocketing demand for natural gas from the electric power sector. (See Figure 3.6.) Because supply could not keep up with demand, natural gas prices rose. The industry responded with greater production, and prices began to come down. By 2013 the citygate price was down to $4.88 per thousand cubic feet.

FUTURE TRENDS IN THE NATURAL GAS INDUSTRY

The EIA predicts that domestic natural gas production will greatly increase in the coming decades to keep pace with rising demand. The agency believes that much of the new production will be gas obtained from unconventional geological sources—that is, shale gas and tight gas. (See Figure 3.5.) In fact, by 2040 shale gas is projected to supply more than half of the nation's natural gas supply.

ENVIRONMENTAL ISSUES

The natural gas industry is associated with far fewer environmental concerns than are the oil and coal industries for two main reasons. First, leaks of natural gas (which do occur) do not contaminate ecosystems in the same way that oil spills do. Second, natural gas burns much cleaner than oil and coal. Nevertheless, leaks and the combustion of natural gas release large amounts of carbon into the atmosphere, which, as explained in Chapter 1, contributes to global warming and climate change.

CHAPTER 4

COAL

Although it had been a source of energy for many centuries, coal was first used on a large scale during the Industrial Revolution (1760–1848). Its use expanded over the following decades with the building of railroads across the country. Coal eventually replaced wood as the fuel for steam engines, which became the new workhorses of the modern age. However, coal's widespread use in industry waned during the latter 20th century as petroleum became more popular. Coal found a new niche in electricity generation, a field it now dominates. Coal's strong appeal is driven by its high abundance and easy accessibility in the United States. Nevertheless, coal has its problems, chiefly environmental ones.

UNDERSTANDING COAL

Coal is a dark, combustible, mineral solid. Coalbeds, or seams, are found in the earth between beds of sandstone, shale, and limestone. Like oil and thermogenic natural gas, coal developed underground over millions of years as organic (carbon-containing) material was subjected to intense temperatures and pressures. Oil and thermogenic natural gas originated from microscopic organisms, whereas coal is believed to have developed from vegetation, particularly plant fibers. These materials were first transformed into peat, a fibrous sodlike mass of partially disintegrated organic material. Peat is typically found near the ground surface and is very moist; however, once dried it can be burned as fuel. Peat created several millennia ago was baked and squeezed by the earth and eventually turned into coal.

Measuring Coal

In the United States coal amounts are measured in tons, which are also known as short tons. One ton is equivalent to 2,000 pounds (907.2 kg). In countries that rely on the metric system, the metric tonne (t) is the preferred unit for measuring coal amounts. One ton is equivalent to 0.9 t.

Coal Ranks

There are different coal ranks (classifications), which are based on coal maturity. Stanley P. Schweinfurth of the U.S. Geological Survey explains in *An Introduction to Coal Quality* (July 2009, http://pubs.usgs.gov/pp/1625f/downloads/ChapterC.pdf) that coal rank depends on heat, moisture, carbon, and volatile matter contents. Heat content is the amount of heat that can be produced from a given unit of fuel. In general, more mature coal has a higher heat content and less moisture than younger coal. Moisture content is very important because drier coals are easier to handle and burn hotter than wetter coals.

In *Monthly Energy Review: June 2014* (June 2014, http://www.eia.gov/totalenergy/data/monthly/archive/00351406.pdf), the U.S. Energy Information Administration (EIA) within the U.S. Department of Energy (DOE) explains that the United States uses four coal ranks:

- Lignite (brown coal) is the lowest-ranked coal and the first true coal produced by the earth from peat. As such, it is relatively soft and moist compared with other coals. Lignite is brownish-black in color and has a high moisture content (as much as 45%). Lignite's heat content is about 9 million to 17 million British thermal units (Btu) per ton.

- Subbituminous coal ranks above lignite. Subbituminous coal ranges from dark brown to jet black in color and typically contains 20% to 30% moisture. Its heat content is approximately 17 million to 24 million Btu per ton.

- Bituminous coal is more mature than subbituminous coal and is the most abundant type of coal in the United States. Bituminous coal is dense and usually black, with a moisture content of less than 20%. It has a heat content of approximately 21 million to 30 million Btu per ton.

- Anthracite is the highest-ranked coal and the most mature. It is hard, brittle, and lustrous and typically jet-black in color, with a moisture content of less than 15%. Its heat content is approximately 22 million to 28 million Btu per ton. Anthracite is highly valued for its low moisture content and high heat content, but is very rare.

Coal Grades

Coal is also divided into grades based on its quality and intended end use. Two of the most common grades are metallurgical (or coking) coal and thermal (or steam) coal. The EIA (2014, http://www.eia.gov/tools/glossary/index.cfm?id=C) notes that coking coal has low sulfur and ash contents and is typically drawn from the bituminous rank. It is used to make coke, a high-value solid substance that is used in certain industrial processes, such as steelmaking. According to the EIA, all coal not classified as coking coal is steam coal, which is mostly used to generate steam to produce electricity or for heating purposes.

COAL DEPOSITS

The locations of coal deposits around the world are driven solely by geology. Regions and countries known to have large coal deposits include the United States, Eurasia (particularly China, Russia, and India), Australia, South Africa, and northern South America.

Geologists divide U.S. coalfields into the Appalachian, interior, and western regions. The Appalachian region encompasses the Appalachian Mountains in the eastern United States and stretches from Pennsylvania south to Alabama. The interior region covers parts of the Midwest and deep South, including Texas. The western region includes Alaska and a huge swath of territory from Montana and North Dakota in the north to the upper portions of Arizona and New Mexico in the south.

Like oil and natural gas, coal is located both onshore and offshore (i.e., beneath the earth's oceans). Offshore coal deposits were first mined during the 1800s, and some offshore mining is still conducted. However, huge offshore coal deposits remain almost entirely untouched because of the difficulties and costs involved in extracting them.

Estimates of the amounts of coal deposits around the world and in the United States that have not yet been extracted are provided in Chapter 7, along with information about coal exploration and development activities.

COAL EXTRACTION

Coal exists in the earth in solid form. As such, it is typically mined out of the ground. The method used to mine coal depends on the terrain and depth of the coal.

Surface mining is used for deposits that lie relatively near the ground surface—that is, less than about 200 feet (61 m) deep. Surface mines can be developed in flat or hilly terrain. On large plots of relatively flat ground, workers use a technique known as area surface mining. Rock and soil that lie above the coal—called overburden or spoil—are loosened by drilling and blasting and then dug away.

Underground mining is required when the coal lies more than about 200 feet (61 m) below ground. The depth of most underground mines is less than 1,000 feet (305 m), but a few are 2,000 feet (610 m) deep. In underground mines, some coal must be left untouched to form pillars that prevent the mines from caving in. It should be noted that underground cave mining is inherently dangerous. The U.S. Department of Labor notes in the fact sheet "Injury Trends in Mining" (2014, http://www.msha.gov/MSHAINFO/FactSheets/MSHAFCT2.HTM#.U71L455dWra) that more than 3,200 coal miners died on the job in 1907, the deadliest year for the industry. Since then stricter regulations and improved safety measures have dramatically lowered the casualty rates. In 2012, 19 coal miners lost their lives in U.S. mines. Coal mining death tolls have been much higher in other parts of the world. For example, more than 300 miners died in a mine explosion in Turkey in May 2014.

Table 4.1 shows regional and U.S. totals for 2012 for the number of mining operations, number of employees, and productivity (tons extracted per hour worked). There were 1,695 coal mining operations around the country that employed 89,838 people. Average productivity in 2012 was 5.2 tons (4.7 t) per employee hour. Nearly all (1,559) of the mining operations were located east of the Mississippi River. Only 91 operated west of the river; however, their average productivity of 15 tons (13.6 t) per employee hour was much higher than that for the eastern mines, which was 2.7 tons (2.4 t) per employee hour.

PROCESSING AND TRANSPORTING COAL

Coal seams can contain noncoal materials, such as rock, ash, and other minerals. These impurities are removed at processing facilities (typically located at the mines) to meet the requirements of the coal buyers. One of the targeted impurities is sulfur, which is found mostly in the form of pyrite, an iron sulfide mineral. Impurity removal helps improve coal's heat content, lowers transportation costs, and makes the coal burn cleaner—that is, it generates less air pollutants, particularly sulfur dioxide. Coal may be crushed, either before or after cleaning, for easier handling. It can also be pulverized into a fine dust.

Coal cleaning is not a perfect process; thus, some of the removed rock and mineral materials still contain enough hydrocarbons to make them useful combustible

TABLE 4.1

Coal mining operations, employees, and productivity, 2012

Coal-producing state, region and mine type	Number of mining operations[a]	Number of employees[b]	Average production per employee hour[c] (short tons)
Alabama	54	5,041	1.68
Underground	11	3,190	1.64
Surface	43	1,851	1.75
Alaska	1	143	5.98
Surface	1	143	5.98
Arizona	1	432	7.38
Surface	1	432	7.38
Arkansas	2	73	0.58
Underground	1	70	0.59
Surface	1	3	0.37
Colorado	14	2,505	5.79
Underground	11	2,032	5.93
Surface	3	473	5.21
Illinois	34	4,512	4.76
Underground	21	3,938	4.83
Surface	13	574	4.31
Indiana	39	3,935	4.19
Underground	13	2,054	3.23
Surface	26	1,881	5.37
Kansas	1	6	0.99
Surface	1	6	0.99
Kentucky total	484	16,351	2.56
Underground	213	11,181	2.37
Surface	271	5,170	2.97
Kentucky (east)	443	11,847	1.99
Underground	192	7,335	1.61
Surface	251	4,512	2.58
Kentucky (west)	41	4,504	3.82
Underground	21	3,846	3.55
Surface	20	658	5.59
Louisiana	2	270	6.86
Surface	2	270	6.86
Maryland	23	476	2.28
Underground	4	213	1.80
Surface	19	263	2.66
Mississippi	1	211	6.73
Surface	1	211	6.73
Missouri	2	32	6.73
Surface	2	32	6.73
Montana	6	1,233	14.46
Underground	1	320	7.47
Surface	5	913	17.47
New Mexico	4	1,291	8.14
Underground	1	435	5.19
Surface	3	856	9.70
North Dakota	4	1,228	11.57
Surface	4	1,228	11.57
Ohio	51	3,191	3.69
Underground	14	1,969	4.01
Surface	37	1,222	3.13
Oklahoma	7	199	2.21
Underground	1	55	2.37
Surface	6	144	2.14
Pennsylvania total	328	8,927	2.81
Underground	81	6,120	3.22
Surface	247	2,807	1.75
Pennsylvania (anthracite)	113	1,146	1.02
Underground	23	128	0.50
Surface	90	1,018	1.08
Pennsylvania (bituminous)	215	7,781	3.04
Underground	58	5,992	3.27
Surface	157	1,789	2.16
Tennessee	20	363	1.58
Underground	7	175	1.63
Surface	13	188	1.53
Texas	12	2,918	6.93
Surface	12	2,918	6.93
Utah	16	1,611	5.08
Underground	14	1,576	5.04
Surface	2	35	6.54
Virginia	137	4,998	1.74
Underground	79	3,763	1.51

TABLE 4.1

Coal mining operations, employees, and productivity, 2012 [CONTINUED]

Coal-producing state, region and mine type	Number of mining operations[a]	Number of employees[b]	Average production per employee hour[c] (short tons)
Surface	58	1,235	2.44
West Virginia total	388	22,786	2.38
Underground	227	17,085	2.15
Surface	161	5,701	3.04
West Virginia (northern)	52	5,891	3.17
Underground	31	5,590	3.17
Surface	21	301	3.22
West Virginia (southern)	336	16,895	2.10
Underground	196	11,495	1.64
Surface	140	5,400	3.03
Wyoming	19	7,004	27.74
Underground	1	250	7.81
Surface	18	6,754	28.59
Appalachia total	1,444	57,629	2.32
Underground	615	39,850	2.22
Surface	829	17,779	2.56
Appalachia (central)	936	34,103	2.01
Underground	474	22,768	1.61
Surface	462	11,335	2.77
Appalachia (northern)	454	18,485	3.07
Underground	130	13,892	3.30
Surface	324	4,593	2.30
Appalachia (southern)	54	5,041	1.68
Underground	11	3,190	1.64
Surface	43	1,851	1.75
Interior Basin total	141	16,660	4.73
Underground	57	9,963	3.94
Surface	84	6,697	6.01
Illinois Basin	114	12,951	4.25
Underground	55	9,838	3.97
Surface	59	3,113	5.20
Interior	27	3,709	6.50
Underground	2	125	1.43
Surface	25	3,584	6.70
Western total	65	15,447	17.09
Underground	28	4,613	5.79
Surface	37	10,834	21.95
Powder River Basin	17	6,983	29.35
Surface	17	6,983	29.35
Uinta Region	24	3,771	5.67
Underground	21	3,315	5.75
Surface	3	456	5.01
Western	24	4,693	8.22
Underground	7	1,298	5.89
Surface	17	3,395	9.13
East of Mississippi River	1,559	70,791	2.70
Underground	670	49,688	2.58
Surface	889	21,103	2.99
West of Mississippi River	91	18,945	15.03
Underground	30	4,738	5.65
Surface	61	14,207	18.15
U.S. subtotal	1,650	89,736	5.19
Underground	700	54,426	2.84
Surface	950	35,310	8.97
Refuse recovery	45	102	6.97
U.S. Total	**1,695**	**89,838**	**5.19**

[a]Mining operations that consist of a mine and preparation plant or preparation plant processing both underground and surface coal are reported as two operations.
[b]Includes all employees engaged in production, processing, development, maintenance, repair shop, or yard work at mining operations, including office workers.
[c]Calculated by dividing total coal production by the total labor hours worked by all employees engaged in production, processing, development, maintenance, repair shop, or yard work at mining operations, including office workers.

SOURCE: Adapted from "Table 21. Coal Productivity by State and Mine Type, 2012 and 2011," in *Annual Coal Report 2012*, U.S. Energy Information Administration, December 2013, http://www.eia.gov/coal/annual/pdf/acr.pdf (accessed July 7, 2014)

fuels. The EIA refers to these processing by-products as waste coal. Technological advances in combustion equipment have made waste coal a marketable energy product.

Cleaned coal is transported from mine sites to customer locations. In the United States the primary transportation modes are freight trains and, to a lesser extent, barges and trucks. Crushed coal can also be mixed with water and piped as a slurry to its destination.

DOMESTIC PRODUCTION
Traditional Coal

Table 4.2 shows domestic coal production between 1950 and 2013. During the 1950s and 1960s production hovered around 500 million tons (450 million t) per year. Demand for coal began increasing during the 1970s as a result of the oil embargo, which is described in Chapter 2. Domestic coal production rose over subsequent decades, reaching 1 billion tons (900 million t) per year by the early 1990s. Production has leveled off and even declined since then. In 2013 the United States produced nearly 984 million tons (893 million t) of coal. Table 4.3 provides a breakdown of coal production by state and region. Wyoming produced more coal than any other state with 388.3 million tons (352.3 million t) and accounting for nearly 40% of the total. Other major producing states included West Virginia, Kentucky, Pennsylvania, and Illinois. The western region produced the most coal in 2013—529.7 million tons (480.5 million t)—which was more than half (54%) of the nation's total. (See Figure 4.1.)

Until the 21st century bituminous coal was the most produced rank in the United States. (See Figure 4.2.) Subbituminous coal production has soared since the 1970s, and by around 2008 the two coal types were produced in near equal amounts. As shown in Figure 4.3, in 2013 production by coal rank was:

- Bituminous coal—461.7 million tons (418.8 million t)
- Subbituminous coal—443.2 million tons (402.1 million t)
- Lignite—77 million tons (69.9 million t)
- Anthracite—2.1 million tons (1.9 million t)

Figure 4.4 provides a historical production breakdown by mining method. During the 1970s surface mining first surpassed underground mining in terms of coal volume. Surface mining is easier, cheaper, and more efficient in terms of productivity than underground mining.

Before 1999 most of the nation's coal was mined east of the Mississippi River. (See Figure 4.5.) Miners had been digging deeper and deeper into the Appalachian Mountains for years before bulldozers began cutting open rich coal seams in the west. Since the mid-1990s more coal has been produced annually west of the Mississippi

River than east of the river. The growth in coal production in the western states has resulted, in part, because of increased demand for low-sulfur coal, which is concentrated there. Low-sulfur coal burns cleaner than other coals and is less harmful to the environment. In addition, western coal is closer to the surface, so it can be extracted by surface mining, rather than by underground mining. Improved rail service has also made it easier to deliver coal mined in the western part of the country to electric power plants located in the eastern United States.

Waste Coal

As shown in Table 4.2, waste coal amounts have increased dramatically since 1990, when the EIA first began tracking this material. In 2013 mining operations supplied 10.2 million tons (9.2 million t) of waste coal to the electric power and industrial sectors.

Coal Products

Like crude oil, raw coal can be processed to produce other marketable commodities. For example, coal dust can be blended with binding agents, such as asphalt, to produce briquettes, pellets, or other materials with industrial uses. Coke is a high-value product made from coal at specialized facilities. The coal is heated to a high temperature to eliminate volatile impurities and fuse together certain carbon and ash materials within the coal. The result is a solid material with a high heat content of 24.8 million Btu per ton, according to the EIA (2014, http://www.eia.gov/tools/glossary/index.cfm?id=C). Coke is combusted as a fuel and used in certain industrial processes, particularly steelmaking.

Coal can also be processed into fuels called coal synfuels. These may be either liquid or gaseous and can be manufactured by subjecting extracted coal to high temperatures and pressures. Another method is called in situ (in place) coal gasification (ISCG) or underground coal gasification. ISCG processes burn coal while it is still in the ground to produce gas that can be pumped to the surface. Although such technologies have been tried in the past, modern innovations have made ISCG a more viable alternative for fuel production. It could conceivably produce huge amounts of energy from the earth's vast coal seams that are too deep to mine, under the oceans, or otherwise untapped because of technological or economic reasons. For example, in "Newly Discovered North Sea Coal 'Could Power Britain for Centuries'" (IBTimes.co.uk, March 30, 2014), Jack Moore notes that British researchers believe that trillions of tons of coal lying underneath the North Sea could be exploited using ISCG. Likewise, Neil Reynolds describes in "Cape Breton's Undersea Coal Field a Vein to Energy Wealth" (GlobeandMail.com, September 12, 2013) the billions of tons of coal believed to be lying under the waters of the North Atlantic near Nova Scotia, Canada. Traditional

TABLE 4.2

Coal production, trade, and consumption statistics, selected years 1950–2013

[Thousand short tons]

	Production[a]	Waste coal supplied[b]	Trade			Stock change[d, e]	Losses and unaccounted for[d, f]	Consumption
			Imports	Exports	Net imports[c]			
1950 Total	560,388	NA	365	29,360	−28,995	27,829	9,462	494,102
1955 Total	490,838	NA	337	54,429	−54,092	−3,974	−6,292	447,012
1960 Total	434,329	NA	262	37,981	−37,719	−3,194	1,722	398,081
1965 Total	526,954	NA	184	51,032	−50,848	1,897	2,244	471,965
1970 Total	612,661	NA	36	71,733	−71,697	11,100	6,633	523,231
1975 Total	654,641	NA	940	66,309	−65,369	32,154	−5,522	562,640
1980 Total	829,700	NA	1,194	91,742	−90,548	25,595	10,827	702,730
1985 Total	883,638	NA	1,952	92,680	−90,727	−27,934	2,796	818,049
1990 Total	1,029,076	3,339	2,699	105,804	−103,104	26,542	−1,730	904,498
1995 Total	1,032,974	8,561	9,473	88,547	−79,074	−275	632	962,104
2000 Total	1,073,612	9,089	12,513	58,489	−45,976	−48,309	938	1,084,095
2001 Total	1,127,689	10,085	19,787	48,666	−28,879	41,630	7,120	1,060,146
2002 Total	1,094,283	9,052	16,875	39,601	−22,726	10,215	4,040	1,066,355
2003 Total	1,071,753	10,016	25,044	43,014	−17,970	−26,659	−4,403	1,094,861
2004 Total	1,112,099	11,299	27,280	47,998	−20,718	−11,462	6,887	1,107,255
2005 Total	1,131,498	13,352	30,460	49,942	−19,482	−9,702	9,092	1,125,978
2006 Total	1,162,750	14,409	36,246	49,647	−13,401	42,642	8,824	1,112,292
2007 Total	1,146,635	14,076	36,347	59,163	−22,816	5,812	4,085	1,127,998
2008 Total	1,171,809	14,146	34,208	81,519	−47,311	12,354	5,740	1,120,548
2009 Total	1,074,923	13,666	22,639	59,097	−36,458	39,668	14,985	997,478
2010 Total	1,084,368	13,651	19,353	81,716	−62,363	−13,039	182	1,048,514
2011 Total	1,095,628	13,209	13,088	107,259	−94,171	211	11,506	1,002,948
2012 Total	1,016,458	11,196	9,159	125,746	−116,586	6,902	14,980	889,185
2013 Total	983,964	10,194	8,906	117,659	−108,753	−41,386	1,684	925,106

[a]Beginning in 2001, includes a small amount of refuse recovery (coal recaptured from a refuse mine and cleaned to reduce the concentration of noncombustible materials).

[b]Waste coal (including fine coal, coal obtained from a refuse bank or slurry dam, anthracite culm, bituminous gob, and lignite waste) consumed by the electric power and industrial sectors. Beginning in 1989, waste coal supplied is counted as a supply-side item to balance the same amount of waste coal included in "Consumption."

[c]Net imports equal imports minus exports. A minus sign indicates exports are greater than imports.

[d]A negative value indicates a decrease in stocks and a positive value indicates an increase.

[e]In 1949, stock change is included in "Losses and Unaccounted for."

[f]The difference between calculated coal supply and disposition, due to coal quantities lost or to data reporting problems.

NA = Not available.

SOURCE: Adapted from "Table 6.1. Coal Overview (Thousand Short Tons)," in *Monthly Energy Review: June 2014*, U.S. Energy Information Administration, June 25, 2014, http://www.eia.gov/totalenergy/data/monthly/archive/00351406.pdf (accessed June 27, 2014)

TABLE 4.3

Coal production, by state and region, 2013

[Thousand short tons]

Coal-producing region and state	2013
Alabama	18,411
Alaska	1,550
Arizona	7,603
Arkansas	59
Colorado	23,789
Illinois	52,124
Indiana	38,945
Kansas	22
Kentucky total	**79,949**
Eastern (Kentucky)	39,048
Western (Kentucky)	40,901
Louisiana	2,835
Maryland	1,797
Mississippi	3,575
Missouri	414
Montana	42,231
New Mexico	21,969
North Dakota	27,639
Ohio	25,762
Oklahoma	1,117
Pennsylvania total	**54,215**
Anthracite (Pennsylvania)	2,028
Bituminous (Pennsylvania)	52,187
Tennessee	1,271
Texas	42,559
Utah	16,568
Virginia	16,710
West Virginia total	**112,910**
Northern (West Virginia)	42,468
Southern (West Virginia)	70,442
Wyoming	388,345
Appalachia total	**270,124**
Appalachia central	127,365
Appalachia northern	124,242
Appalachia southern	18,517
Interior Basin total	**182,549**
Illinois Basin	131,970
Interior	50,579
Western total	**529,695**
Powder River Basin	407,567
Uinta Region	38,665
Western	83,463
East of Mississippi River	405,669
West of Mississippi River	576,699
U.S. subtotal	**982,368**
Refuse recovery	1,596
U.S. total	**983,964**

Note: Total may not equal sum of components because of independent rounding.

SOURCE: Adapted from "Table 2. Coal Production by State (Thousand Short Tons)," in *Quarterly Coal Report: October–December 2013*, U.S. Energy Information Administration, March 2014, http://www.eia.gov/coal/production/quarterly/pdf/0121134q.pdf (accessed July 7, 2014)

mining methods were used in the past to extract undersea coal from the area, but any future extraction will likely be based on ISCG.

Many ISCG demonstration projects have been conducted around the world to gather design data for larger-scale applications. As of October 2014, one of the most watched projects was the Swan Hills Synfuel project (http://swanhills-synfuels.com) in Alberta, Canada, which is scheduled to begin commercial operation in 2017.

DOMESTIC COAL CONSUMPTION

After rising for many decades, domestic coal consumption dipped dramatically during the latter part of the first decade of the 21st century. (See Figure 4.6.) As shown in Table 3.6 in Chapter 3, this period saw lowering natural gas prices, which made natural gas a more attractive fuel than coal to industrial users and electric power producers.

Coal Consumption by Sector

Figure 4.7 provides a historical breakdown of coal consumption by sector. Since the early 1960s the electric power sector has been the dominant consumer of coal. In 2013 it used 858.4 million tons (778.7 million t) and accounted for 93% of total consumption, up from only 19% in 1950. (See Table 4.4.) In the electric power sector, coal is pulverized and either burned directly or gasified. Steam from boilers or the hot coal gases turn turbines, which power generators that create electricity. According to the EIA, in *Monthly Energy Review: June 2014*, coal-fired plants produced 1.6 trillion kilowatt-hours of electricity in 2013, or 40% of the nation's total net generation from the electric power sector. Net generation refers to the power available to the system—it does not include power used at the generating plants themselves.

The industrial sector was the second-largest coal consumer in 2013. (See Figure 4.7 and Table 4.4.) It used 64.8 million tons (58.8 million t), which was 7% of total consumption, down from 45% in 1950. Coal is used in many industrial applications, including the chemical, cement, paper, synthetic fuels, metals, and food-processing industries. In addition, some industrial facilities burn coal in their own electricity plants or combined heat and power plants. As noted earlier, coal is also used to make coke and other products. As shown in Table 4.4, coke plants were large coal consumers during the 1950s and 1960s; however, the U.S. steel industry declined over subsequent decades, which substantially reduced demand for coking coal.

Coal was once a significant fuel source in the residential and commercial sectors. (See Figure 4.7 and Table 4.4.) After the early 1950s, however, coal was replaced by oil, natural gas, and electricity. Thus, the residential and commercial sectors have become minor consumers of coal, as has the transportation sector.

COAL IMPORTS AND EXPORTS

As shown in Figure 4.6, domestic coal consumption was slightly lower than domestic production for most years dating back to 1949. As a result, the United States

FIGURE 4.1

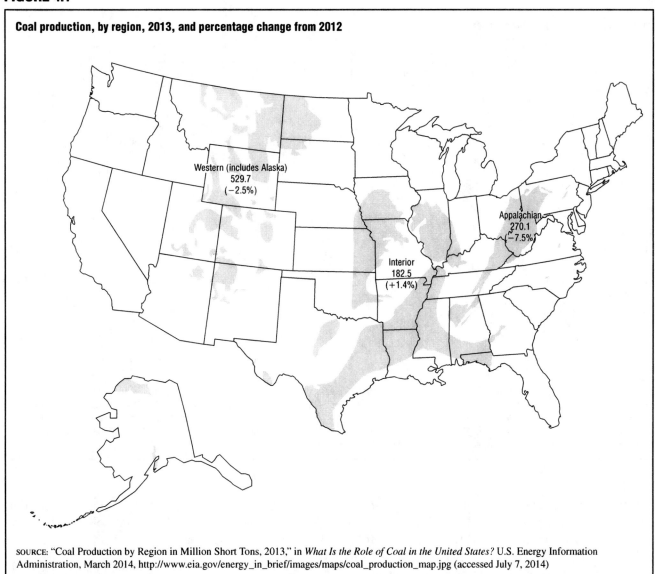

Coal production, by region, 2013, and percentage change from 2012

Western (includes Alaska)
529.7
(−2.5%)

Appalachian
270.1
(−7.5%)

Interior
182.5
(+1.4%)

SOURCE: "Coal Production by Region in Million Short Tons, 2013," in *What Is the Role of Coal in the United States?* U.S. Energy Information Administration, March 2014, http://www.eia.gov/energy_in_brief/images/maps/coal_production_map.jpg (accessed July 7, 2014)

has exported small amounts of coal annually. (See Table 4.2.) In 2013 exports totaled 117.7 million tons (106.7 million t), which was considerably higher than annual levels from the latter 20th century. According to the EIA, in *Quarterly Coal Report: October–December 2013* (March 2014, http://www.eia.gov/coal/production/quarterly/pdf/0121134q.pdf), the major destinations for U.S. coal in 2013 were:

• United Kingdom—13.5 million tons (12.3 million t)

• Netherlands—12.7 million tons (11.5 million t)

• Brazil—8.6 million tons (7.8 million t)

• South Korea—8.4 million tons (7.6 million t)

• China—8.2 million tons (7.4 million t)

• Canada—7.1 million tons (6.5 million t)

The United States has historically imported small amounts of coal each year. (See Table 4.2.) In 2013

imports totaled 8.9 million tons (8.1 million t). The EIA notes in *Quarterly Coal Report: October–December 2013* that nearly three-fourths (74%) of the imported coal came from Colombia. Other source countries included Canada, Indonesia, Ukraine, China, and Venezuela.

THE DOMESTIC OUTLOOK

In *Annual Energy Outlook 2014 with Projections to 2040* (April 2014, http://www.eia.gov/forecasts/aeo/pdf/0383(2014).pdf), the EIA considers various scenarios for future domestic coal demand. Figure 4.8 shows the expected production levels through 2040 for a middle-of-the-road reference case. The EIA predicts that domestic coal production will continue to decline through the second decade of the 21st century and then modestly increase over the following decades. Competition from natural gas and rising coal costs due to more

FIGURE 4.2

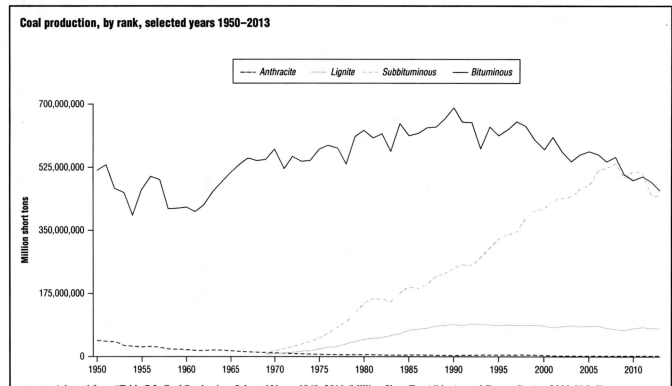

Coal production, by rank, selected years 1950–2013

SOURCE: Adapted from "Table 7.2. Coal Production, Selected Years, 1949–2011 (Million Short Tons)," in *Annual Energy Review 2011*, U.S. Energy Information Administration, September 27, 2012, http://www.eia.gov/totalenergy/data/annual/pdf/aer.pdf (accessed July 7, 2014); "U.S. Coal Flow, 2012 (Million Short Tons)," in *Energy Flow Diagrams 2012*, U.S. Energy Information Administration, http://www.eia.gov/totalenergy/data/annual/archive/flowimages/2012/coal.pdf (accessed July 7, 2014); and "U.S. Coal Flow, 2013 (Million Short Tons)," in *Diagrams: Energy Flows*, U.S. Energy Information Administration, http://www.eia.gov/totalenergy/data/monthly/pdf/flow/coal.pdf (accessed July 7, 2014)

stringent environmental standards are forecast to dampen future coal production. In addition, the coal industry is expected to face increasing competition from renewable energy sources for electricity generation. The EIA anticipates that stricter regulations on emissions, such as of sulfur dioxide and mercury, will force companies to retire older coal-fired power plants that cannot be economically outfitted with pollution-control technologies. These closures are expected to reduce coal demand through 2015; however, after that date the agency expects that growing demand for electricity, coupled with rising natural gas prices, will increase the demand for coal.

WORLD COAL PRODUCTION AND CONSUMPTION

Table 4.5 shows total coal production for 2012 for the world, by region, and for the top-20 producers. Total production was 8,695 million tons (7,888 million t). Asia and Oceania was the largest producing region, accounting for 5,802 million tons (5,263 million t), or 67% of world production. North America was second with 1,107 million tons (1,004 million t), or 13% of the total. China led all countries with 4,025 million tons (3,651 million t), or 46% of world production. The

United States was second with 1,016 million tons (921.7 million t), or 12% of the total, followed by India, Indonesia, and Australia.

The total world coal consumption in 2012 was 8,449 million tons (7,665 million t). (See Table 4.6.) China was the leading consumer, at 4,151 million tons (3,766 million t) and accounting for 49% of the world total. Other top consumers in 2012 included the United States, India, Russia, and Germany.

U.S. COAL PRICES

The EIA tracks various types of coal prices, one of which is the sales price at the coal mine (the first point of sale). Table 4.7 lists coal prices by coal rank between 1949 and 2011. The prices are expressed in nominal dollars (current to that year) and in real dollars (inflation adjusted). The real dollar amounts assume that the value of a dollar was constant over time. Thus, changes in real prices reflect actual market variations and not inflationary effects. Real coal prices experienced considerable up and down movement over the decades. The price peaked in 1975 at nearly $58 per ton and then began to decline. Around the start of the 21st century the price dipped to less than $19 per ton. It then rose slowly to around $33

FIGURE 4.3

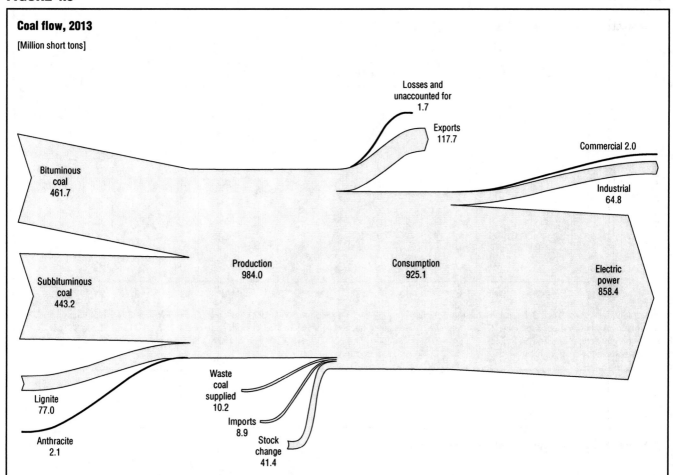

Coal flow, 2013

[Million short tons]

Notes: Production categories are estimated; all data are preliminary. Values are derived from source data prior to rounding for publication. Totals may not equal sum of components due to independent rounding.

SOURCE: "U.S. Coal Flow, 2013 (Million Short Tons)," in *Diagrams: Energy Flows*, U.S. Energy Information Administration, http://www.eia.gov/ totalenergy/data/monthly/pdf/flow/coal.pdf (accessed July 7, 2014)

FIGURE 4.4

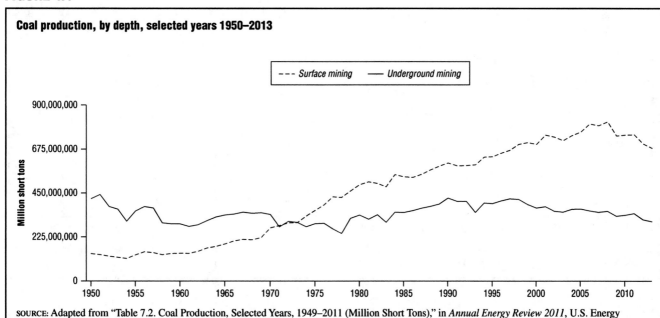

Coal production, by depth, selected years 1950–2013

SOURCE: Adapted from "Table 7.2. Coal Production, Selected Years, 1949–2011 (Million Short Tons)," in *Annual Energy Review 2011*, U.S. Energy Information Administration, September 27, 2012, http://www.eia.gov/totalenergy/data/annual/pdf/aer.pdf (accessed July 7, 2014) and "Table 2. Coal Production by State (Thousand Short Tons)," in *Quarterly Coal Report: October–December 2013*, U.S. Energy Information Administration, March 2014, http://www.eia.gov/coal/production/quarterly/pdf/0121134q.pdf (accessed July 7, 2014)

FIGURE 4.5

Coal production, by location, selected years 1950–2013

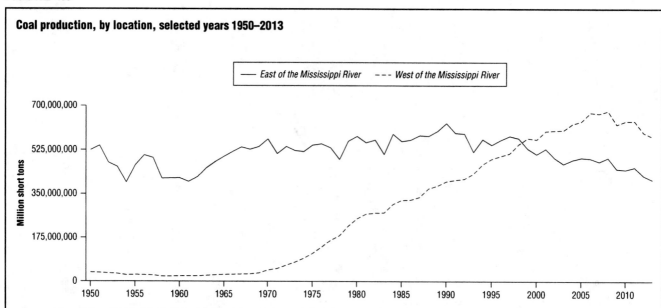

SOURCE: Adapted from "Table 7.2. Coal Production, Selected Years, 1949–2011 (Million Short Tons)," in *Annual Energy Review 2011*, U.S. Energy Information Administration, September 27, 2012, http://www.eia.gov/totalenergy/data/annual/pdf/aer.pdf (accessed July 7, 2014) and "Table 2. Coal Production by State (Thousand Short Tons)," in *Quarterly Coal Report: October–December 2013*, U.S. Energy Information Administration, March 2014, http://www.eia.gov/coal/production/quarterly/pdf/0121134q.pdf (accessed July 7, 2014)

FIGURE 4.6

Coal production, consumption, and net exports, 1949–2013

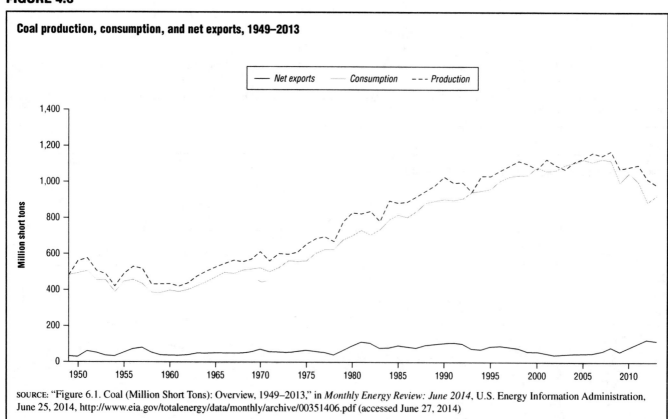

SOURCE: "Figure 6.1. Coal (Million Short Tons): Overview, 1949–2013," in *Monthly Energy Review: June 2014*, U.S. Energy Information Administration, June 25, 2014, http://www.eia.gov/totalenergy/data/monthly/archive/00351406.pdf (accessed June 27, 2014)

per ton in 2011. Anthracite has historically been the highest-priced coal rank, followed by bituminous, lignite, and subbituminous coal.

In *Annual Coal Report 2012* (December 2013, http://www.eia.gov/coal/annual/pdf/acr.pdf), the EIA provides 2012 sales prices by rank as follows:

FIGURE 4.7

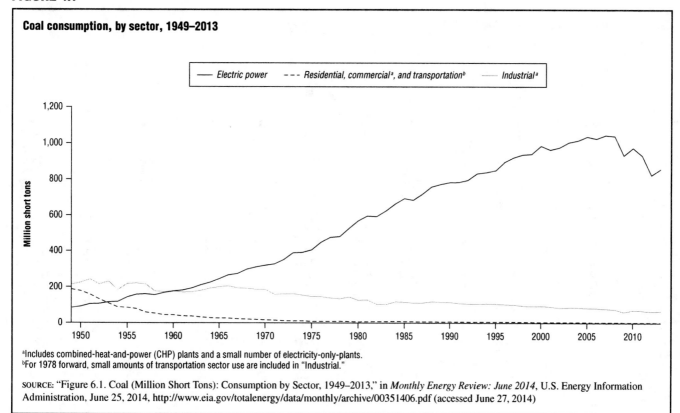

Coal consumption, by sector, 1949–2013

— Electric power   - - - Residential, commercial[a], and transportation[b]   ········ Industrial[a]

[a]Includes combined-heat-and-power (CHP) plants and a small number of electricity-only-plants.
[b]For 1978 forward, small amounts of transportation sector use are included in "Industrial."

SOURCE: "Figure 6.1. Coal (Million Short Tons): Consumption by Sector, 1949–2013," in *Monthly Energy Review: June 2014*, U.S. Energy Information Administration, June 25, 2014, http://www.eia.gov/totalenergy/data/monthly/archive/00351406.pdf (accessed June 27, 2014)

- Anthracite—$80.21 per ton

- Bituminous—$66.04 per ton

- Lignite—$19.60 per ton

- Subbituminous—$15.34 per ton

The average sales price in 2012 was $39.95 per ton. Surface-mined coal ($26.43 per ton) was less expensive than underground-mined coal ($66.56 per ton).

Another way to look at coal prices is on a Btu basis. Figure 4.9 shows coal prices per million Btu between 1990 and 2012 and projected by the EIA to 2040 for its reference case. Coal prices have been rising steadily since the dawn of the 21st century. Price differences by mining location are expected to grow considerably as Appalachian coal becomes more expensive. It is largely extracted by underground mining and is typically higher in sulfur content than coal from other parts of the country. By contrast, the price of western coal is expected to increase more modestly.

Coal Pricing Factors

The pricing for coal, like for oil and natural gas, is dependent on various supply and demand factors and weather. Coal demand is particularly sensitive to weather conditions because the vast majority of production goes to electric power generation. Electricity demand varies strongly with outdoor temperature, given that heating and cooling homes and buildings are top electricity uses. Because the United States produces nearly all the coal it consumes, coal pricing in the United States is not dependent on foreign events and manipulation as is oil pricing.

As noted earlier, the electric power sector accounted for the vast majority of coal consumption in 2013. Thus, demand changes in that sector have a big impact on coal prices. Chapter 8 explains that natural gas is the chief competitor against coal in electricity production. When natural gas becomes cheaper than coal, the electric power sector uses more of its existing natural gas–burning units than its existing coal-burning units. This fuel switching greatly reduces the demand for coal and puts downward pressure on coal prices.

GOVERNMENT INTERVENTION. Coal pricing is also influenced by government actions. These include financial incentives, taxes, and regulations. Financial incentives put downward pressure on coal prices, whereas taxes and regulations push prices upward. The federal government and some state governments impose various kinds of taxes on domestically produced coal. The collected monies often go into trust funds that help offset some of the external costs of coal mining. (As explained in Chapter 1, external costs are costs outside market costs.) The Black Lung Disability Fund has been operated since the late 1970s by the federal government and pays benefits under certain

TABLE 4.4

Coal consumption, by sector, selected years 1950–2013

[Thousand short tons]

| | | Commercial | | | Industrial | | | | | | | Electric power sector[e,f] | |
| | | | | | | Other industrial | | | | | | | |
	Residential	CHP[a]	Other[b]	Total	Coke plants	CHP[c]	Non-CHP[d]	Total	Total	Transportation		Total
1950 Total	51,562	g	63,021	63,021	104,014	h	120,623	120,623	224,637	63,011	91,871	494,102
1955 Total	35,590	g	32,852	32,852	107,743	h	110,096	110,096	217,839	16,972	143,759	447,012
1960 Total	24,159	g	16,789	16,789	81,385	h	96,017	96,017	177,402	3,046	176,685	398,081
1965 Total	14,635	g	11,041	11,041	95,286	h	105,560	105,560	200,846	655	244,788	471,965
1970 Total	9,024	g	7,090	7,090	96,481	h	90,156	90,156	186,637	298	320,182	523,231
1975 Total	2,823	g	6,587	6,587	83,598	h	63,646	63,646	147,244	24	405,962	562,640
1980 Total	1,355	g	5,097	5,097	66,657	h	60,347	60,347	127,004	h	569,274	702,730
1985 Total	1,711	g	6,068	6,068	41,056	h	75,372	75,372	116,429	h	693,841	818,049
1990 Total	1,345	1,191	4,189	5,379	38,877	27,781	48,549	76,330	115,207	h	782,567f	904,498
1995 Total	755	1,419	3,633	5,052	33,011	29,363	43,693	73,055	106,067	h	850,230	962,104
2000 Total	454	1,547	2,126	3,673	28,939	28,031	37,177	65,208	94,147	h	985,821	1,084,095
2001 Total	481	1,448	2,441	3,888	26,075	25,755	39,514	65,268	91,344	h	964,433	1,060,146
2002 Total	533	1,405	2,506	3,912	23,656	26,232	34,515	60,747	84,403	h	977,507	1,066,355
2003 Total	551	1,816	1,869	3,685	24,248	24,846	36,415	61,261	85,509	h	1,005,116	1,094,861
2004 Total	512	1,917	2,693	4,610	23,670	26,613	35,582	62,195	85,865	h	1,016,268	1,107,255
2005 Total	378	1,922	2,420	4,342	23,434	25,875	34,465	60,340	83,774	h	1,037,485	1,125,978
2006 Total	290	1,886	1,050	2,936	22,957	25,262	34,210	59,472	82,429	h	1,026,636	1,112,292
2007 Total	353	1,927	1,247	3,173	22,715	22,537	34,078	56,615	79,331	h	1,045,141	1,127,998
2008 Total	i	2,021	1,485	3,506	22,070	21,902	32,491	54,393	76,463	h	1,040,580	1,120,548
2009 Total	i	1,798	1,412	3,210	15,326	19,766	25,549	45,314	60,641	h	933,627	997,478
2010 Total	i	1,720	1,361	3,081	21,092	24,638	24,650	49,289	70,381	h	975,052	1,048,514
2011 Total	i	1,668	1,125	2,793	21,434	22,319	23,919	46,238	67,671	h	932,484	1,002,948
2012 Total	i	1,450	595	2,045	20,751	20,065	22,773	42,838	63,589	h	823,551	889,185
2013 Total	i	1,412	539	1,951	21,474	19,613	23,717	43,331	64,805	h	858,351	925,106

[a]Commercial combined-heat-and-power (CHP) and a small number of commercial electricity-only plants, such as those at hospitals and universities.
[b]All commercial sector fuel use other than that in "Commercial CHP."
[c]Industrial combined-heat-and-power (CHP) and a small number of industrial electricity-only plants.
[d]All industrial sector fuel use other than that in "Coke Plants" and "Industrial CHP."
[e]The electric power sector comprises electricity-only and combined-heat-and-power (CHP) plants within the NAICS 22 category whose primary business is to sell electricity, or electricity and heat, to the public.
[f]Through 1988, data are for electric utilities only. Beginning in 1989, data are for electric utilities and independent power producers.
[g]Included in "Commercial Other."
[h]Included in "Industrial Non-CHP."
[i]Beginning in 2008, residential coal consumption data are no longer collected by the U.S. Energy Information Administration (EIA).
Notes: Data values preceded by "F" are derived from EIA's Short-Term Integrated Forecasting System.
Totals may not equal sum of components due to independent rounding. Geographic coverage is the 50 states and the District of Columbia.

SOURCE: Adapted from "Table 6.2. Coal Consumption by Sector (Thousand Short Tons)," in *Monthly Energy Review: June 2014*, U.S. Energy Information Administration, June 25, 2014, http://www.eia.gov/totalenergy/data/monthly/archive/00351406.pdf (accessed June 27, 2014)

conditions to miners with black lung disease (a lung disease that is associated with coal mining). Federal and state taxes and fees are also used to clean up abandoned coal mines.

ENVIRONMENTAL ISSUES

Environmental concerns related to the coal industry primarily involve the mining and combustion stages. Coal is laden with heavy hydrocarbons and naturally occurring elements, such as mercury and sulfur. Combustion, even with pollution-control equipment, releases chemicals into the atmosphere that can negatively impact air and water quality, ecosystems, and human health. Coal combustion annually produces billions of tons of emissions of carbon dioxide, sulfur dioxide, and nitrogen oxides. The latter two gases are associated with air pollution problems, such as smog and acid rain (precipitation containing abnormally

high levels of acids, particularly sulfuric acids). As explained in Chapter 1, carbon emissions are blamed for enhancing global warming and related climate changes. Emissions from coal-fired power plants can also contain mercury, a toxin that settles in water bodies and is absorbed by fish and other aquatic creatures that humans ingest.

Fuel combustion is heavily regulated in the United States. Since 1970, when the Clean Air Act was passed, the government has imposed ever tighter restrictions on combustion emissions and invested money in making coal a cleaner burning fuel. For example, in 1984 Congress established the Clean Coal Technology program and directed the DOE to administer projects designed to demonstrate more environmentally friendly and economically efficient coal uses. Mechanical and chemical control measures have been developed through industry and government investment that have substantially reduced

FIGURE 4.8

Coal production, by region, 1970–2012 and predicted through 2040

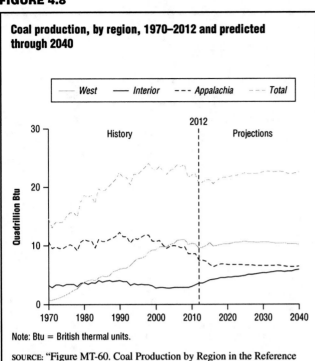

Note: Btu = British thermal units.

SOURCE: "Figure MT-60. Coal Production by Region in the Reference Case, 1970–2040 (Quadrillion Btu)," in *Annual Energy Outlook 2014 with Projections to 2040*, U.S. Energy Information Administration, April 2014, http://www.eia.gov/forecasts/aeo/ (accessed June 26, 2014)

TABLE 4.5

World production of coal, by region and selected country, 2012

[Million short tons]

	2012
World	**8,695**
Regions	
Asia & Oceania	5,802
North America	1,107
Europe	774
Eurasia	607
Africa	295
Central & South America	110
Middle East	1
Countries	
China	4,025
United States	1,016
India	650
Indonesia	488
Australia	464
Russia	390
South Africa	286
Germany	217
Poland	158
Kazakhstan	139
Colombia	99
Turkey	77
Canada	73
Ukraine	71
Greece	68
Czech Republic	61
Vietnam	46
Korea, North	43
Serbia	42
Romania	38

SOURCE: Adapted from "Table. Total Primary Coal Production (Thousand Short Tons)," in *International Energy Statistics*, U.S. Energy Information Administration, 2014, http://www.eia.gov/cfapps/ipdbproject/iedindex3.cfm?tid=1&pid=7&aid=1&cid=regions&syid=2012&eyid=2012&unit=TST (accessed July 8, 2014)

TABLE 4.6

World consumption of coal, by region and selected country, 2012

[Million short tons]

	2012
World	**8,449**
Regions	
Asia & Oceania	5,707
Europe	1,027
North America	956
Eurasia	465
Africa	221
Central & South America	52
Middle East	23
Countries	
China	4,151
United States	889
India	745
Russia	274
Germany	269
South Africa	206
Japan	202
Australia	151
Poland	147
Korea, South	138
Turkey	108
Kazakhstan	105
Ukraine	77
Taiwan	72
Greece	70
United Kingdom	70
Indonesia	66
Czech Republic	55
Canada	46
Serbia	43

SOURCE: Adapted from "Table. Total Coal Consumption (Thousand Short Tons)," in *International Energy Statistics*, U.S. Energy Information Administration, 2014, http://www.eia.gov/cfapps/ipdbproject/iedindex3.cfm?tid=1&pid=1&aid=2&cid=regions&syid=2012&eyid=2012&unit=TST (accessed July 8, 2014)

the emissions from coal combustion and improved the nation's air quality.

Ever stricter emissions standards, however, have been implemented or proposed in the 21st century. For example, in 2011 the U.S. Environmental Protection Agency (EPA) finalized its mercury and air toxics standards (MATS). The agency notes in "Cleaner Power Plants" (February 11, 2014, http://www.epa.gov/airquality/powerplanttoxics/powerplants.html) that the standards apply to approximately 1,400 coal- and oil-fired electric generating units located at 600 power plants around the country. The MATS program covers emissions of mercury, nonmercury metallic toxics, acid gases, and organic air toxics including dioxin. As is described in Chapter 8, the EPA has struggled to implement tougher regulations on other air contaminants associated with coal combustion, specifically sulfur dioxide and carbon. More information about pollution-control regulations and global warming mitigation techniques (such as carbon sequestration), which are related to electric power generation from coal, is included in Chapter 8.

TABLE 4.7

Coal prices, by type, selected years 1949–2011

[Dollars per short ton]

Year	Bituminous coal		Subbituminous coal		Lignite[a]		Anthracite		Total	
	Nominal[b]	Real[c]	Nominal[b]	Real[c]	Nominal[b]	Real[c]	Nominal[b]	Real[c]	Nominal[b]	Real[c]
1949	4.90[d]	33.80[d, R]	[d]	[d]	2.37	16.35[R]	8.90	61.38[R]	5.24	36.14[R]
1950	4.86[d]	33.16[d, R]	[d]	[d]	2.41	16.44[R]	9.34	63.73[R]	5.19	35.41[R]
1955	4.51[d]	27.17[d, R]	[d]	[d]	2.38	14.34[R]	8.00	48.19[R]	4.69	28.25[R]
1960	4.71[d]	25.31[d, R]	[d]	[d]	2.29	12.30[R]	8.01	43.04[R]	4.83	25.95[R]
1965	4.45[d]	22.32[d, R]	[d]	[d]	2.13	10.68[R]	8.51	42.69[R]	4.55	22.82[R]
1970	6.30[d]	25.89[d, R]	[d]	[d]	1.86	7.64[R]	11.03	45.32[R]	6.34	26.05[R]
1975	19.79[d]	58.91[d, R]	[d]	[d]	3.17	9.44	32.26	96.04[R]	19.35	57.60[R]
1976	20.11[d]	56.62[d, R]	[d]	[d]	3.74	10.53[R]	33.92	95.50[R]	19.56	55.07[R]
1977	20.59[d]	54.50[d, R]	[d]	[d]	4.03	10.67[R]	34.86	92.26[R]	19.95	52.80[R]
1978	22.64[d]	55.99[d, R]	[d]	[d]	5.68	14.05[R]	35.25	87.18[R]	21.86	54.06[R]
1979	27.31	62.35[R]	9.55	21.80[R]	6.48	14.80[R]	41.06	93.75[R]	23.75	54.23[R]
1980	29.17	61.04[R]	11.08	23.18[R]	7.60	15.90[R]	42.51	88.95[R]	24.65	51.58[R]
1981	31.51	60.28[R]	12.18	23.30[R]	8.85	16.93[R]	44.28	84.71[R]	26.40	50.51[R]
1982	32.15	57.97[R]	13.37	24.11[R]	9.79	17.65[R]	49.85	89.89[R]	27.25	49.14[R]
1983	31.11	53.96[R]	13.03	22.60[R]	9.91	17.19[R]	52.29	90.70[R]	25.98	45.06[R]
1984	30.63	51.21[R]	12.41	20.75[R]	10.45	17.47[R]	48.22	80.61[R]	25.61	42.81[R]
1985	30.78	49.94[R]	12.57	20.40[R]	10.68	17.33[R]	45.80	74.32[R]	25.20	40.89[R]
1986	28.84	45.78[R]	12.26	19.46[R]	10.64	16.89[R]	44.12	70.04[R]	23.79	37.77[R]
1987	28.19	43.49[R]	11.32	17.46[R]	10.85	16.74[R]	43.65	67.34[R]	23.07	35.59[R]
1988	27.66	41.26[R]	10.45	15.59[R]	10.06	15.00[R]	44.16	65.87[R]	22.07	32.92[R]
1989	27.40	39.38[R]	10.16	14.60[R]	9.91	14.24[R]	42.93	61.70[R]	21.82	31.36[R]
1990	27.43	37.96[R]	9.70	13.42[R]	10.13	14.02[R]	39.40	54.52[R]	21.76	30.11[R]
1991	27.49	36.74[R]	9.68	12.94[R]	10.89	14.55[R]	36.34	48.57[R]	21.49	28.72[R]
1992	26.78	34.96[R]	9.68	12.64[R]	10.81	14.11[R]	34.24	44.70[R]	21.03	27.46[R]
1993	26.15	33.40[R]	9.33	11.92[R]	11.11	14.19[R]	32.94	42.07[R]	19.85	25.35[R]
1994	25.68	32.12[R]	8.37	10.47[R]	10.77	13.47[R]	36.07	45.12[R]	19.41	24.28[R]
1995	25.56	31.32[R]	8.10	9.93	10.83	13.27[R]	39.78	48.75[R]	18.83	23.07[R]
1996	25.17	30.27[R]	7.87	9.46[R]	10.92	13.13[R]	36.78	44.23[R]	18.50	22.25[R]
1997	24.64	29.12[R]	7.42	8.77[R]	10.91	12.89[R]	35.12	41.50[R]	18.14	21.43[R]
1998	24.87	29.06[R]	6.96	8.13[R]	11.08	12.95[R]	42.91	50.14[R]	17.67	20.65[R]
1999	23.92	27.54[R]	6.87	7.91[R]	11.04	12.71[R]	35.13	40.45[R]	16.63	19.15[R]
2000	24.15	27.22[R]	7.12	8.02[R]	11.41	12.86[R]	40.90	46.10[R]	16.78	18.91[R]
2001	25.36	27.95[R]	6.67	7.35[R]	11.52	12.70[R]	47.67	52.54[R]	17.38	19.16[R]
2002	26.57	28.82[R]	7.34	7.96[R]	11.07	12.01[R]	47.78	51.82[R]	17.98	19.50[R]
2003	26.73	28.40[R]	7.73	8.21	11.20	11.90	49.87	52.98[R]	17.85	18.96[R]
2004	30.56	31.57[R]	8.12	8.39	12.27	12.68	39.77	41.09[R]	19.93	20.59[R]
2005	36.80	36.80	8.68	8.68	13.49	13.49	41.00	41.00	23.59	23.59
2006	39.32	38.09[R]	9.95	9.64	14.00	13.56	43.61	42.25[R]	25.16	24.37
2007	40.80	38.41[R]	10.69	10.06	14.89	14.02[R]	52.24	49.18[R]	26.20	24.66[R]
2008	51.39	47.33[R]	12.31	11.34[R]	16.50	15.20[R]	60.76	55.96[R]	31.25	28.78[R]
2009	55.44	50.52[R]	13.35	12.17[R]	17.26	15.73[R]	57.10	52.04[R]	33.24	30.29[R]
2010	60.88[R]	54.85[R]	14.11[R]	12.71[R]	18.76[R]	16.90[R]	59.51[R]	53.62[R]	35.61[R]	32.08[R]
2011[E]	57.64	50.85	15.80	13.94	19.38	17.10	70.99	62.62	36.91	32.56

[a]Because of withholding to protect company confidentiality, lignite prices exclude Texas for 1955–1977 and Montana for 1974–1978. As a result, lignite prices for 1974–1977 are for North Dakota only.
[b]Nominal costs represent costs at time of transaction.
[c]In chained (2005) dollars, calculated by using gross domestic product implicit price deflators.
[d]Through 1978, subbituminous coal is included in "Bituminous coal."
R = Revised. E = Estimate.
Note: Prices are free-on-board (F.O.B.) rail/barge prices, which are the F.O.B. prices of coal at the point of first sale, excluding freight or shipping and insurance costs. For 1949–2000, prices are for open market and captive coal sales; for 2001–2007, prices are for open market coal sales; for 2008 forward, prices are for open market and captive coal sales.

SOURCE: "Table 7.9. Coal Prices, Selected Years, 1949–2011 (Dollars per Short Ton)," in *Annual Energy Review 2011*, U.S. Energy Information Administration, September 27, 2012, http://www.eia.gov/totalenergy/data/annual/pdf/aer.pdf (accessed June 26, 2014)

FIGURE 4.9

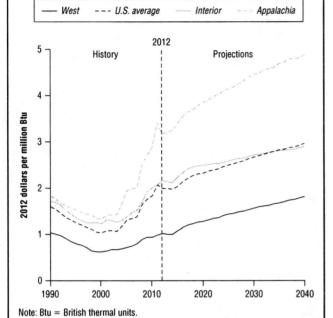

Coal prices, by region, 1990–2012 and predicted through 2040

Note: Btu = British thermal units.

SOURCE: "Figure MT-62. Average Annual Minemouth Coal Prices by Region in the Reference Case, 1990–2040 (2012 Dollars per Million Btu)," in *Annual Energy Outlook 2014 with Projections to 2040*, U.S. Energy Information Administration, April 2014, http://www.eia.gov/forecasts/aeo/ (accessed June 26, 2014)

CHAPTER 5
NUCLEAR ENERGY

During the early 20th century scientists succeeded in releasing energy that was bound up in the atom. Using a process called fission, they split apart the nucleus of a heavy atom (an atom containing many protons and neutrons) into two lighter nuclei. (See Figure 5.1.) The two resulting nuclei contained less mass than the original nucleus because some of the original atomic mass was converted into energy in the form of heat and radiation. Scientists knew that the key to harnessing this energy was setting up a chain reaction in which numerous heavy nuclei could be split apart in a confined space under controlled conditions. In 1942 the physicist Enrico Fermi (1901–1954) achieved this feat at the University of Chicago in Illinois by creating the first self-sustaining nuclear fission chain reaction. His work transformed energy production as the techniques were quickly refined to produce electricity using the heat that was generated during controlled fission reactions.

At first, nuclear power was hailed as a super energy source that could provide huge amounts of electricity without the need for burning air-polluting fossil fuels. Nuclear power's potential, however, has been tempered by the logistical, environmental, and safety considerations involved. Controlling chain reactions and disposing of the radioactive materials that result from them have proven to be massive challenges.

UNDERSTANDING NUCLEAR ENERGY

Radiation is a form of energy transfer that naturally results from the spontaneous emission of energy and/or high-energy particles from the nucleus of an atom. The earth is bombarded by radiation from the sun and other sources in outer space. In addition, many naturally radioactive elements, such as uranium, are found within the earth's crust and oceans. Scientists first produced nuclear energy by bombarding the nuclei of an isotope of uranium called uranium 235 (U-235). (Isotopes are atoms of

an element that have the usual number of protons but different numbers of neutrons in their nuclei.)

Under proper conditions, the fission of a U-235 atom creates the needed cascading chain of nuclear reactions. If this series of reactions is regulated to occur slowly, as it is in nuclear power plants, the energy emitted can be captured for generating electricity. If this series of reactions is allowed to occur all at once, as in an atomic bomb, the energy emitted is explosive. (Plutonium 239 can also be used to generate a chain reaction similar to that of U-235.)

Figure 5.2 shows a pressurized-water nuclear reactor, the most common type of reactor in commercial use. Bombardment of uranium in the core of the reactor (shown as "1" in Figure 5.2) generates a nuclear reaction (fission) that produces heat. The heat from the reaction is carried away by water under high pressure ("2") to a steam generator ("3"). This heat vaporizes the water in the steam generator, producing steam. The steam is carried by a steamline ("4") to a turbine, making the attached generator spin, which produces electricity. The large cooling towers that are associated with nuclear plants cool the steam after it has run through the turbines. A boiling-water reactor works much the same way, except that the water surrounding the core boils and directly produces the steam, which is then piped to the turbine generator.

Commercial nuclear power reactors exclusively produce electrical power, which is measured by a basic unit called a watt. Because the watt is a relatively small unit, power plant capacities are typically measured in a multiple of watts, such as the kilowatt (10^3 watts), megawatt (MW; 10^6 watts), gigawatt (GW; 10^9), or terawatt (10^{12} watts). Electrical power production is often expressed in multiples of a kilowatt-hour (kWh; the amount of work done by a kilowatt over a period of one hour).

FIGURE 5.1

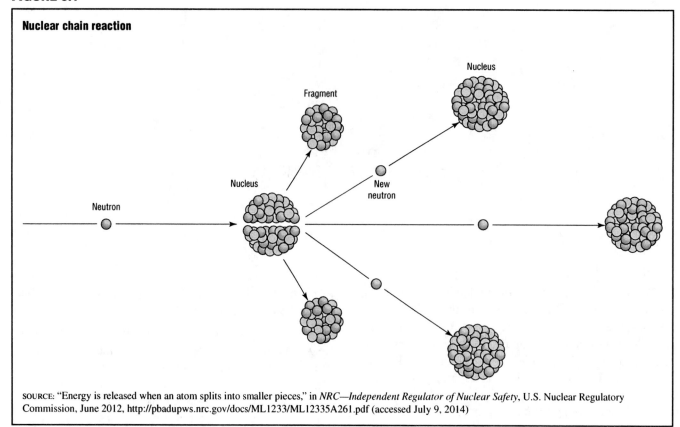

Nuclear chain reaction

SOURCE: "Energy is released when an atom splits into smaller pieces," in *NRC—Independent Regulator of Nuclear Safety*, U.S. Nuclear Regulatory Commission, June 2012, http://pbadupws.nrc.gov/docs/ML1233/ML12335A261.pdf (accessed July 9, 2014)

DOMESTIC URANIUM PRODUCTION, CONSUMPTION, AND PRICING

Uranium is a natural substance consisting almost entirely (greater than 99%) of U-238, which is not easily fissionable. Natural uranium contains only about 0.7% U-235 and a trace (extremely small) quantity of U-234. Uranium is present in low concentrations throughout the earth's soils, rocks, and water bodies. It is most highly concentrated in certain rock and mineral deposits called uranium ore. In "Where Our Uranium Comes From" (August 12, 2014, http://www.eia.gov/energyexplained/index.cfm?page=nuclear_where), the U.S. Energy Information Administration (EIA) within the U.S. Department of Energy (DOE) explains that domestic uranium ore deposits are located primarily in the western United States. Uranium removal (recovery) from the deposits is regulated by the U.S. Nuclear Regulatory Commission (NRC).

Uranium Ore Recovery Methods

Uranium can be recovered by mining uranium ore from the ground. A typical uranium milling operation is shown in Figure 5.3. Mined ore is crushed and ground and then treated with liquid chemicals in a process called leaching. This separates the uranium from the other ore materials (or tailings). The uranium undergoes further chemical processing while the tailings go to disposal.

An alternative option for uranium recovery from ores is in situ (in place) leaching. (See Figure 5.4.) During in situ leaching a chemical solution is pumped through the underground ore deposits, and the separated uranium is pumped to the surface for processing.

There is a third recovery option called heap leaching. In *2013–2014 Information Digest* (August 2013, http://pbadupws.nrc.gov/docs/ML1324/ML13241A207.pdf), the NRC describes heap leaching as a process in which acid is dripped over aboveground piles (heaps) of uranium ore to separate the uranium. The agency notes that as of 2013 it had not licensed any heap leach facilities but expected to begin receiving applications for them in the future.

Recovered uranium is processed into a powder called uranium concentrate, which has the chemical formula U_3O_8 (uranium oxide) and is commonly called yellowcake, although it may be yellow or brown in color.

Domestic Uranium Ore Mines and Production

The U.S. Environmental Protection Agency (EPA) indicates in *Uranium Location Database Compilation* (August 2006, http://www.epa.gov/radiation/docs/tenorm/402-r-05-009.pdf) that from the 1940s through the 1990s thousands of uranium ore mines operated in the United States, mostly in Arizona, Colorado, New

FIGURE 5.2

Pressurized-water reactor

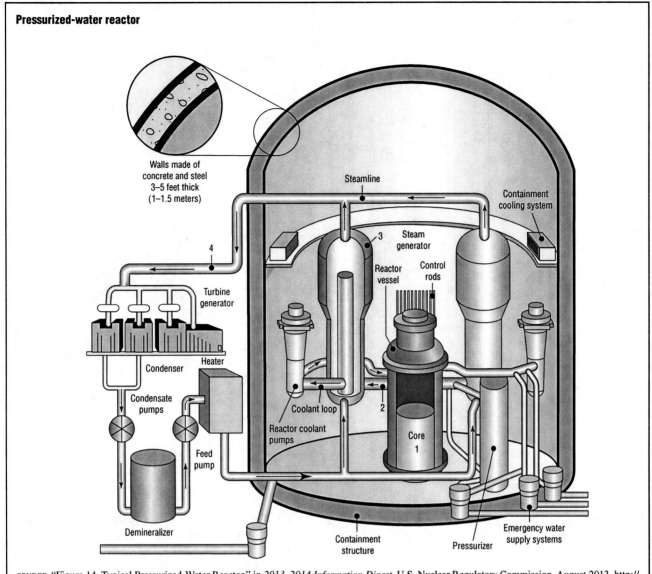

Walls made of concrete and steel 3–5 feet thick (1–1.5 meters)

Steamline

Containment cooling system

3 Steam generator

Reactor vessel

Control rods

4

Turbine generator

Heater

Condenser

Condensate pumps

Coolant loop

Reactor coolant pumps

2

Core 1

Feed pump

Demineralizer

Containment structure

Pressurizer

Emergency water supply systems

SOURCE: "Figure 14. Typical Pressurized-Water Reactor," in *2013–2014 Information Digest*, U.S. Nuclear Regulatory Commission, August 2013, http://pbadupws.nrc.gov/docs/ML1324/ML13241A207.pdf (accessed June 27, 2014)

Mexico, Utah, and Wyoming. Uranium ore is mined using mechanical methods that are similar to those used for other metal ores. A major difference is that uranium ore mining exposes workers to radioactivity. Uranium atoms naturally split by themselves at a slow rate, causing radioactive substances such as radon to accumulate slowly in the deposits.

Figure 5.5 shows domestic yellowcake production between 1949 and 2013. Production was very high from the 1950s through 1980, when it peaked at 43.7 million pounds (19.8 million kg). Since that time domestic production has plummeted. It was 4.7 million pounds (2.1 million kg) in 2013.

According to the EIA, in *2013 Domestic Uranium Production Report* (May 2014, http://www.eia.gov/uranium/production/annual/pdf/dupr.pdf), only 10 uranium

mines were in operation in the United States in 2013. Three of the mines extracted ore and the other seven used in situ leaching. In addition, some uranium was recovered at other facilities from mining waste materials and by-products, such as mill tailings and mine water.

Uranium Consumption and Trade

Uranium has a variety of industrial applications. It is also used to produce nuclear weapons and as a fuel source for nuclear-powered submarines and ships. However, uranium is primarily used for electricity production. For this purpose yellowcake is made into a suitable fuel through processes called conversion and enrichment. During conversion, yellowcake is combined with fluorine to produce uranium hexafluoride (UF_6). In "Uranium Hexafluoride (UF_6)" (2014, http://web.ead.anl.gov/uranium/guide/uf6), the Argonne National Laboratory

FIGURE 5.3

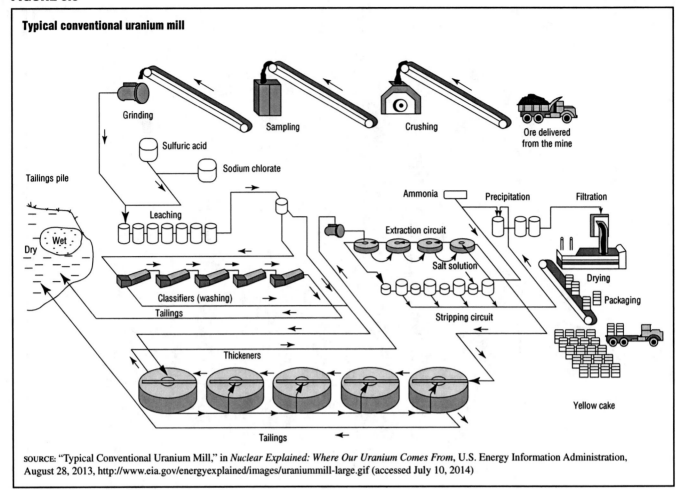

Typical conventional uranium mill

SOURCE: "Typical Conventional Uranium Mill," in *Nuclear Explained: Where Our Uranium Comes From*, U.S. Energy Information Administration, August 28, 2013, http://www.eia.gov/energyexplained/images/uraniummill-large.gif (accessed July 10, 2014)

explains that UF_6 provides a convenient means for storing uranium and can be handled in solid, liquid, or gaseous form.

Nuclear reactor fuel requires a higher concentration of U-235 than what exists in natural uranium ore, yellowcake, or UF_6. These materials must be enriched to make the uranium more concentrated. According to the NRC, in "Uranium Enrichment" (October 21, 2014, http://www.nrc.gov/materials/fuel-cycle-fac/ur-enrichment.html), there are various means for enriching uranium; however, gaseous diffusion is the primary method used in the United States. UF_6 gas is fed through porous membranes that separate the lighter gas containing U-235 and U-234 molecules from the heavier gas containing U-238 molecules. The U-235/U-234–enriched UF_6 gas is then cooled and solidified for transport to fuel fabrication facilities. There, the solid UF_6 is vaporized and chemically transferred into uranium dioxide (UO_2) powder. (See Figure 5.6.) The powder is pressed into pellets that are stacked inside rods, which are tubes about 12 feet (3.7 m) long. (See Figure 5.7.) Many rods (see "control rods" in Figure 5.2) are bundled together in assemblies, and hundreds of these assemblies make up the core of a nuclear reactor.

In "The U.S. Relies on Foreign Uranium, Enrichment Services to Fuel Its Nuclear Power Plants" (August 28, 2013, http://www.eia.gov/todayinenergy/detail.cfm?id=12731), the EIA notes that U.S. commercial nuclear power plants purchase uranium in three forms: U_3O_8, UF6, and enriched uranium. These materials are referenced in terms of million pounds of U_3O_8 equivalent.

As shown in Figure 5.5, domestic yellowcake production plummeted during the early 1980s. As a result, the United States has become heavily reliant on imported uranium. Table 5.1 lists U.S. uranium purchases for civilian nuclear power reactors between 1994 and 2013. Foreign-origin uranium made up the vast majority of the total. In 2013 U.S. nuclear power plants purchased 47.9 million pounds (21.7 million kg) U_3O_8 equivalent of foreign-origin uranium. This accounted for 83% of the total 57.4 million pounds (26 million kg) purchased that year.

Table 5.2 provides the amounts and prices for foreign-origin uranium delivered between 2009 and 2013. Australia and Russia were the largest suppliers in 2013. The United States obtained 10.7 million pounds

FIGURE 5.4

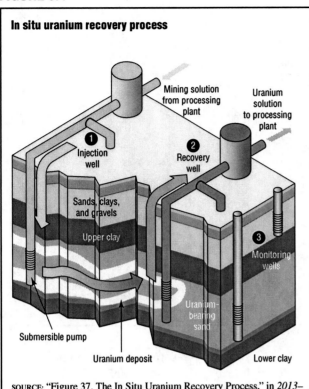

In situ uranium recovery process

SOURCE: "Figure 37. The In Situ Uranium Recovery Process," in *2013–2014 Information Digest*, U.S. Nuclear Regulatory Commission, August 2013, http://pbadupws.nrc.gov/docs/ML1324/ML13241A207.pdf (accessed June 27, 2014)

(4.9 million kg) U_3O_8 equivalent from Australia. This was 19% of the total imported. Another 10.6 million pounds (4.8 million kg), or 18%, of the total came from Russia. Smaller percentages were obtained from Canada, Kazakhstan, Namibia, Uzbekistan, Niger, Malawi, and South Africa. An unknown amount was imported from Portugal in 2013.

SECONDARY SOURCES. Nuclear power fuels are primarily produced from uranium taken from the ground (i.e., natural uranium) that is enriched to low levels. There are other methods that incorporate what are known as secondary sources of uranium: depleted uranium, highly enriched uranium (HEU), and reprocessed uranium. In addition, plutonium can be used as a nuclear power fuel.

Depleted uranium is a generic term for uranium that has been depleted of its U-235 content. It is a by-product of enrichment processes, such as gaseous diffusion. In the United States depleted uranium is produced in the form of UF_6 gas in which U-238 has been highly concentrated. This isotope is not easily fissionable; thus, depleted uranium has long been considered a waste material called "tails." It does, however, contain tiny amounts of U-235. The U.S. Government Accountability Office (GAO) notes in *Nuclear Material: DOE's Depleted Uranium Tails Could Be a Source of Revenue for the Government* (June 13, 2011, http://www.gao.gov/assets/130/126405.pdf) that tails contain up to about 0.7% U-235. Conceivably, they could be re-enriched to provide suitable

FIGURE 5.5

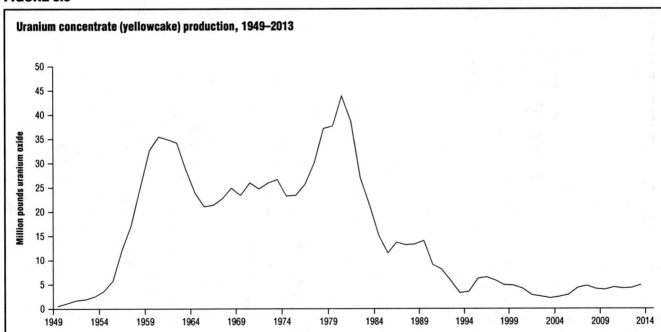

Uranium concentrate (yellowcake) production, 1949–2013

SOURCE: Adapted from "Figure 9.3. Uranium Overview: Production and Trade, 1949–2011," in *Annual Energy Review 2011*, U.S. Energy Information Administration, September 27, 2012, http://www.eia.gov/totalenergy/data/annual/pdf/aer.pdf (accessed July 8, 2014) and "Table 9. Summary Production Statistics of the U.S. Uranium Industry, 1993–2013," in *2013 Domestic Uranium Production Report*, U.S. Energy Information Administration, May 2014, http://www.eia.gov/uranium/production/annual/pdf/dupr.pdf (accessed July 8, 2014)

FIGURE 5.6

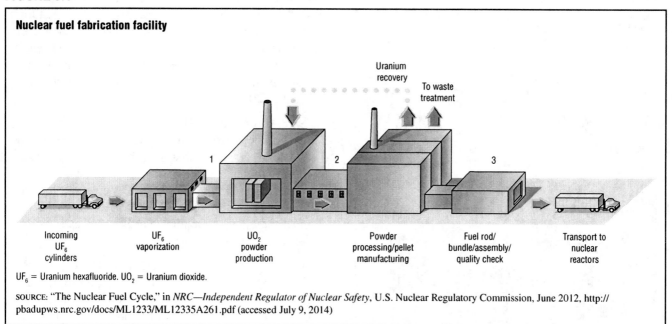

Nuclear fuel fabrication facility

Incoming UF₆ cylinders

UF₆ vaporization

UO₂ powder production

Powder processing/pellet manufacturing

Fuel rod/ bundle/assembly/ quality check

Transport to nuclear reactors

UF₆ = Uranium hexafluoride. UO₂ = Uranium dioxide.

SOURCE: "The Nuclear Fuel Cycle," in *NRC—Independent Regulator of Nuclear Safety*, U.S. Nuclear Regulatory Commission, June 2012, http://pbadupws.nrc.gov/docs/ML1233/ML12335A261.pdf (accessed July 9, 2014)

FIGURE 5.7

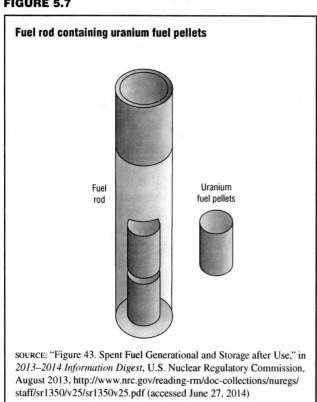

Fuel rod containing uranium fuel pellets

Fuel rod

Uranium fuel pellets

SOURCE: "Figure 43. Spent Fuel Generational and Storage after Use," in *2013–2014 Information Digest*, U.S. Nuclear Regulatory Commission, August 2013, http://www.nrc.gov/reading-rm/doc-collections/nuregs/staff/sr1350/v25/sr1350v25.pdf (accessed June 27, 2014)

nuclear fuel. As of 2014, the United States did not conduct re-enrichment due to the high costs involved; however, higher uranium prices in the future could render the process economically viable.

The uranium meant for nuclear power production is enriched to a relatively low level of about 3% to 5% U-235 concentration. This is called low-enriched uranium (LEU). By contrast, HEU contains greater than 20% U-235. Nuclear weapons require uranium enriched to a very high level (in excess of 90% U-235). The U.S. stockpile of nuclear weapons is overseen by the DOE's National Nuclear Security Administration (NNSA). In "U.S. HEU Disposition Program" (2014, http://nnsa.energy.gov/aboutus/ourprograms/dnn/fmd/heu), the NNSA indicates that HEU can be chemically down-blended to LEU suitable for use in nuclear power plants. The process has been performed in the United States since the late 1990s using surplus HEU from dismantled U.S. nuclear weapons. Until 2013 Russian-supplied HEU was also used through a program called Megatons to Megawatts. The program expired in 2013 and has not been renewed.

Plutonium, like uranium, is a radioactive metal. It is found in nature only in trace quantities. Plutonium can be created when uranium is subjected to fission, as in a nuclear power plant. According to the NRC, in "Plutonium" (May 2014, http://www.nrc.gov/reading-rm/doc-collections/fact-sheets/plutonium.pdf), U.S. nuclear reactors create plutonium, some of which undergoes fission and helps produce nuclear power. The NRC states, "Any plutonium that does not fission before the fuel is removed from the reactor remains in the spent fuel." Some other countries conduct reprocessing—that is, recover the still viable fuel (U-235 and any remaining plutonium) from the spent rods. The United States has long rejected reprocessing, primarily because the technique separates plutonium from uranium. Plutonium can be used to build nuclear bombs.

Nuclear fuel rods can be packed with a fuel called mixed oxide (MOX), which contains a mixture of oxides, typically uranium mixed with plutonium. In 2007

TABLE 5.1

Uranium amounts purchased by owners and operators of U.S. civilian nuclear power reactors, 1994–2013

[Million pounds U₃O₈ equivalent]

Delivery year	Total purchased	Purchased from U.S. producers	Purchased from U.S. brokers and traders	Purchased from other owners and operators of U.S. civilian nuclear power reactors, other U.S. suppliers, (and U.S. government for 2007)*	Purchased from foreign suppliers	U.S.-origin uranium	Foreign-origin uranium
1994	38.3	5.4	15.3	1.1	16.5	7.7	30.6
1995	43.4	5.3	16.2	0.6	21.4	5.2	38.2
1996	47.3	5.8	13.3	1.9	26.4	8.3	39.0
1997	42.0	5.7	9.9	3.0	23.4	8.1	33.9
1998	42.7	6.5	10.5	4.5	21.3	7.2	35.6
1999	47.9	5.2	10.4	5.6	26.8	11.4	36.5
2000	51.8	3.6	9.1	8.8	30.4	13.3	38.6
2001	55.4	2.3	11.7	11.4	30.0	13.2	42.2
2002	52.7	1.5	13.4	5.7	32.2	6.2	46.5
2003	56.6	0.6	10.5	8.3	37.2	10.2	46.4
2004	64.1	0.0	13.2	12.2	38.7	12.3	51.8
2005	65.7	W	10.4	W	39.4	11.0	54.7
2006	66.5	0.0	13.9	12.6	40.0	10.8	55.7
2007	51.0	0.0	9.8	7.6	33.5	4.0	47.0
2008	53.4	0.6	9.4	6.3	37.2	7.7	45.6
2009	49.8	W	11.1	W	36.8	7.1	42.8
2010	46.6	0.4	11.7	1.9	32.6	3.7	42.9
2011	54.8	0.6	14.8	1.1	38.4	5.2	49.6
2012	57.5	W	11.5	W	37.6	9.8	47.7
2013	57.4	W	12.8	W	37.4	9.5	47.9

W = Data withheld to avoid disclosure of individual company data.
U₃O₈ = Uranium oxide.
*Includes purchases between owners and operators of U.S. civilian nuclear power reactors along with purchases from other U.S. suppliers which are U.S. converters, enrichers, and fabricators.
Notes: "Other U.S. suppliers" are U.S. converters, enrichers, and fabricators. Totals may not equal sum of components because of independent rounding.

SOURCE: Adapted from "Table S1a. Uranium Purchased by Owners and Operators of U.S. Civilian Nuclear Power Reactors, 1994–2013," in *2013 Uranium Marketing Annual Report*, U.S. Energy Information Administration, May 2014, http://www.eia.gov/uranium/marketing/pdf/2013umar.pdf (accessed July 8, 2014)

construction began on a MOX facility near Augusta, Georgia. It was supposed to be operational by around 2015; however, schedule delays and cost overruns have hampered the project's completion. In March 2014 President Barack Obama (1961–) submitted his budget proposal for the NNSA for fiscal year 2015. (The federal government's fiscal year runs from October to September; thus, FY 2015 covers October 1, 2014, to September 30, 2015.) In "FY2015 Budget Request: Preserving President Obama's Nuclear Security Vision" (March 4, 2014, http://nnsa .energy.gov/mediaroom/pressreleases/fy15budget), the NNSA notes that the budget request "reflects the decision to place the MOX project in cold standby to further study more efficient options for plutonium disposition." As of October 2014, the future of the MOX facility was uncertain.

Uranium Prices

Table 5.3 shows the annual price per pound U₃O₈ equivalent paid by U.S. civilian nuclear power plants between 1994 and 2013 for uranium from various sellers. The average price was around $10 per pound U₃O₈ equivalent in 1994. It remained relatively flat for more than a decade and then increased dramatically, peaking in 2011 at $55.64 per pound U₃O₈ equivalent. By 2013 the average price had declined to $51.99 per pound U₃O₈ equivalent.

Overall, foreign-origin uranium has been cheaper than domestically sourced uranium. (See Table 5.3.) For example, in 2013 the average price for foreign-origin uranium was $51.13 per pound U₃O₈ equivalent, compared with $56.37 per pound U₃O₈ equivalent for U.S.-origin uranium.

DOMESTIC NUCLEAR ENERGY PRODUCTION

Table 5.4 shows the number of operable nuclear generating units in the United States dating back to the late 1950s. The number peaked in 1990 at 112 units and then declined. As of December 2013, 100 nuclear generating units were operable. According to the NRC, in *2013–2014 Information Digest*, the units were located in 31 states, but heavily concentrated in the eastern United States. Most (65) of the reactors were the pressurized-water type (the type illustrated in Figure 5.2). The remaining 35 reactors were boiling-water reactors.

The EIA notes in *Annual Energy Review 2011* (September 2012, http://www.eia.gov/totalenergy/data/ annual/pdf/aer.pdf) that between 1980 and 2011 no new

TABLE 5.2

Uranium purchased by owners and operators of U.S. civilian nuclear power reactors, by origin country, 2009–13

[Thousand pounds U_3O_8 equivalent. Dollars per pound U_3O_8 equivalent.]

| Origin country | Deliveries in 2009 | | Deliveries in 2010 | | Deliveries in 2011 | | Deliveries in 2012 | | Deliveries in 2013 | |
	Purchases	Weighted-average price	Purchases	Weighted-average price	Purchases	Weighted-average price	Purchases	Weighted-average price	Purchases	Weighted-average price
Australia	11,164	52.25	7,112	51.35	6,001	57.47	6,724	51.17	10,741	49.92
Brazil	W	W	W	W	W	W	W	W	W	W
Canada	8,975	42.25	10,238	50.35	10,832	56.08	13,584	56.75	7,808	52.61
China	0	—	0	—	W	W	W	W	W	W
Czech Republic	W	W	W	W	0	—	0	—	W	W
Germany	0	—	W	W	0	—	0	—	W	W
Hungary	0	—	W	W	0	—	0	—	W	W
Kazakhstan	4,985	43.41	6,830	47.81	9,728	53.71	6,234	51.69	6,454	46.73
Malawi	0	—	W	W	780	65.44	W	W	1,277	59.89
Namibia	5,732	47.30	4,913	47.90	6,199	56.74	5,986	54.56	5,677	49.78
Niger	2,001	47.55	587	49.00	1,744	54.38	2,133	50.45	1,666	51.26
Portugal	0	—	0	—	0	—	0	—	W	W
Russia	7,938	37.98	10,544	50.28	10,199	56.57	7,643	54.40	10,580	53.73
South Africa	W	W	W	W	1,524	53.62	1,243	56.45	186	46.72
Ukraine	0	—	W	W	W	W	W	W	0	—
Uzbekistan	1,424	46.65	1,865	48.57	1,808	55.99	2,576	52.80	3,064	50.02
Unknown	0	—	0	—	0	—	0	—	W	W
Foreign Total	**42,777**	**45.35**	**42,895**	**49.64**	**49,626**	**55.98**	**47,713**	**54.07**	**47,919**	**51.13**
United States	7,053	48.92	3,687	45.25	5,205	52.12	9,807	59.44	9,484	56.37
Total Purchases	**49,830**	**45.86**	**46,582**	**49.29**	**54,831**	**55.64**	**57,520**	**54.99**	**57,403**	**51.99**

W = Data withheld to avoid disclosure of individual company data.
— = Not applicable.
U_3O_8 = Uranium oxide.
Notes: Totals may not equal sum of components because of independent rounding. Weighted-average prices are not adjusted for inflation.

SOURCE: "Table 3. Uranium Purchased by Owners and Operators of U.S. Civilian Nuclear Power Reactors by Origin Country and Delivery Year, 2009–2013," in *2013 Uranium Marketing Annual Report*, U.S. Energy Information Administration, May 2014, http://www.eia.gov/uranium/marketing/pdf/2013umar.pdf (accessed July 8, 2014)

construction permits were issued for nuclear power plants in the United States. In addition, some plants were permanently shut down. The decline in nuclear power plants stems from several related issues. Financing is difficult to find, and construction has become more expensive, partly because of longer delays for licensing, but also because of regulations that were instituted following an accident at the Three Mile Island nuclear power plant in Pennsylvania in 1979. As will be explained later in this chapter, that accident allowed nuclear fuel to overheat to a dangerous level. No large-scale releases or explosions resulted; however, much stricter controls were put into place to regulate nuclear power plant operations.

Although no new nuclear power plants have been built for decades, the output of electricity at existing plants has increased. The net summer capacity of operable units has generally increased. It was 99.1 million kilowatts in December 2013. (See Table 5.4.) A capacity factor is the proportion of electricity produced compared with what could have been produced at full-power operation. As shown in Table 5.4, the average capacity factor for U.S. nuclear power plants in 2013 was 90.1%, near the all-time annual high of 91.8% set in 2007, and far greater than the value of 55.9% reported in 1975. Better training for operators, longer operating cycles between

refueling, and control-system improvements have contributed to increased plant performance and an increase in the capacity factor.

As shown in Table 5.4, nuclear power supplied only 1.4% of the total electricity generated in the United States in 1970. The percentage grew considerably during the 1970s and early to mid-1980s and then leveled off. (See Figure 5.8.) Nuclear power's share has hovered around 19% to 20% since 1990. (See Table 5.4.) Net electricity generation varied greatly from state to state in 2013. (See Figure 5.9.) Nineteen states, mostly in the interior west, generated no net electricity from nuclear power, while 16 others generated up to 24% of their electricity in this manner. Eleven states generated 25% to 50% of their electricity using nuclear power. Four states—New Hampshire, New Jersey, South Carolina, and Vermont—generated more than 50% of their electricity using nuclear power in 2013.

OUTLOOK FOR DOMESTIC NUCLEAR ENERGY

As noted earlier, no new nuclear power units were built in the United States for decades. However, some existing units increased their power production over their originally permitted levels. The NRC calls this uprating. In *2013–2014 Information Digest*, the commission notes

TABLE 5.3

Prices for uranium purchased by owners and operators of U.S. civilian nuclear power reactors, 1994–2013

[Dollars per pound U_3O_8 equivalent]

Delivery year	Total purchased (weighted-average price)	Purchased from U.S. producers	Purchased from U.S. brokers and traders	Purchased from other owners and operators of U.S. civilian nuclear power reactors, other U.S. suppliers, (and U.S. government for 2007)*	Purchased from foreign suppliers	U.S.-origin uranium (weighted-average price)	Foreign-origin uranium (weighted-average price)
1994	10.40	13.72	9.34	8.04	10.43	12.08	9.97
1995	11.25	14.84	9.83	12.52	11.40	14.20	10.84
1996	14.12	14.20	13.36	14.98	14.45	14.62	14.02
1997	12.88	13.60	12.31	W	12.91	13.36	12.78
1998	12.14	13.61	11.95	W	11.97	13.37	11.90
1999	11.63	13.93	11.54	W	11.47	12.24	11.47
2000	11.04	14.81	11.28	10.45	10.65	11.52	10.88
2001	10.15	13.26	10.44	9.98	9.86	10.50	10.05
2002	10.36	13.03	10.21	W	10.37	10.89	10.29
2003	10.81	14.17	11.05	10.16	10.82	10.81	10.81
2004	12.61	—	12.08	11.30	13.15	11.87	12.76
2005	14.36	W	13.76	W	14.70	15.11	14.21
2006	18.61	—	20.49	W	18.62	17.85	18.75
2007	32.78	—	34.10	W	32.36	28.89	33.05
2008	45.88	75.16	39.62	W	48.49	59.55	43.47
2009	45.86	W	41.88	W	46.68	48.92	45.35
2010	49.29	47.13	44.98	42.24	51.30	45.25	49.64
2011	55.64	58.12	53.29	52.50	56.60	52.12	55.98
2012	54.99	W	54.44	W	54.40	59.44	54.07
2013	51.99	W	50.44	W	51.93	56.37	51.13

— = Not applicable.
W = Data withheld to avoid disclosure of individual company data.
U_3O_8 = Uranium oxide.
*Includes purchases between owners and operators of U.S. civilian nuclear power reactors along with purchases from other U.S. suppliers which are U.S. converters, enrichers, and fabricators.
Notes: "Other U.S. suppliers" are U.S. converters, enrichers, and fabricators. Totals may not equal sum of components because of independent rounding. Weighted-average prices are not adjusted for inflation.

SOURCE: Adapted from "Table S1b. Weighted-Average Price of Uranium Purchased by Owners and Operators of U.S. Civilian Nuclear Power Reactors, 1994–2013," in *2013 Uranium Marketing Annual Report*, U.S. Energy Information Administration, May 2014, http://www.eia.gov/uranium/marketing/pdf/2013umar.pdf (accessed July 8, 2014)

that between 1977 and 2012 completed uprates resulted in 6,823 MW of additional electricity production. Between 2013 and 2017 the NRC projects that uprates will introduce another 1,563 MW.

The NRC lists in "Combined License Applications for New Reactors" (July 1, 2014, http://www.nrc.gov/reactors/new-reactors/col.html) the applications it has received for the construction and operation of nuclear power plants in the United States. These are called combined license (COL) applications. As of July 1, 2014, eight of the COL applications had been withdrawn or suspended for various reasons. Eight other applications were under review for a total of 12 units in the following states: Florida (four units at two separate sites), Maryland (one unit), Michigan (one unit), Pennsylvania (one unit), South Carolina (two units), Texas (two units), and Virginia (one unit).

As of July 1, 2014, the NRC had issued COL permits to two applicants for four units. These are the first new units permitted since the late 1970s. In February 2012 the NRC announced that it had approved a COL permit for two new units at an existing nuclear power plant in

Georgia. The Southern Company, the plant's owner, notes in "Southern Company Subsidiary, DOE Finalize Vogtle Nuclear Project Loan Guarantees" (February 20, 2014, http://www.southerncompany.com/news/dyn_pressroom.cshtml?s=43&item=3048) that the new units at the Alvin W. Vogtle Electric Generation Plant near Augusta, Georgia, are expected to begin operating in 2017 or 2018.

In March 2012 the NRC approved a COL permit for two new units at the existing Virgil C. Summer nuclear power plant in South Carolina. In a status update for the first quarter of 2014, the plant's owner, SCANA Corporation (March 31, 2014, http://www.scana.com/NR/rdonlyres/BA56733F-139C-462C-9242-B8962F5D5495/0/BLRAQuarterlyReport2014Q1.pdf), notes that construction of the units is expected to be completed by 2019.

In *Annual Energy Outlook 2014 with Projections to 2040* (April 2014, http://www.eia.gov/forecasts/aeo/pdf/0383(2014).pdf), the EIA predicts energy production in the future for various supply and demand scenarios. As shown in Figure 5.10, the agency forecasts rather flat U.S. nuclear electricity generation under the reference case. Generation is expected to hover around 800 billion

TABLE 5.4

Nuclear power units and generation, selected years 1957–2011 and monthly, January 2012–December 2013

	Total operable units[a, b]	Net summer capacity of operable units[b, c]	Nuclear electricity net generation	Nuclear share of electricity net generation	Capacity factor[d]
	Number	Million kilowatts	Million kilowatthours	Percent	Percent
1957 Total	1	0.055	10	(s)	NA
1960 Total	3	0.411	518	0.1	NA
1965 Total	13	0.793	3,657	0.3	NA
1970 Total	20	7.004	21,804	1.4	NA
1975 Total	57	37.267	172,505	9.0	55.9
1980 Total	71	51.810	251,116	11.0	56.3
1985 Total	96	79.397	383,691	15.5	58.0
1990 Total	112	99.624	576,862	19.0	66.0
1995 Total	109	99.515	673,402	20.1	77.4
2000 Total	104	97.860	753,893	19.8	88.1
2001 Total	104	98.159	768,826	20.6	89.4
2002 Total	104	98.657	780,064	20.2	90.3
2003 Total	104	99.209	763,733	19.7	87.9
2004 Total	104	99.628	788,528	19.9	90.1
2005 Total	104	99.988	781,986	19.3	89.3
2006 Total	104	100.334	787,219	19.4	89.6
2007 Total	104	100.266	806,425	19.4	91.8
2008 Total	104	100.755	806,208	19.6	91.1[d]
2009 Total	104	101.004	798,855	20.2	90.3
2010 Total	104	101.167	806,968	19.6	91.1
2011 Total	104	101.419[c]	790,204	19.3	89.1
2012					
January	104	101.602	72,381	21.3	95.8
February	104	101.602	63,847	20.6	90.3
March	104	101.602	61,729	20.0	81.7
April	104	101.602	55,871	18.9	76.4
May	104	101.625	62,081	18.4	82.1
June	104	101.625	65,140	18.1	89.0
July	104	101.747	69,129	16.7	91.3
August	104	101.856	69,602	17.6	91.8
September	104	101.856	64,511	19.3	88.0
October	104	101.856	59,743	19.2	78.8
November	104	101.885	56,713	18.5	77.3
December	104	101.885	68,584	20.5	90.5
Total	**104**	**101.885**	**769,331**	**19.0**	**86.1**
2013					
January	104	101.923[E]	71,406	20.5	94.2[E]
February	103	101.063[E]	61,483	19.9	90.5[E]
March	103	101.172[E]	62,947	19.4	83.6[E]
April	103	101.468[E]	56,767	19.0	77.7[E]
May	102	101.147[E]	62,848	19.5	83.4[E]
June	100	98.997[E]	66,430	18.6	93.2[E]
July	100	98.997[E]	70,539	17.9	95.8[E]
August	100	98.997[E]	71,344	18.6	96.9[E]
September	100	98.997[E]	65,799	19.3	92.3[E]
October	100	98.997[E]	63,184	20.1	85.8[E]
November	100	98.997[E]	64,975	20.7	91.2[E]
December	100	99.105[E]	71,294	20.2	96.7[E]
Total	**100**	**99.105[E]**	**789,017**	**19.4**	**90.1[E]**

[a]Total of nuclear generating units holding full-power licenses, or equivalent permission to operate, at end of period.
[b]At end of period.
[c]Beginning in 2011, monthly capacity values are estimated in two steps: (1) uprates and derates reported on Form EIA-860M are added to specific months; and (2) the difference between the resulting year-end capacity and final capacity is allocated to the month of January.
[d]Beginning in 2008, capacity factor data are calculated using a new methodology.
E = Estimate. NA = Not available. (s) = Less than 0.05.
Notes: Nuclear electricity net generation totals may not equal sum of components due to independent rounding. Geographic coverage is the 50 states and the District of Columbia.

SOURCE: Adapted from "Table 8.1. Nuclear Energy Overview," in *Monthly Energy Review: June 2014*, U.S. Energy Information Administration, June 25, 2014, http://www.eia.gov/totalenergy/data/monthly/archive/00351406.pdf (accessed June 27, 2014)

kWh through 2040. Figure 5.11 shows domestic electricity generation by fuel type between 1990 and 2012 and predicted through 2040. Nuclear energy is projected to provide around 17% of the national total in 2040. More information about projected future electricity supply and demand is included in Chapter 8.

WORLD NUCLEAR POWER PRODUCTION

The NRC notes in *2013–2014 Information Digest* that as of 2013, 440 nuclear power units were in operation in 34 countries. The nations with the most units were the United States (102), France (58), Japan (50), Russia (33), and South Korea (23). Total world nuclear

FIGURE 5.8

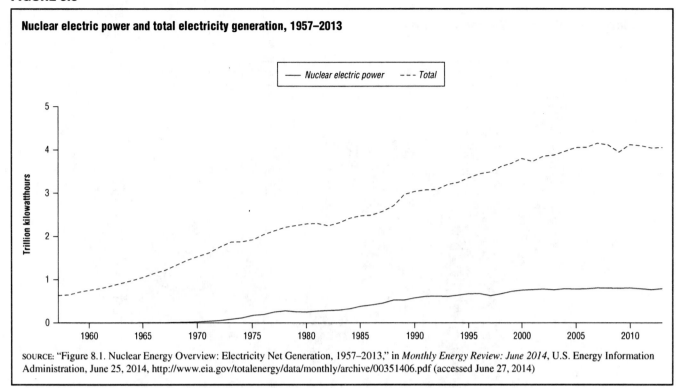

Nuclear electric power and total electricity generation, 1957–2013

SOURCE: "Figure 8.1. Nuclear Energy Overview: Electricity Net Generation, 1957–2013," in *Monthly Energy Review: June 2014*, U.S. Energy Information Administration, June 25, 2014, http://www.eia.gov/totalenergy/data/monthly/archive/00351406.pdf (accessed June 27, 2014)

power production was 2.3 million gigawatt-hours (GWh) in 2011. The United States had the highest production, at 770,719 GWh. Other countries with substantial production included France, with 407,438 GWh, and Russia, with 166,293 GWh.

France produced 75% of its electricity from nuclear power in 2013, the largest percentage of any nation. Other major producers included Slovakia (54%), Belgium (51%), Hungary (46%), and Ukraine (46%). The United States produced 19% of its electrical power using nuclear energy in 2013. Sixty-eight additional nuclear power units were under construction or on order worldwide in 2013. China was expected to install the most new units (28), followed by Russia (11 units) and India (7 units).

NUCLEAR SAFETY ISSUES

Safety is a concern in all energy industries, but the nuclear power industry has unique safety concerns. The consequences of a destructive accident or terrorist attack at a nuclear power plant could be quite calamitous due to radiation release. One troubling scenario involves a meltdown of the reactor core following the failure of the cooling system. In this event, all the control rods holding the uranium fuel get so hot they melt, releasing their radioactive contents. As shown in Figure 5.2, a typical U.S. reactor is encased in a containment structure with walls that are made of concrete and steel several feet thick. Thus, a partial or even complete meltdown does not necessarily mean that radiation will escape from the reactor. It depends on the structural integrity of the containment walls.

Nuclear power has been generated commercially since only the late 1950s. Three major incidents, however, that have severely affected the industry's safety reputation have occurred in three different countries.

Three Mile Island

On March 28, 1979, the Three Mile Island nuclear facility near Harrisburg, Pennsylvania, was the site of the worst nuclear accident in U.S. history when one of its reactors overheated and suffered a partial meltdown. The emergency system was designed to dump water on the hot core of the reactor and spray water into the reactor building to stop the production of steam. During the accident, however, the valves leading to the emergency water pumps closed. Another valve was stuck in the open position, drawing water away from the core, which then became partially uncovered and began to melt.

The accident did not result in any deaths or injuries to plant workers or to people in the nearby community. On average, area residents were exposed to less radiation than that of a chest X-ray. Nevertheless, the incident raised concerns about nuclear safety, which resulted in more rigorous safety standards in the nuclear power industry. Antinuclear sentiment was fueled as well, heightening Americans' wariness of nuclear power as an energy source.

FIGURE 5.9

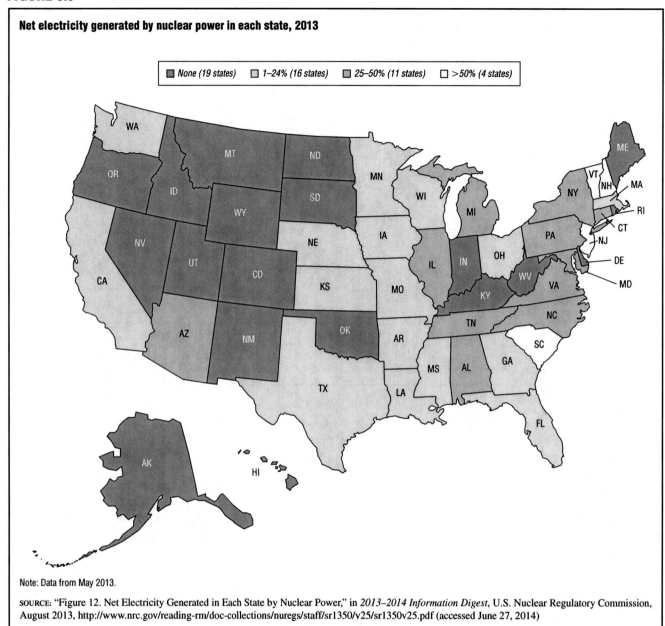

Net electricity generated by nuclear power in each state, 2013

■ None (19 states)　□ 1–24% (16 states)　▨ 25–50% (11 states)　□ >50% (4 states)

Note: Data from May 2013.

SOURCE: "Figure 12. Net Electricity Generated in Each State by Nuclear Power," in *2013–2014 Information Digest*, U.S. Nuclear Regulatory Commission, August 2013, http://www.nrc.gov/reading-rm/doc-collections/nuregs/staff/sr1350/v25/sr1350v25.pdf (accessed June 27, 2014)

The damaged nuclear reactor at Three Mile Island was permanently shut down after it underwent cleanup. An undamaged reactor at the plant, however, continued to operate as of October 2014.

Chernobyl

On April 26, 1986, the most serious nuclear accident in history occurred at Chernobyl, a nuclear plant in what is now Ukraine (then part of the Soviet Union). At least 31 people died and hundreds were injured when one of the four reactors exploded during a badly run test. Millions of people were exposed to some levels of radiation when radioactive particles were released into the atmosphere. About 350,000 people were eventually evacuated from the area.

The cleanup was a huge project. Helicopters dropped tons of limestone, sand, clay, lead, and boron on the smoldering reactor to stop the radiation leakage and reduce the heat. Meanwhile, workers built a giant steel and cement sarcophagus to entomb the remains of the reactor and contain the radioactive waste.

The International Atomic Energy Agency indicates in *Chernobyl's Legacy: Health, Environmental and Socio-economic Impacts* (April 2006, http://www.iaea .org/sites/default/files/chernobyl.pdf) that about 1,000 people involved in the initial cleanup, including emergency workers and the military, received high doses of radiation. Eventually, over 600,000 people were involved in decontamination and containment activities. The long-term effects of whatever exposure they received are being monitored.

Although some of the evacuated land in Chernobyl has been declared fit for habitation again, several areas

FIGURE 5.10

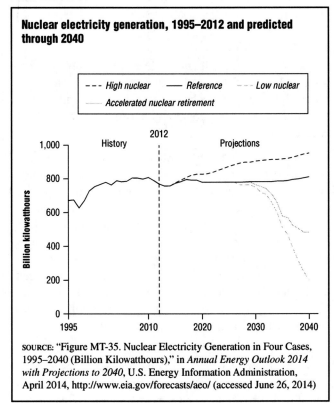

Nuclear electricity generation, 1995–2012 and predicted through 2040

SOURCE: "Figure MT-35. Nuclear Electricity Generation in Four Cases, 1995–2040 (Billion Kilowatthours)," in *Annual Energy Outlook 2014 with Projections to 2040*, U.S. Energy Information Administration, April 2014, http://www.eia.gov/forecasts/aeo/ (accessed June 26, 2014)

FIGURE 5.11

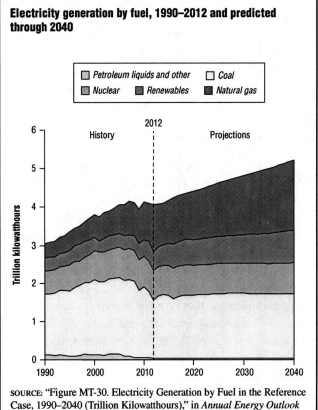

Electricity generation by fuel, 1990–2012 and predicted through 2040

SOURCE: "Figure MT-30. Electricity Generation by Fuel in the Reference Case, 1990–2040 (Trillion Kilowatthours)," in *Annual Energy Outlook 2014 with Projections to 2040*, U.S. Energy Information Administration, April 2014, http://www.eia.gov/forecasts/aeo/ (accessed June 26, 2014)

that received heavy concentrations of radiation are expected to be closed for decades.

Fukushima Daiichi

On March 11, 2011, an underwater earthquake triggered a tsunami that flooded the northeastern coast of Japan and killed nearly 20,000 people. The Fukushima Daiichi nuclear power plant is located on the northeastern coast approximately 150 miles (240 km) north of Tokyo. Three of the plant's six reactors suffered meltdowns after their cooling systems became inoperable following the earthquake and tsunami. Over subsequent days the reactors were plagued by partial and complete meltdowns and small hydrogen gas explosions. Some radioactive gases were released into the atmosphere from the damaged containment structures. The overheated reactors were finally cooled with seawater to prevent further releases.

Kevin Krolicki reports in "Fukushima Radiation Higher than First Estimated" (Reuters.com, May 24, 2012) that more than a year after the accident occurred officials estimated that "the amount of radiation released in the first three weeks of the accident [was] about one-sixth the radiation released during the 1986 Chernobyl disaster." The Fukushima incident dampened the enthusiasm that had been building around the world for greater reliance on nuclear power. In *Annual Energy Outlook 2012* (June 2012, http://www.eia.gov/forecasts/aeo/pdf/0383(2012).pdf), the EIA notes "in the aftermath, governments in several countries that previously had planned

to expand nuclear capacity—including Japan, Germany, Switzerland, and Italy—reversed course." In fact, the agency notes that Germany decided to phase out all of its nuclear power by 2025.

The United States has continued to cautiously embrace nuclear power. The Fukushima accident did spur some changes in the U.S. nuclear power industry. The Nuclear Energy Institute (NEI) explains in "Nuclear Industry Opens Memphis Response Center" (June 30, 2014, http://www.nei.org/News-Media/News/News-Archives/Nuclear-Industry-Opens-Memphis-Response-Center) that the industry has established a safety program that includes the positioning of emergency equipment at strategic locations around the country. As of October 2014, equipment such as portable backup generators, pumps, couplings, and hoses had been stationed in Phoenix, Arizona, and Memphis, Tennessee. The NEI notes the equipment can be transported "to any U.S. nuclear plant within 24 hours."

NUCLEAR WASTE ISSUES

Another safety (and environmental) issue related to nuclear power production is the creation of radioactive waste. Radioactive waste is produced at all stages of the nuclear fuel cycle, from the initial mining of the uranium to the final disposal of the spent fuel from the reactor. The term *radioactive waste* encompasses a broad range of material with widely varying characteristics. Some is barely radioactive and safe to handle, whereas other types are intensely hot and highly radioactive. Some waste decays to safe levels of radioactivity in a matter of days or weeks, whereas other types will remain dangerous for thousands of years. The DOE and the NRC have defined the major types of radioactive waste that are associated with nuclear power generation in the United States.

Disposing of radioactive waste is unquestionably one of the major problems associated with the development of nuclear power. The highly toxic wastes must be isolated from the environment until the radioactivity decays to a safe level. That period can last from several years to several millennia, depending on the radioactivity of the waste. Although U.S. policy is based on the assumption that radioactive waste can be disposed of safely, new storage and disposal facilities for all types of radioactive waste have frequently been delayed or blocked by concerns about safety, health, and the environment.

Uranium Mill Tailings

Uranium mill tailings are sandlike wastes produced in uranium refining operations. Although they emit low levels of radiation, their large volume poses a hazard, particularly from radon emissions and groundwater contamination. Mill tailings are usually deposited in large piles next to the mill that processed the ore and must be covered to prevent radiation problems.

Low-Level Waste

Low-level waste (LLW) includes trash (such as wiping rags, swabs, and syringes), contaminated clothing (such as shoe covers and protective gloves), and hardware (such as luminous dials, filters, and tools). This waste comes from nuclear reactors, industrial users, government users (but not nuclear weapons sites), research universities, and medical facilities. In general, LLW decays relatively quickly (in 10 to 100 years). According to the NRC, in *2013–2014 Information Digest*, as of 2013 four licensed LLW facilities were operating in the United States: in Barnwell, South Carolina; in Richland, Washington; in Clive, Utah; and in Andrews, Texas.

The Low-Level Radioactive Waste Policy Amendments Act of 1985 encouraged states to enter into compacts, which are legal agreements among states for low-level radioactive waste disposal. Each compact is responsible for the development of disposal capacity for the LLW generated within the compact; however, as of October 2014 new disposal sites had yet to be built. Nuclear power facilities that are located in compacts without existing LLW disposal sites must petition the compact to export their low-level radioactive waste to one of the four operating LLW disposal sites.

Spent Nuclear Fuel

As noted earlier, spent nuclear fuel is fuel that has exhausted its usefulness in a nuclear power reactor. It is called high-level waste because it is highly radioactive and requires very long containment times, typically thousands of years.

For decades the United States has pursued development of a national repository for its high-level wastes; however, finding a suitable site acceptable to all parties involved has proven impossible. In 1987 the federal government began investigating Yucca Mountain, a barren wind-swept mountain in the desert about 100 miles (161 km) northwest of Las Vegas, Nevada. The project was highly controversial from the start and has been fought bitterly by the state of Nevada and environmentalists. After years of court challenges and political wrangling the Obama administration dropped the site in 2010 as a repository candidate.

Thus, as of October 2014 the United States had no central repository for spent nuclear fuel. The fuel continued to be stored either at the nuclear power plants that generated it or at other secure locations. In *Commercial Spent Nuclear Fuel: Observations on the Key Attributes and Challenges of Storage and Disposal Options* (April 11, 2013, http://www.gao.gov/assets/660/653731.pdf), the GAO states that "commercial reactors have generated nearly 70,000 metric tons [77,200 tons] of spent fuel, which is currently stored at 75 reactor sites in 33 states, and this inventory is expected to more than double by 2055."

A NEW STRATEGY STALLS. In 2010, after President Obama refused to provide further federal funding toward licensing Yucca Mountain, the Blue Ribbon Commission on America's Nuclear Future (BRC) was established to recommend alternative options for consideration. In January 2012 the BRC issued its final report, *Report to the Secretary of Energy* (http://brc.gov/sites/default/files/documents/brc_finalreport_jan2012.pdf), in which it pointed out "this nation's failure to come to grips with the nuclear waste issue has already proved damaging and costly and it will be more damaging and more costly the longer it continues."

The BRC recommended numerous legislative and policy changes as first steps toward finding a permanent solution. One of those recommendations was the creation of a new federal agency called the Nuclear Waste Administration to handle the disposal problem. In January 2013 the DOE published *Strategy for the Management and Disposal of Used Nuclear Fuel and High-Level Radioactive Waste* (http://energy.gov), noting that "the [Obama] Administration endorses the key principles that underpin the BRC's recommendations." The DOE also urged Congress to make "the appropriate authorizations" for implementing the new strategy. In June 2013 the Nuclear Waste Administration Act was introduced in Congress to create the new agency and implement some of the other BRC recommendations; however, as of October 2014 the bill had not been passed.

REPROCESSING SPENT NUCLEAR FUEL. As noted earlier, some other countries reprocess spent nuclear fuel to recycle uranium. Reprocessing also reduces the amount of spent fuel requiring disposal. The United States has rejected this approach because of the security dangers posed by plutonium. Presently, the plutonium within spent nuclear fuel in the United States is dispersed among large amounts of uranium and other contaminants, such as americium, curium, and neptunium. Thus, the plutonium is not a tempting target for terrorists or other parties seeking weapons-grade plutonium.

NUCLEAR POWER COST FACTORS

The commercial nuclear power industry is devoted entirely to electricity production. In the United States electricity is also produced by the combustion of fossil fuels, mainly coal and natural gas. Because electricity producers feed their electricity to the nation's electrical grid for consumption by consumers, it is difficult to distinguish between the prices for electricity produced from various fuel sources. However, there are specific supply and demand factors that affect nuclear power pricing.

Analysts agree that one cost differential between nuclear-based electricity and electricity from other sources is capital costs. Construction of a nuclear power plant is extremely expensive. Most of the United States' nuclear power plants were built decades ago. Thus, the high capital costs associated with building the reactors have long been absorbed by the industry and are not a significant factor in current pricing. The same holds true for initial licensing costs and other costs that are incurred before plants begin operating. Nuclear power plant operators also incur fuel, operating, and maintenance costs. Fuel costs can vary considerably from year to year as shown in Table 5.3. The nuclear power industry must also pay into the Nuclear Waste Fund, which is administered by the federal government.

According to the DOE, in *U.S. Department of Energy Nuclear Waste Fund Fee Adequacy Report* (January 2013, http://energy.gov), the fund was established by law in 1983 and requires civilian nuclear power producers to pay a fee of one-tenth cent per kilowatt-hour of electricity generated. As of August 2012, the fund balance totaled approximately $28.2 billion.

The Nuclear Waste Fund represents an expense that is imposed by the government on the nuclear power industry; however, the government has also taken actions to financially support and promote the industry. These actions help lower the production price of electricity that is generated by nuclear power. Chapter 1 describes the federal tax breaks, research and development funds, and other types of financial assistance that are provided to energy suppliers.

CHAPTER 6
RENEWABLE ENERGY

Renewable energy is energy that is virtually unlimited. As explained in Chapter 1, under the right circumstances renewable energy sources are constantly produced and can be tapped again and again by humans without eliminating them. Examples include flowing water, wood, wind, biologically based waste materials, sunlight, and geothermal energy (i.e., the heat stored beneath the earth's crust).

Until the early 1970s most Americans were content to rely on fossil fuels for their energy needs. However, an embargo on imported oil ended this carefree approach. Throughout the United States people waited in line to fill their gas tanks—in some places gasoline was rationed—and lower heat settings for offices and homes were encouraged. In a country where mobility and convenience were highly valued, the 1970s oil crisis was a shock to the system. Developing alternative sources of energy to supplement and perhaps eventually replace fossil fuels suddenly became important. Over the following decades financial incentives and technological advancements helped alternative energy providers build their industries.

Renewable energy sources are relative newcomers to the energy marketplace and, in many cases, must compete directly with fossil fuels for consumers. This is a difficult task. The systems and infrastructure for fossil fuel production and delivery have long been in place, and Americans are accustomed to them. As a result, renewables must overcome logistical, technological, and economical challenges to get to consumers.

It is also important to understand that although renewables begin as natural sources, they may be heavily processed before they actually provide energy to consumers. Industrial processing requires energy—that is, it has an energy price. For example, chipping wood into small pieces so it is easier to burn is energy intensive. Likewise, converting crops, such as corn, into liquid fuel is a highly industrial process. Because U.S. industry is heavily dependent on fossil fuels, the reality is that fossil fuels are burned during the processing of many renewable sources. This energy price has to be considered when evaluating the relative advantages and disadvantages of alternative fuels.

As noted in previous chapters, fossil fuels are forecast to maintain their prominent role as energy sources for decades to come. Even so, renewable sources have carved out a niche in the market, and that niche seems destined to grow.

MARKET FACTORS

The renewables market is driven by concerns about energy production from nuclear energy and fossil fuels. One major concern relates to environmental impacts. Nuclear power generates radioactive waste that can be hazardous for thousands of years. The combustion of fossil fuels releases emissions that degrade air quality and contribute to global warming and climate change. Renewable fuels do not generate radioactive waste. The noncombustible renewables (solar, wind, tides, hydropower, and geothermal) do not emit the air pollutants that are associated with fossil fuels. The combustible renewables, by virtue of their organic makeup, do contribute such emissions, but to a lesser extent than fossil fuels. Energy self-sufficiency is another concern that drives interest in renewable fuels because they can be produced domestically.

Although environmental impacts and self-sufficiency are powerful motivators for developing alternative fuels, both concerns pale in comparison to economic considerations. Many renewable energy source technologies are relatively immature and still in the research and development (R&D) stage. As such, they are more expensive to produce commercially than fossil fuels. When fossil fuels drop in price, interest wanes in the business world for developing alternative fuels because there is less profit to be made. In addition, the impetus for renewables development declines when "new" domestic sources of fossil fuels become available. As described in Chapters 2 and 3, domestic production of oil and natural gas from unconventional geological sources, such as shale and tar sands, has skyrocketed. These sources will likely help keep domestic fossil fuel prices low, further damaging the economic competitiveness of renewables.

Renewable Energy Providers

Renewable energy is a focus of investment for companies both large and small. Large energy companies may operate renewables facilities themselves or invest in smaller renewables companies. Chapter 2 describes the so-called supermajor fossil fuel companies that are collectively dubbed "Big Oil." One of these companies is Total, which is based in France. SunPower Inc. is a solar energy provider headquartered in California. According to SunPower (http://investors.sunpower.com), as of 2014 Total owned a 66% share in the company. Chevron (May 2014, http://www.chevron.com/delivering energy/geothermal), another of the Big Oil companies, indicates that it is "one of the world's leading producers of geothermal energy."

Smaller players in the fossil fuel industry, such as Valero Energy Corporation, have invested heavily in the production of transportation fuels, such as ethanol, which are derived from corn and other biological sources. According to Valero (2014, http://www.valero.com/products/renewables/Pages/Home.aspx), it was the first traditional oil refiner to begin producing ethanol. In addition, the company has teamed with Darling International Inc. to produce renewable (or green) diesel fuel from recycled animal fat, used cooking oil and distiller's corn oil.

Excluding ethanol and other biofuels, renewable energy sources are almost entirely devoted to electricity generation. The federal government, by virtue of its control of large hydropower dams, is the leading provider of renewables-derived electricity. Electric utilities, both public owned and investor owned, use renewable sources to varying degrees. For example, Ceres and Clean Edge are nonprofit organizations devoted to sustainability. In July 2014 the two organizations published a report rating the nation's largest investor-owned electric utilities in terms of their renewables utilization. In *Benchmarking Utility Clean Energy Deployment 2014* (http://www.ceres.org/resources/reports/benchmarking-utility-clean-energy-deployment-2014/view), Ceres and Clean Edge note that NV Energy, a utility based in Nevada, used renewable sources for 21% of the electricity it sold in 2012. Other major providers of renewables-derived electricity included Edison International, PG&E, Sempra Energy, and Xcel Energy. The electric power sector also includes independent power producers (IPPs). NRG Energy, Inc. (2014, http://www.nrg.com/about/who-we-are/our-assets), the nation's largest IPP as of 2014, operates dozens of power plants that are fueled by solar and wind in addition to its fossil fuel–fired fleet.

Government Involvement

When interest in developing renewable energy sources became keen during the 1970s, the government began providing financial support to the fledgling industry. As described in Chapter 1, the federal government uses a variety of incentives to encourage domestic energy development. Figure 1.14 in Chapter 1 shows the costs of energy-related tax preferences between 1977 and 2013. The fossil fuel industry has historically been the major beneficiary; however, preferences for the renewable energy industry began increasing dramatically during the first decade of the 21st century. Legislative changes, particularly the Energy Policy Act of 2005, helped turn the focus toward renewables.

As shown in Table 1.6 in Chapter 1, the federal government gave $16.4 billion in total energy-related tax preferences during fiscal year (FY) 2013. (The federal government's fiscal year runs from October to September; thus, FY 2013 covered October 1, 2012, to September 30, 2013.) Renewable energy enjoyed around $7.3 billion in tax preferences in FY 2013, or 45% of the total. However, as noted in Chapter 1, most renewable energy provisions are temporary, whereas those given to fossil fuels and nuclear energy are mostly permanent.

Critics complain that the incentives granted to the renewable energy sector pale in comparison with the many billions of dollars that have been pumped into the fossil fuel industry for nearly a century. Government support is particularly important during the initial R&D stages of an industry. The fossil fuel industry is extremely mature, whereas the renewables industry is still largely doing initial R&D tasks. (It should be noted that this is not true for the hydroelectric sector, which has operated for many decades.) Some analysts believe the government should provide more funding support for renewables at this crucial time in their development and make their tax preferences permanent to boost the competitiveness of the industry.

As noted earlier, government entities are substantial suppliers of renewable energy through their role as electricity utility operators. As is explained in Chapter 8, the U.S. electric power sector includes power plants that are owned and operated by municipalities, federal agencies (such as the Bonneville Power Administration), and federally owned corporations (such as the Tennessee Valley Authority).

The government also supports renewables development through mandates and standards. For example, the Energy Independence and Security Act of 2007 includes a Renewable Fuels Standard that mandates the use of specified amounts of biofuels by 2022. This standard will be explained in more detail later in this chapter. State governments also issue renewables mandates. The U.S. Energy Information Administration (EIA) indicates in *Annual Energy Outlook 2014 with Projections to 2040* (April 2014, http://www.eia.gov/forecasts/aeo/pdf/0383(2014).pdf) that as of April 2014, 29 states and the District of Columbia had mandatory (enforceable) renewable portfolio standards or similar laws. The agency notes that "under such standards, each state determines its own levels of renewable generation, eligible technologies, and noncompliance penalties." For example, Nevada requires that renewables account for 25% of electricity sales in the state by 2025.

THE EXECUTIVE BRANCH. As described in Chapter 1, President Barack Obama (1961–) has championed renewable energy usage as part of his "all-of-the-above" energy policy. One major driver is concern about the contribution of fossil fuel combustion to global warming and climate change. Congress has proved reluctant to pass laws that could encumber the nation's oil and gas industry and hence boost usage of renewable fuels. As a result, Obama has furthered his renewables agenda by taking actions that affect the executive branch (the offices and agencies under the control of the president). Some of the major initiatives are described in "Fact Sheet: Building on Progress—Supporting Solar Deployment and Jobs" (April 17, 2014, http://www.whitehouse.gov/the-press-office/2014/04/17/fact-sheet-building-progress-supporting-solar-deployment-and-jobs).

The Obama administration has concentrated on increasing renewable energy usage by federal agencies, such as the U.S. Department of Defense, which has committed to deploying 3 gigawatts of renewable energy on military installations by 2025. Likewise, federal buildings across the country are required to obtain 20% of their energy from renewable sources by 2020. Agencies such as the U.S. Department of the Interior's Bureau of Land Management (BLM) control huge swaths of government-owned land in the West. As of August 2014, the BLM (http://www.blm.gov/wo/st/en/prog/energy/renewable_energy/Renewable_Energy_Projects_Approved_to_Date.html) had allowed dozens of companies to develop utility-scale renewable energy projects on public lands under its control. The projects rely on solar, wind, or geothermal resources.

The Obama administration has been particularly keen to encourage solar power generation. In April 2014 the White House hosted a Solar Summit to convene and honor leading firms in the solar industry. The honorees and new presidential initiatives devoted to solar energy are described in "Fact Sheet: President Obama Announces Commitments and Executive Actions to Advance Solar Deployment and Energy Efficiency" (May 9, 2014, http://www.whitehouse.gov/the-press-office/2014/05/09/fact-sheet-president-obama-announces-commitments-and-executive-actions-a). The White House notes that about one-fourth of the nation's power generating capacity added in 2013 was solar based. Declining equipment costs are helping drive consumer demand for solar energy. In 2014 the Obama administration implemented measures to facilitate greater use of solar power within the federal government and to make the solar industry more attractive financially to private investors.

The U.S. Environmental Protection Agency (EPA) encourages use of renewables-derived electricity through its Green Power Partnership program. In "National Top 100" (October 27, 2014, http://www.epa.gov/greenpower/toplists/top100.htm), the EPA ranks 100 of its commercial partners in terms of their usage of renewables-derived electricity. As of October 2014, the top-five companies were Intel Corporation, Kohl's Department Stores, Microsoft Corporation, Google Inc., and Wal-Mart Stores, Inc. The 100 companies obtained green power from numerous providers, including utilities and IPPs. In addition, some of them generated their own green power on-site. The EPA (April 15, 2014, http://www.epa.gov/greenpower/awards/winners.htm) also annually recognizes green power suppliers. The winners of the agency's 2013 Green Power Supplier Award were 3Degrees, Dominion Virginia Power, and Sterling Planet.

PRODUCTION AND CONSUMPTION

Figure 6.1 shows total U.S. energy consumption by major energy source between 1949 and 2013. Historically, fossil fuels have dominated domestic consumption. As shown in Table 1.2 in Chapter 1, renewable sources accounted for 9.3 quadrillion British thermal units (Btu) of consumption in 2013, or 11% of the total of 81.7 quadrillion Btu. In 2013 hydroelectric power was the most consumed renewable source, followed by wood and biofuels. (See Table 6.1.) The EIA lumps wood and biofuels together with waste under the biomass category. (Waste refers to municipal solid waste from biogenic [biologically derived] sources, landfill gas, sludge waste, agricultural by-products [such as stalks and husks], and other biologically based waste.) Biomass is either directly combustible or is used to produce other combustible fuels, such as ethanol and biodiesel. As indicated in Figure 6.2, biomass and hydroelectric power have been the two most commonly used renewables for decades. Biomass consumption has increased noticeably since around 2000.

Figure 6.3 provides a breakdown of renewables consumption in 2013 by end-use sectors. The electric power sector accounted for 4.8 quadrillion Btu, which was more than half (52%) of the total consumption of

FIGURE 6.1

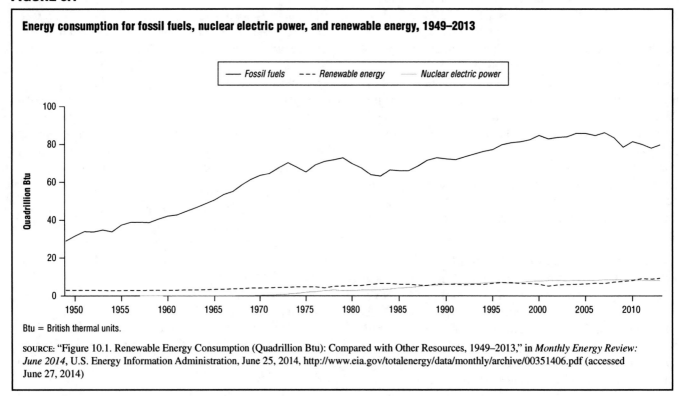

Energy consumption for fossil fuels, nuclear electric power, and renewable energy, 1949–2013

Btu = British thermal units.

SOURCE: "Figure 10.1. Renewable Energy Consumption (Quadrillion Btu): Compared with Other Resources, 1949–2013," in *Monthly Energy Review: June 2014*, U.S. Energy Information Administration, June 25, 2014, http://www.eia.gov/totalenergy/data/monthly/archive/00351406.pdf (accessed June 27, 2014)

9.3 quadrillion Btu. The industrial and transportation sectors were the next biggest consumers of renewable energy sources in 2013. The residential and commercial sectors were much smaller users.

Biomass Energy

Biomass provided 4.6 quadrillion Btu in 2013, or 50% of the total renewables consumed. (See Table 6.1.) Wood was the largest biomass source providing 2.1 quadrillion Btu, or nearly half (46%) of the biomass total. It was followed by biofuels (2 quadrillion Btu, or 43% of the biomass total) and waste (0.5 quadrillion Btu, or 10% of the biomass total).

The biofuels category includes fuel ethanol and biodiesel. Fuel ethanol is ethanol intended for fuel use, rather than for human consumption. Fuel ethanol is denatured (made unfit for human consumption) by the addition of petroleum products. Fuel ethanol can be manufactured from various vegetative feedstocks, including starchy/sugary crops, such as corn (which is primarily used in the United States), and cellulosic sources, such as trees and grasses.

Fuel ethanol can be blended at low concentrations into motor gasoline. For example, gasohol is a gasoline blend that contains up to 10% fuel ethanol by volume and can be used just like gasoline in conventional vehicles. At high concentrations, ethanol is blended with gasoline to make fuels that are suitable only for specially designed vehicles called alternative-fuel vehicles. For example,

E85 is the short name for a fuel that contains 85% ethanol and 15% motor gasoline. Biodiesel is a fuel made from biological sources, such as soybeans or animal fats, and is used in vehicles that ordinarily run on petroleum-derived diesel fuel.

As shown in the footnotes for Table 6.1, annual domestic production equals annual domestic consumption for all renewables except biofuels. Biofuels are heavily processed, and some losses and coproducts result during processing. In addition, the United States imports and exports small amounts of biofuels. In 2013 fuel ethanol feedstocks (corn and other biomass inputs) totaled 1,827 trillion Btu. (See Table 6.2.) Losses and coproducts totaled 728 trillion Btu. After denaturant addition, the heat content of the final product was 1,128 trillion Btu. Overall, fuel ethanol production in 2013 was 13.3 billion gallons (50.4 billion L), whereas consumption was 13.2 billion gallons (49.9 billion L). Consumption of fuel ethanol increased dramatically during the first decade of the 21st century.

As shown in Table 6.3, biodiesel production totaled 1.3 billion gallons (5.1 billion L) in 2013, whereas consumption was nearly 1.4 billion gallons (5.2 billion L). The consumption of biodiesel was only around 300 million gallons (1.1 billion L) from 2007 to 2010 and then grew considerably.

GOVERNMENT INVOLVEMENT. Growth in biofuels consumption has been driven largely by government mandates for biofuels use. Janet McGurty and Matthew

TABLE 6.1

Renewable energy production and consumption by major source, selected years 1949–2013

[Trillion Btu]

	Production[a]			Consumption								
	Biomass		Total renewable energy[d]	Hydroelectric power[e]	Geo-thermal[f]	Solar/PV[g]	Wind[h]	Biomass				Total renewable energy
	Biofuels[b]	Total[c]						Wood[i]	Waste[j]	Biofuels[k]	Total	
1950 Total	NA	1,562	2,978	1,415	NA	NA	NA	1,562	NA	NA	1,562	2,978
1955 Total	NA	1,424	2,784	1,360	NA	NA	NA	1,424	NA	NA	1,424	2,784
1960 Total	NA	1,320	2,928	1,608	(s)	NA	NA	1,320	NA	NA	1,320	2,928
1965 Total	NA	1,335	3,396	2,059	2	NA	NA	1,335	NA	NA	1,335	3,396
1970 Total	NA	1,431	4,070	2,634	6	NA	NA	1,429	2	NA	1,431	4,070
1975 Total	NA	1,499	4,687	3,155	34	NA	NA	1,497	2	NA	1,499	4,687
1980 Total	NA	2,475	5,428	2,900	53	NA	NA	2,474	2	NA	2,475	5,428
1985 Total	93	3,016	6,084	2,970	97	(s)	(s)	2,687	236	93	3,016	6,084
1990 Total	111	2,735	6,041	3,046	171	59	29	2,216	408	111	2,735	6,041
1995 Total	198	3,099	6,558	3,205	152	69	33	2,370	531	200	3,101	6,560
2000 Total	233	3,006	6,104	2,811	164	66	57	2,262	511	236	3,008	6,106
2001 Total	254	2,624	5,164	2,242	164	64	70	2,006	364	253	2,622	5,163
2002 Total	308	2,705	5,734	2,689	171	63	105	1,995	402	303	2,701	5,729
2003 Total	402	2,805	5,947	2,793	173	62	113	2,002	401	404	2,807	5,948
2004 Total	487	2,998	6,069	2,688	178	63	142	2,121	389	499	3,010	6,081
2005 Total	564	3,104	6,229	2,703	181	63	178	2,137	403	577	3,117	6,242
2006 Total	720	3,216	6,599	2,869	181	68	264	2,099	397	771	3,267	6,649
2007 Total	978	3,480	6,528	2,446	186	76	341	2,089	413	990	3,492	6,541
2008 Total	1,387	3,881	7,219	2,511	192	89	546	2,059	435	1,370	3,865	7,202
2009 Total	1,584	3,967	7,655	2,669	200	98	721	1,931	452	1,568	3,950	7,638
2010 Total	1,884	4,332	8,128	2,539	208	126	923	1,981	468	1,837	4,285	8,081
2011 Total	2,044	4,516	9,170	3,103	212	171	1,168	2,010	462	1,948	4,420	9,074
2012 Total	1,942	4,419	8,826	2,629	212	227	1,340	2,010	467	1,902	4,379	8,786
2013 Total	2,001	4,614	9,298	2,561	221	307	1,595	2,138	476	1,993	4,607	9,291

[a]Production equals consumption for all renewable energy sources except biofuels.
[b]Total biomass inputs to the production of fuel ethanol and biodiesel.
[c]Wood and wood-derived fuels, biomass waste, and total biomass inputs to the production of fuel ethanol and biodiesel.
[d]Hydroelectric power, geothermal, solar thermal/photovoltaic, wind, and biomass.
[e]Conventional hydroelectricity net generation (converted to Btu using the fossil-fuels heat rate).
[f]Geothermal electricity net generation (converted to Btu using the fossil-fuels heat rate), and geothermal heat pump and direct use energy.
[g]Solar thermal and photovoltaic (PV) electricity net generation (converted to Btu using the fossil-fuels heat rate), and solar thermal direct use energy.
[h]Wind electricity net generation (converted to Btu using the fossil-fuels heat rate).
[i]Wood and wood-derived fuels.
[j]Municipal solid waste from biogenic sources, landfill gas, sludge waste, agricultural byproducts, and other biomass. Through 2000, also includes non-renewable waste (municipal solid waste from non-biogenic sources, and tire-derived fuels).
[k]Fuel ethanol (minus denaturant) and biodiesel consumption, plus losses and co-products from the production of fuel ethanol and biodiesel.
NA = Not available. (s) = Less than 0.5 trillion Btu.
Notes: Most data for the residential, commercial, industrial, and transportation sectors are estimates.
Totals may not equal sum of components due to independent rounding. Geographic coverage is the 50 states and the District of Columbia.

SOURCE: Adapted from "Table 10.1 Renewable Energy Production and Consumption by Source (Trillion Btu)," in *Monthly Energy Review: June 2014*, U.S. Energy Information Administration, June 25, 2014, http://www.eia.gov/totalenergy/data/monthly/archive/00351406.pdf (accessed June 27, 2014)

Robinson report in "Analysis: U.S. Government Mandate or No, Fuel Ethanol Is Here to Stay" (Reuters.com, August 24, 2012) that in 1990 the Clean Air Act was amended to require the motor gasoline industry to sell reformulated gasoline (RFG) that burns cleaner (i.e., produces less air pollutants) than regular gasoline. RFG burns cleaner because it contains an oxygenate additive. Although the RFG requirement originally applied to only a handful of U.S. cites with air pollution problems, by 2012 approximately 30% of the nation's gasoline stations were required to sell RFG. Fuel ethanol has become the primary oxygenate used to produce RFG.

The Energy Independence and Security Act of 2007 includes a Renewable Fuel Standard (RFS) that mandates biofuel use. Specifically, the RFS requires that by 2022 U.S. refineries will blend 36 billion gallons (136.3 billion L) of biofuels into their transportation fuel annually. Figure 6.4 shows the total amount required each year through 2022 and the required breakdown by renewable fuel. When the law was passed it was expected that cellulosic biofuel use would grow dramatically during the second decade of the 21st century and the early 2020s; however, this view is now considered overly optimistic. In *The Renewable Fuel Standard: Issues for 2014 and Beyond* (June 2014, http://www.cbo.gov/sites/default/files/cbofiles/attachments/45477-Biofuels2.pdf), the Congressional Budget Office notes that "the supply of cellulosic biofuels is limited because such fuels are complex and expensive to produce." Meanwhile, there are practical limits on the amount of ethanol that can be blended into gasoline, particularly for older vehicles. These issues pose significant challenges to the future success of the RFS mandates.

FIGURE 6.2

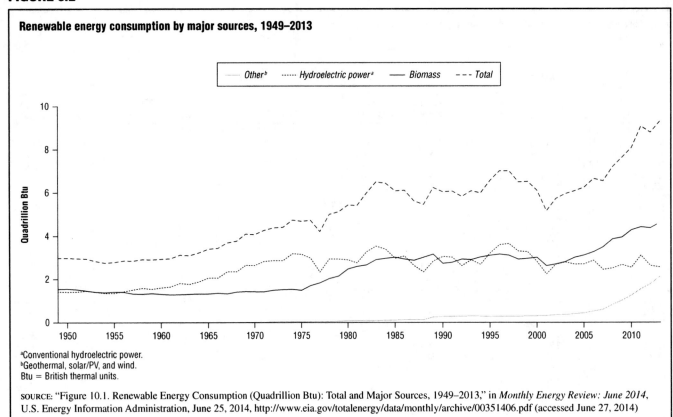

Renewable energy consumption by major sources, 1949–2013

⋯⋯ Other[b]   ⋯⋯ Hydroelectric power[a]   —— Biomass   - - - Total

[a]Conventional hydroelectric power.
[b]Geothermal, solar/PV, and wind.
Btu = British thermal units.

SOURCE: "Figure 10.1. Renewable Energy Consumption (Quadrillion Btu): Total and Major Sources, 1949–2013," in *Monthly Energy Review: June 2014*, U.S. Energy Information Administration, June 25, 2014, http://www.eia.gov/totalenergy/data/monthly/archive/00351406.pdf (accessed June 27, 2014)

FIGURE 6.3

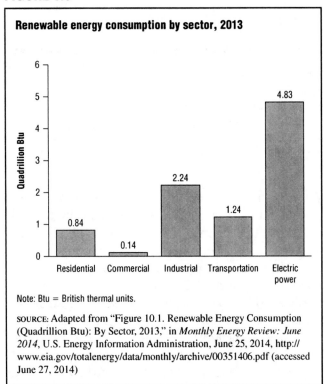

Renewable energy consumption by sector, 2013

Note: Btu = British thermal units.

SOURCE: Adapted from "Figure 10.1. Renewable Energy Consumption (Quadrillion Btu): By Sector, 2013," in *Monthly Energy Review: June 2014*, U.S. Energy Information Administration, June 25, 2014, http://www.eia.gov/totalenergy/data/monthly/archive/00351406.pdf (accessed June 27, 2014)

As explained in Chapter 1, energy producers, including the biomass industries, benefit from financial incentives that are provided by the federal government. Government incentives for fuel ethanol production have long been controversial because corn is a food crop. Critics fear that strong demand for corn-derived fuel ethanol since 1990 has driven up prices for food corn for humans, pets, and livestock. At the end of 2011 the federal government let a long-standing subsidy for corn ethanol expire. The article "Congress Ends Era of Ethanol Subsidies" (NPR.org, January 3, 2012) notes that the subsidy had been in place for three decades and amounted to around $20 billion total.

ENVIRONMENTAL ISSUES. In general, biomass sources are hailed as more environmentally friendly than fossil fuels. However, the use of biomass is not without environmental problems. Deforestation can occur from widespread use of wood, especially if forests are clear-cut, which can result in soil erosion and mudslides. In addition, burning biomass produces air emissions that degrade air quality. Although biomass is less energy intensive (has a lower heat content) than fossil fuels, the combustion of any carbon-containing fuel releases carbon into the atmosphere that contributes to problems with global warming and climate change.

Hydropower

Hydropower provided 2.6 quadrillion Btu in 2013, or 28% of the renewables total of 9.3 quadrillion Btu. (See Table 6.1.)

TABLE 6.2

Fuel ethanol production and consumption, selected years 1981–2013

	Feedstock[a] TBtu	Losses and co-products[b] TBtu	Denaturant[c] Mbbl	Production[d] Mbbl	Production[d] MMgal	Production[d] TBtu	Trade[d] Net imports[e] Mbbl	Stocks[d,f] Mbbl	Stock change[d,g] Mbbl	Consumption[d] Mbbl	Consumption[d] MMgal	Consumption[d] TBtu	Consumption minus denaturant[h] TBtu
1981 Total	13	6	40	1,978	83	7	NA	NA	NA	1,978	83	7	7
1985 Total	93	42	294	14,693	617	52	NA	NA	NA	14,693	617	52	51
1990 Total	111	49	356	17,802	748	63	NA	NA	NA	17,802	748	63	62
1995 Total	198	86	647	32,325	1,358	115	387	2,186	−207	32,919	1,383	117	114
2000 Total	233	99	773	38,627	1,622	138	116	3,400	−624	39,367	1,653	140	137
2001 Total	253	108	841	42,028	1,765	150	315	4,298	898	41,445	1,741	148	144
2002 Total	307	130	1,019	50,956	2,140	182	306	6,200	1,902	49,360	2,073	176	171
2003 Total	400	169	1,335	66,772	2,804	238	292	5,978	−222	67,286	2,826	240	233
2004 Total	484	203	1,621	81,058	3,404	289	3,542	6,002	24	84,576	3,552	301	293
2005 Total	552	230	1,859	92,961	3,904	331	3,234	5,563	−439	96,634	4,059	344	335
2006 Total	688	285	2,326	116,294	4,884	414	17,408	8,760	3,197	130,505	5,481	465	453
2007 Total	914	376	3,105	155,263	6,521	553	10,457	10,535	1,775	163,945	6,886	584	569
2008 Total	1,300	531	4,433	221,637	9,309	790	12,610	14,226	3,691	230,556	9,683	821	800
2009 Total	1,517	616	5,688	260,424	10,938	928	4,720	16,594	2,368	262,776	11,037	936	910
2010 Total	1,839	742	6,506	316,617	13,298	1,127	−9,115	17,941	1,347	306,155	12,858	1,090	1,061
2011 Total	1,919	769	6,649	331,646	13,929	1,181	−24,365	18,238	297	306,984	12,893	1,093	1,065
2012 Total	1,814	722	6,264	314,714	13,218	1,120	−5,891	20,350	2,112	306,711	12,882	1,092	1,064
2013 Total	1,827	728	6,184	316,964	13,312	1,128	−7,508	16,419	−4,258	313,714	13,176	1,117	1,089

[a]Total corn and other biomass inputs to the production of undenatured ethanol used for fuel ethanol.
[b]Losses and co-products from the production of fuel ethanol. Does not include natural gas, electricity, and other non-biomass energy used in the production of fuel ethanol—these are included in the industrial sector consumption statistics for the appropriate energy source.
[c]The amount of denaturant in fuel ethanol produced.
[d]Includes denaturant.
[e]Through 2009, data are for fuel ethanol imports only; data for fuel ethanol exports are not available. Beginning in 2010, data are for fuel ethanol imports minus fuel ethanol (including industrial alcohol) exports.
[f]Stocks are at end of period.
[g]A negative value indicates a decrease in stocks and a positive value indicates an increase.
[h]Consumption of fuel ethanol minus denaturant.
NA = Not available.
Notes: Mbbl = thousand barrels. MMgal = million U.S. gallons. TBtu = trillion Btu. Fuel ethanol data in thousand barrels are converted to million gallons by multiplying by 0.042, and are converted to Btu by multiplying by the approximate heat content of fuel ethanol. Through 1980, data are not available. For 1981–1992, data are estimates. For 1993–2008, only data for feedstock, losses and co-products, and denaturant are estimates. Beginning in 2009, only data for feedstock, and losses and co-products, are estimates. Totals may not equal sum of components due to independent rounding. Geographic coverage is the 50 states and the District of Columbia.

SOURCE: Adapted from "Table 10.3. Fuel Ethanol Overview," in *Monthly Energy Review: June 2014*, U.S. Energy Information Administration, June 25, 2014, http://www.eia.gov/totalenergy/data/monthly/archive/00351406.pdf (accessed June 27, 2014)

Hydropower has been used for decades in the United States to generate electricity. Hydropower facilities convert the energy of flowing water into mechanical energy, turning turbines to create electricity. In "Hydroelectric Power Resources Form Regional Clusters" (June 10, 2011, http://www.eia.gov/todayinenergy/detail.cfm?id=1750), the EIA divides hydropower into two broad categories: conventional and nonconventional.

Conventional hydropower plants use either flowing water (a run-of-river plant) or water backed up behind a dam (a storage plant) to produce electricity. A run-of-river plant produces electricity as river flows allow. The flows can be quite variable and depend heavily on weather events, such as rainfall and snowmelt. By contrast, a storage plant relies on a dam to create an ever-ready reservoir of water that can be tapped as needed. (See Figure 6.5.) The dam creates a height from which water can flow at a fast rate. When the water reaches the power plant at the bottom of the dam, it pushes the turbine blades that are attached to the electrical generator. Whenever power is needed, the valves are opened, the moving water spins the turbines, and the generator produces electricity.

There are various nonconventional hydropower means for generating electricity. The most common method is called pumped storage. In these systems water is pumped from a low elevation to a high elevation within the plant during times of low demand for electricity. In essence, some of the water that has already been used to generate electricity is reused. Because pumping is an energy-intensive process, more energy can be used during the pumping than is generated from the pumped water.

There are hundreds of conventional and pumped-storage hydroelectric plants around the United States. (The EIA provides a map of their locations at http://www.eia.gov/todayinenergy/detail.cfm?id=1750.) They are heavily concentrated in the river valleys of the central Atlantic states, the Pacific Northwest, and California. Most of the dams were built decades ago as part of massive federal programs designed to decrease flooding and provide freshwater supplies and electricity to the

TABLE 6.3

Biodiesel production, trade, and consumption, 2001–13

	Feed-stock[a]	Losses and co-products[b]	Production			Trade Imports	Exports	Net imports[c]	Stocks[d]	Stock change[e]	Balancing item[f]	Consumption		
	TBtu	TBtu	Mbbl	MMgal	TBtu	Mbbl	Mbbl	Mbbl	Mbbl	Mbbl	Mbbl	Mbbl	MMgal	TBtu
2001 Total	1	(s)	204	9	1	81	41	40	NA	NA	NA	244	10	1
2002 Total	1	(s)	250	10	1	197	57	140	NA	NA	NA	390	16	2
2003 Total	2	(s)	338	14	2	97	113	−17	NA	NA	NA	322	14	2
2004 Total	4	(s)	666	28	4	101	128	−27	NA	NA	NA	639	27	3
2005 Total	12	(s)	2,162	91	12	214	213	1	NA	NA	NA	2,163	91	12
2006 Total	32	(s)	5,963	250	32	1,105	856	250	NA	NA	NA	6,213	261	33
2007 Total	63	1	11,662	490	62	3,455	6,696	−3,241	NA	NA	NA	8,422	354	45
2008 Total	88	1	16,145	678	87	7,755	16,673	−8,918	NA	NA	NA	7,228	304	39
2009 Total	67	1	12,281	516	66	1,906	6,546	−4,640	711	711	733	7,663	322	41
2010 Total	44	1	8,177	343	44	564	2,588	−2,024	672	−39	0	6,192	260	33
2011 Total	125	2	23,035	967	123	890	1,799	−908	2,012	1,035[g]	0	21,092	886	113
2012 Total	128	2	23,588	991	126	853	3,056	−2,203	2,083	72	0	21,314	895	114
2013 Total	173	2	31,887	1,339	171	7,497	4,477	3,020	4,509	2,340	0	32,567	1,368	175

[a]Total vegetable oil and other biomass inputs to the production of biodiesel.
[b]Losses and co-products from the production of biodiesel. Does not include natural gas, electricity, and other non-biomass energy used in the production of biodiesel—these are included in the industrial sector consumption statistics for the appropriate energy source.
[c]Net imports equal imports minus exports.
[d]Stocks are at end of period. Through 2010, includes stocks at bulk terminals only. Beginning in 2011, includes stocks at bulk terminals and biodiesel production plants.
[e]A negative value indicates a decrease in stocks and a positive value indicates an increase.
[f]Beginning in 2009, because of incomplete data coverage and different data sources, "Balancing Item" is used to balance biodiesel supply and disposition.
[g]Derived from the final 2010 stocks value for bulk terminals and biodiesel production plants (977 thousand barrels), not the final 2010 value for bulk terminals only (672 thousand barrels) that is shown under "Stocks."
NA = Not available. Btu = British thermal units.
(s) = Less than 0.5 trillion Btu.
Notes: Mbbl = thousand barrels. MMgal = million U.S. gallons. TBtu = trillion Btu. Biodiesel data in thousand barrels are converted to million gallons by multiplying by 0.042, and are converted to Btu by multiplying by 5.359 million Btu per barrel (the approximate heat content of biodiesel. Through 2000, data are not available. Beginning in 2001, data not from U.S. Energy Information Administration (EIA) surveys are estimates. Beginning in 2014, biodiesel production data are estimated by EIA, and are only partially based on survey data. Totals may not equal sum of components due to independent rounding. Geographic coverage is the 50 states and the District of Columbia.

SOURCE: "Table 10.4. Biodiesel Overview," in *Monthly Energy Review: June 2014*, U.S. Energy Information Administration, June 25, 2014, http://www.eia.gov/totalenergy/data/monthly/archive/00351406.pdf (accessed June 27, 2014)

public. The EIA indicates in "Hydropower Explained: Where Hydropower Is Generated" (April 18, 2014, http://www.eia.gov/energyexplained/index.cfm?page=hydropower_where) that more than half of the U.S. hydroelectric capacity is concentrated in Washington, Oregon, and California. In *State Electricity Profiles 2011* (April 2014, http://www.eia.gov/electricity/state/archive/sep2011.pdf), the agency ranks the largest hydroelectric facilities around the country based on their net summer generation capacity in 2011. The five largest facilities were:

- Grand Coulee (Washington)—7,079 megawatts (MW)
- Bath County (Virginia)—3,003 MW
- Chief Joseph (Washington)—2,456 MW
- Robert Moses Niagara (New York)—2,353 MW
- John Day (Oregon)—2,160 MW

The Bath County facility in Virginia is the only pumped-storage facility among the top-five generators. The Grand Coulee facility in Washington is particularly notable because it was not only the nation's largest hydropower generator but also the nation's largest electricity generator overall in 2011.

According to the EIA, in *Monthly Energy Review: June 2014* (June 2014, http://www.eia.gov/totalenergy/data/monthly/archive/00351406.pdf), conventional hydroelectric power accounted for 269 billion kilowatt-hours (kWh), or 7% of the total 4,058 billion kWh of U.S. electricity production in 2013. Among the renewable sources used for electricity production, hydropower was the dominant source. As shown in Table 6.4, nearly all (2,529 trillion Btu) of the 2,561 trillion Btu of hydropower consumed in 2013 was consumed by the electric power sector.

The federal government is the nation's leading provider of hydroelectric power. The Tennessee Valley Authority and the Power Marketing Administration are federally owned corporations that have long provided hydroelectricity to consumers in the south-central and western United States, respectively.

ENVIRONMENTAL ISSUES. Hydroelectric power dams have greatly disrupted natural water flows because they are so large. The structures also impede the migration paths of aquatic creatures, and their spinning turbines can kill and injure creatures unable to escape the blades. Although modern dams typically include fish ladders (stepping-stone waterfalls that provide fish a pathway up and over dam structures), the dams still negatively affect aquatic life by altering natural water flows and temperatures.

FIGURE 6.4

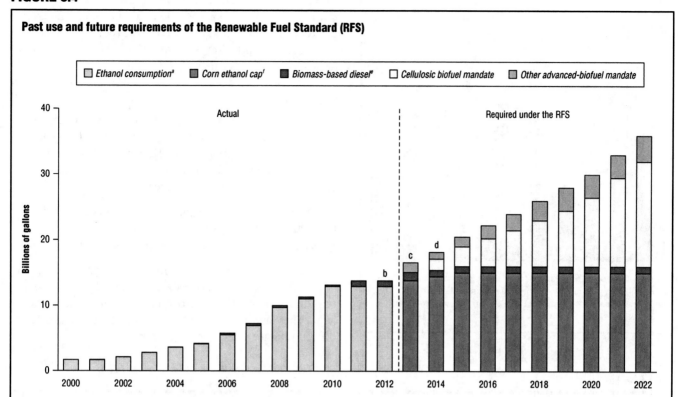

Past use and future requirements of the Renewable Fuel Standard (RFS)

☐ Ethanol consumption[a]   ■ Corn ethanol cap[f]   ■ Biomass-based diesel[e]   ☐ Cellulosic biofuel mandate   ▨ Other advanced-biofuel mandate

[a]Most of the ethanol used in the United States in the past consisted of corn ethanol, although relatively small amounts of sugarcane ethanol and other types of advanced biofuels, either produced domestically or imported, were also used.

[b]Because of high corn prices in 2012, use of renewable fuels was about the same in that year as in 2011. That use was less than the amounts mandated for 2012, but fuel blenders and importers achieved compliance with the RFS by submitting "renewable identification numbers" (or RINs) that they had accumulated from exceeding their obligations in prior years.

[c]For 2013, the Energy Independence and Security Act (EISA) originally required the use of 1 billion gallons each of cellulosic biofuels and biomass-based diesel. In August 2013, the Environmental Protection Agency (EPA) retroactively reduced the cellulosic biofuel requirement for that year to 6 million gallons and raised the mandate for biomass-based diesel to 1.28 billion gallons. Complete data on the actual use of renewable fuels in 2013 were not yet available when this report was published.

[d]The amounts shown here for 2014 are those required under EISA. However, EPA has proposed reducing the 2014 requirement for cellulosic biofuels from 1.75 billion gallons to 17 million gallons, the requirement for advanced biofuels from 3.75 billion gallons to 2.2 billion gallons, and the cap on the amount of corn ethanol that can be used to meet the total requirement for renewable fuels from 14.4 billion gallons to 13.0 billion gallons. EPA has also proposed increasing the requirement for biomass-based diesel from 1 billion gallons to 1.28 billion gallons. Under those proposals, the total requirement for renewable fuels in 2014 would decline from 18.15 billion gallons to 15.21 billion gallons, compared with 16.55 billion gallons in 2013.

[e]The amounts of biomass-based diesel shown here for 2014 and later years reflect the minimum requirement of 1 billion gallons specified in EISA. EPA will set the actual requirement for each year through future rulemaking.

[f]The cap on corn ethanol represents the maximum amount of such ethanol that can used to meet the total requirement for renewable fuels under EISA.

SOURCE: "Figure 1. Past Use of Renewable Fuels and Future Requirements of the Renewable Fuel Standard," in *The Renewable Fuel Standard: Issues for 2014 and Beyond*, Congressional Budget Office, June 2014, http://www.cbo.gov/sites/default/files/cbofiles/attachments/45477-Biofuels2.pdf (accessed July 19, 2014)

Wind Energy

Winds are created by the uneven heating of the atmosphere by the sun, the irregularities of the earth's surface, and the rotation of the planet. They are strongly influenced by bodies of water, weather patterns, vegetation, and other factors. The natural power of wind energy is collected by wind turbines, which resemble airplane propellers. The turbines convert wind energy to mechanical energy and finally to electrical energy. Figure 6.6 shows a wind turbine in which the blades rotate around a horizontal axis. Other types feature vertically aligned blades. Wind turbines are usually clustered on wind farms that may feature dozens or hundreds of individual wind turbines. The most favorable locations for wind turbines are in mountain passes and offshore along coastlines, where wind speeds are generally highest and most consistent.

Wind energy provided 1.6 quadrillion Btu in 2013, or 17% of the total renewables consumed. (See Table 6.1.) Wind was a small energy provider through the 1990s; after the turn of the 21st century, consumption began to grow dramatically. As shown in Table 6.1 and Table 6.4, the electric power sector accounted for 100% of wind power consumption in 2013.

ENVIRONMENTAL ISSUES. In general, wind energy is considered environmentally friendly because it does not involve fuel combustion. Some people find the whirring noise of wind turbines annoying and object to clusters of wind turbines in mountain passes and along shorelines, where they interfere with scenic views. Environmentalists also point out that wind turbines are responsible for the loss of thousands of birds and bats that inadvertently fly into the blades. Birds frequently use windy passages

FIGURE 6.5

Hydroelectric dam

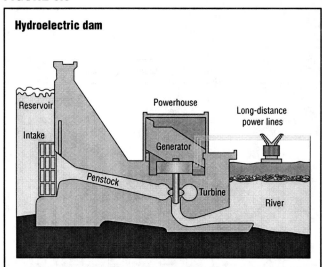

SOURCE: "Hydroelectric Dam," in *Hydropower Explained: Energy from Moving Water*, U.S. Energy Information Administration, May 14, 2014, http://www.eia.gov/energyexplained/index.cfm?page=hydropower_home (accessed July 19, 2014)

in their travel patterns. However, wind farms do not emit climate-altering carbon dioxide and other pollutants, respiratory irritants, or radioactive waste. Furthermore, because wind farms do not require water to operate, they are especially well suited to semiarid and arid regions.

Solar Energy

Solar energy, which comes from the sun, is a renewable, widely available energy source that does not generate pollution or radioactive waste. However, converting solar energy to electricity on a commercial scale has proved to be technologically and economically challenging.

There are two main types of solar systems: passive and active. In both systems the conversion of solar energy into a form of power is made at the site where it is used.

Passive solar energy systems, such as greenhouses or windows with a southern exposure, use heat flow, evaporation, or other natural processes to collect and transfer heat. They are considered to be the least costly and least difficult solar systems to implement.

TABLE 6.4

Renewable energy consumption by electric power sector, by source, selected years 1950–2013

[Trillion Btu]

	Hydroelectric power[a]	Geothermal[b]	Solar/PV[c]	Wind[d]	Biomass Wood[e]	Biomass Waste[f]	Biomass Total	Total
1950 Total	1,346	NA	NA	NA	5	NA	5	1,351
1955 Total	1,322	NA	NA	NA	3	NA	3	1,325
1960 Total	1,569	(s)	NA	NA	2	NA	2	1,571
1965 Total	2,026	2	NA	NA	3	NA	3	2,031
1970 Total	2,600	6	NA	NA	1	2	4	2,609
1975 Total	3,122	34	NA	NA	(s)	2	2	3,158
1980 Total	2,867	53	NA	NA	3	2	4	2,925
1985 Total	2,937	97	(s)	(s)	8	7	14	3,049
1990 Total[g]	3,014	161	4	29	129	188	317	3,524
1995 Total	3,149	138	5	33	125	296	422	3,747
2000 Total	2,768	144	5	57	134	318	453	3,427
2001 Total	2,209	142	6	70	126	211	337	2,763
2002 Total	2,650	147	6	105	150	230	380	3,288
2003 Total	2,749	146	5	113	167	230	397	3,411
2004 Total	2,655	148	6	142	165	223	388	3,339
2005 Total	2,670	147	6	178	185	221	406	3,406
2006 Total	2,839	145	5	264	182	231	412	3,665
2007 Total	2,430	145	6	341	186	237	423	3,345
2008 Total	2,494	146	9	546	177	258	435	3,630
2009 Total	2,650	146	9	721	180	261	441	3,967
2010 Total	2,521	148	12	923	196	264	459	4,064
2011 Total	3,085	149	17	1,167	182	255	437	4,855
2012 Total	2,606	148	40	1,339	190	262	453	4,586
2013 Total	2,529	157	85	1,595	207	258	465	4,831

[a]Conventional hydroelectricity net generation (converted to Btu using the fossil-fuels heat rate).
[b]Geothermal electricity net generation (converted to Btu using the fossil-fuels heat rate).
[c]Solar thermal and photovoltaic (PV) electricity net generation (converted to Btu using the fossil-fuels heat rate).
[d]Wind electricity net generation (converted to Btu using the fossil-fuels heat rate).
[e]Wood and wood-derived fuels.
[f]Municipal solid waste from biogenic sources, landfill gas, sludge waste, agricultural byproducts, and other biomass. Through 2000, also includes non-renewable waste (municipal solid waste from non-biogenic sources, and tire-derived fuels).
[g]Through 1988, data are for electric utilities only. Beginning in 1989, data are for electric utilities and independent power producers.
NA = Not available. (s) = Less than 0.5 trillion Btu. Btu = British thermal units.
Notes: The electric power sector comprises electricity-only and combined-heat-and-power (CHP) plants whose primary business is to sell electricity, or electricity and heat, to the public. Total may not equal sum of components due to independent rounding. Geographic coverage is the 50 states and the District of Columbia.

SOURCE: Adapted from "Table 10.2c. Renewable Energy Consumption: Electric Power Sector (Trillion Btu)," in *Monthly Energy Review: June 2014*, U.S. Energy Information Administration, June 25, 2014, http://www.eia.gov/totalenergy/data/monthly/archive/00351406.pdf (accessed June 27, 2014)

FIGURE 6.6

Horizontal-axis wind machine

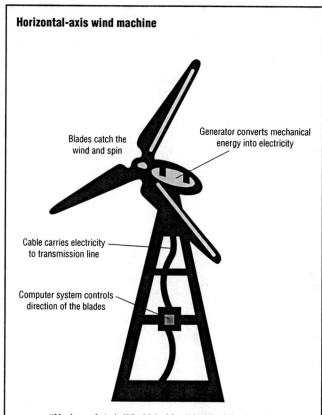

Blades catch the wind and spin

Generator converts mechanical energy into electricity

Cable carries electricity to transmission line

Computer system controls direction of the blades

SOURCE: "Horizontal-Axis Wind Machine," in *Wind Explained: Types of Wind Turbines*, U.S. Energy Information Administration, July 2, 2013, http://www.eia.gov/energyexplained/index.cfm?page=wind_types_of_turbines (accessed July 19, 2014)

Active solar systems require collectors and storage devices as well as motors, pumps, and valves to operate the systems that transfer heat. Some collectors consist of an absorbing plate that transfers the sun's heat to a working fluid (liquid or gas). Photovoltaic cells (which are combined to form solar rooftop panels or collectors) convert sunlight directly to electricity without the use of mechanical generators. Photovoltaic cells do not have moving parts, are easy to install, and require little maintenance. The use of photovoltaic cells is expanding around the world. Because they contain no turbines or other moving parts, operating costs are low and maintenance is minimal. Above all, the fuel source (sunshine) is free and plentiful under the right weather conditions. The main disadvantage of photovoltaic cell systems is the high initial cost, although prices have fallen considerably. Even though toxic materials are often used in the construction of the cells, researchers are investigating new materials, recycling, and disposal.

Solar/photovoltaic energy accounted for 307 trillion Btu of consumption in 2013, or 3% of total domestic renewables consumption. (See Table 6.1.) According to the EIA, in *Monthly Energy Review: June 2014*, most of the solar/photovoltaic energy consumed in 2013 was used by the residential sector. Only a small amount (85 trillion Btu) was consumed by the electric power sector. (See Table 6.4.) This consumption was small in comparison to that of competing renewable sources.

Geothermal Energy

Geothermal energy is the natural, internal heat of the earth trapped in rock formations deep underground. Only a fraction of it can be extracted, usually through large fractures in the earth's crust. Hot springs, geysers, and fumaroles (holes in or near volcanoes from which vapor escapes) are the most easily exploitable sources. Geothermal reservoirs provide hot water or steam that can be used for heating buildings and processing food. Pressurized hot water or steam can also be directed toward turbines, which spin, generating electricity for residential and commercial customers.

Geothermal energy has been a very slow growing source of renewable energy. Greater use is limited by geological constraints. Geothermal energy is usable only when it is concentrated in one spot—in this case, in what is known as a thermal reservoir. Most of the known reservoirs for geothermal power in the United States are located west of the Mississippi River, and the highest-temperature geothermal resources occur for the most part west of the Rocky Mountains.

Geothermal consumption was 221 trillion Btu in 2013, or 2% of the renewables total. (See Table 6.1.) The vast majority of the consumption (157 quadrillion Btu, or 71%) was by the electric power sector. (See Table 6.4.)

DOMESTIC OUTLOOK FOR RENEWABLES

The EIA predicts in *Annual Energy Outlook 2014 with Projections to 2040* domestic capacity and electricity generation by renewable sources in 2040 using 2012 levels as a baseline. The amounts shown in Table 6.5 are for net summer capacity and generation. According to the EIA (2014, http://www.eia.gov/tools/glossary/index.cfm?id=N), net summer capacity is the maximum output of the generating equipment during the peak summer demand time (between June 1 and September 30) less any capacity used by the generating station itself.

In 2040 conventional hydropower is expected to be the largest renewable energy source for electricity generation, providing 297.3 billion kilowatt-hours, or 40% of the total. (See Table 6.5.) Wind is projected to be the second-largest energy source, with 248 billion kilowatt-hours, or 33% of the total.

As shown in Figure 6.7, biofuels consumption is projected to rise only slightly through 2040 and fall far

TABLE 6.5

Renewable energy generating capacity and generation, 2012 and predicted for 2040

Net summer capacity and generation	Reference case		Annual growth 2012–2040 (percent)
	2012	2040	
Electric power sector[a]			
Net summer capacity			
Conventional hydropower	78.10	80.35	0.1%
Geothermal[b]	2.58	8.80	4.5%
Municipal waste[c]	3.57	3.63	0.1%
Wood and other biomass[d]	2.70	3.46	0.9%
Solar thermal	0.48	1.73	4.7%
Solar photovoltaic[e]	2.49	17.07	7.1%
Wind	59.01	85.48	1.3%
Offshore wind	0.00	0.00	—
Total electric power sector capacity	**148.92**	**200.52**	**1.1%**
Generation (billion kilowatthours)			
Conventional hydropower	273.89	297.34	0.3%
Geothermal[b]	15.56	67.26	5.4%
Biogenic municipal waste[f]	16.79	19.21	0.5%
Wood and other biomass	11.04	72.22	6.9%
Dedicated plants	9.84	18.99	2.4%
Cofiring	1.20	53.23	14.5%
Solar thermal	0.90	3.53	5.0%
Solar photovoltaic[e]	3.25	35.24	8.9%
Wind	141.87	248.02	2.0%
Offshore wind	0.00	0.00	—
Total electric power sector generation	**463.29**	**742.82**	**1.7%**
End-use sectors[g]			
Net summer capacity			
Conventional hydropower	0.29	0.29	0.0%
Geothermal	0.00	0.00	—
Municipal waste[h]	0.47	0.47	0.0%
Biomass	4.89	9.62	2.4%
Solar photovoltaic[e]	4.71	29.47	6.8%
Wind	0.15	1.42	8.3%
Total end-use sector capacity	**10.51**	**41.26**	**5.0%**
Generation (billion kilowatthours)			
Conventional hydropower	1.38	1.38	0.0%
Geothermal	0.00	0.00	—
Municipal waste[h]	3.65	3.63	0.0%
Biomass	26.53	53.50	2.5%
Solar photovoltaic[e]	7.35	47.46	6.9%
Wind	0.20	2.01	8.6%
Total end-use sector generation	**39.11**	**107.99**	**3.7%**
Total, all sectors			
Net summer capacity			
Conventional hydropower	78.39	80.63	0.1%
Geothermal	2.58	8.80	4.5%
Municipal waste	4.04	4.10	0.1%
Wood and other biomass[d]	7.59	13.08	2.0%
Solar[e]	7.68	48.26	6.8%
Wind	59.16	86.91	1.4%
Total capacity, all sectors	**159.43**	**241.78**	**1.5%**
Generation (billion kilowatthours)			
Conventional hydropower	275.27	298.72	0.3%
Geothermal	15.56	67.26	5.4%
Municipal waste	20.44	22.84	0.4%
Wood and other biomass	37.57	125.72	4.4%
Solar[e]	11.50	86.23	7.5%
Wind	142.06	250.03	2.0%
Total generation, all sectors	**502.41**	**850.80**	**1.9%**

short of the 36-billion-gallon (136.3-billion-L) RFS requirement described earlier that is to supposed to be met by 2022. The EIA notes that declining gasoline demand and lack of availability of vehicles equipped to burn high ethanol blends are forecast to greatly dampen biofuels consumption.

World Production, Consumption, and Outlook

Figure 6.8 provides EIA estimates of world energy consumption by fuel type between 1990 and 2010 and predicted through 2040. Renewables consumption is forecast to increase dramatically, from around 55 quadrillion Btu in 2010 to around 120 quadrillion Btu in 2040.

TABLE 6.5

Renewable energy generating capacity and generation, 2012 and predicted for 2040 [CONTINUED]

[a]Includes electricity-only and combined heat and power plants that have a regulatory status.
[b]Includes both hydrothermal resources (hot water and steam) and near-field enhanced geothermal systems (EGS). Near-field EGS potential occurs on known hydrothermal sites, however this potential requires the addition of external fluids for electricity generation and is only available after 2025.
[c]Includes municipal waste, landfill gas, and municipal sewage sludge. Incremental growth is assumed to be for landfill gas facilities. All municipal waste is included, although a portion of the municipal waste stream contains petroleum-derived plastics and other non-renewable sources.
[d]Facilities co-firing biomass and coal are classified as coal.
[e]Does not include off-grid photovoltaics (PV). Based on annual PV shipments from 1989 through 2012, EIA estimates that as much as 274 megawatts of remote electricity generation PV applications (i.e., off-grid power systems) were in service in 2012, plus an additional 573 megawatts in communications, transportation, and assorted other non-grid-connected, specialized applications. The approach used to develop the estimate, based on shipment data, provides an upper estimate of the size of the PV stock, including both grid-based and off-grid PV. It will overestimate the size of the stock, because shipments include a substantial number of units that are exported,and each year some of the PV units installed earlier will be retired from service or abandoned.
[f]Includes biogenic municipal waste, landfill gas, and municipal sewage sludge. Incremental growth is assumed to be for landfill gas facilities. Only biogenic municipal waste is included. The U.S. Energy Information Administration estimates that in 2012 approximately 7 billion kilowatthours of electricity were generated from a municipal waste stream containing petroleum-derived plastics and other non-renewable sources.
[g]Includes combined heat and power plants and electricity-only plants in the commercial and industrial sectors that have a non-regulatory status; and small on-site generating systems in the residential, commercial, and industrial sectors used primarily for own-use generation, but which may also sell some power to the grid.
[h]Includes municipal waste, landfill gas, and municipal sewage sludge. All municipal waste is included, although a portion of the municipal waste stream contains petroleum-derived plastics and other non-renewable sources.
— = Not applicable.
Note: Totals may not equal sum of components due to independent rounding. Data for 2012 are model results and may differ from official EIA data reports.
EIA = Energy Information Administration.

SOURCE: Adapted from "Table A16. Renewable Energy Generating Capacity and Generation (Gigawatts, Unless Otherwise Noted)," in *Annual Energy Outlook 2014 with Projections to 2040*, U.S. Energy Information Administration, April 2014, http://www.eia.gov/forecasts/aeo/ (accessed June 26, 2014)

FIGURE 6.7

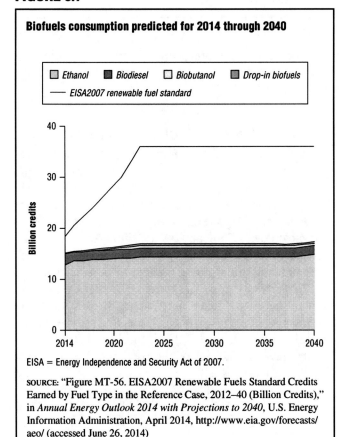

Biofuels consumption predicted for 2014 through 2040

EISA = Energy Independence and Security Act of 2007.

SOURCE: "Figure MT-56. EISA2007 Renewable Fuels Standard Credits Earned by Fuel Type in the Reference Case, 2012–40 (Billion Credits)," in *Annual Energy Outlook 2014 with Projections to 2040*, U.S. Energy Information Administration, April 2014, http://www.eia.gov/forecasts/aeo/ (accessed June 26, 2014)

Figure 6.9 shows EIA projections for world electricity generation from renewable energy sources broken down by country membership in the Organisation for Economic Co-operation and Development (OECD). The OECD is a collection of dozens of mostly Western nations (including the United States) that are devoted to global economic development. The EIA indicates that 4,200 billion kWh were generated from renewables in 2010. By 2040 the value is expected to reach 9,600 billion kWh. Most of the growth is expected from non-OECD members utilizing hydropower resources. Many developing nations see hydropower as an effective means of supplying power to growing populations. These massive public works projects usually require huge amounts of money—most of it borrowed from the developed world. Hydroelectric dams, however, are considered worth the cost and potential environmental threats because they bring cheap electric power to the citizenry.

The Chinese government has constructed the world's largest dam, the Three Gorges Dam, on the Yangtze River in Hubei Province. Five times the size of the Hoover Dam in the United States, the Three Gorges Dam is 607 feet (185 m) tall and 7,575 feet (2,309 m) in length. One decade after the project was launched in 1993, the dam began generating power. The article "China's Three Gorges Dam Reaches Operating Peak" (BBC.com, July 5, 2012) indicates that the dam reached its full operating peak in July 2012, after its 32nd, and final, generator began operating. The addition boosted the dam's generating capacity to 22.5 gigawatts, or around 11% of China's total hydropower capacity at that time. The article notes that the dam cost approximately $40 billion to construct and displaced more than 1 million people from the Yangtze River basin.

In *International Energy Outlook 2014* (September 2014, http://www.eia.gov/forecasts/ieo), the EIA notes that world production of biofuels in 2010 was 1.3 million barrels per day. This value is expected to rise to 3 million

FIGURE 6.8

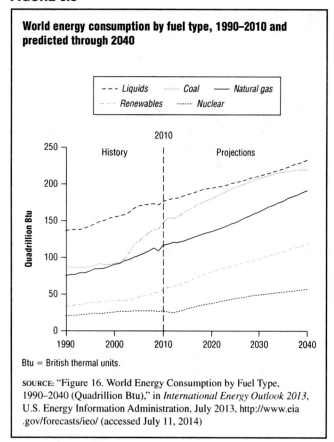

World energy consumption by fuel type, 1990–2010 and predicted through 2040

Btu = British thermal units.

SOURCE: "Figure 16. World Energy Consumption by Fuel Type, 1990–2040 (Quadrillion Btu)," in *International Energy Outlook 2013*, U.S. Energy Information Administration, July 2013, http://www.eia .gov/forecasts/ieo/ (accessed July 11, 2014)

FIGURE 6.9

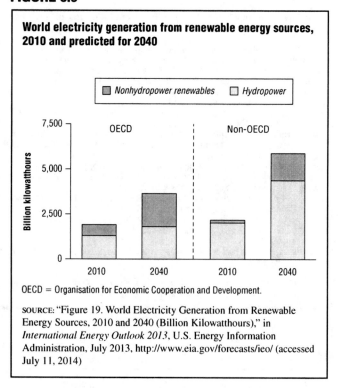

World electricity generation from renewable energy sources, 2010 and predicted for 2040

OECD = Organisation for Economic Cooperation and Development.

SOURCE: "Figure 19. World Electricity Generation from Renewable Energy Sources, 2010 and 2040 (Billion Kilowatthours)," in *International Energy Outlook 2013*, U.S. Energy Information Administration, July 2013, http://www.eia.gov/forecasts/ieo/ (accessed July 11, 2014)

barrels per day by 2040. At that time biofuels will account for about 2.5% of the total world liquid fuels production of 119.4 million barrels per day. Nearly all of that amount (111.8 million barrels per day) is expected to be petroleum liquids.

Several international organizations are devoted to promoting the use of renewable energy sources. In April 2014 the United Nations (http://www.un.org/apps/news/ story.asp?NewsID=47537#.U8q97p5dWrY) launched the initiative Decade of Sustainable Energy for All (2014–2024). The organization notes the initiative has three goals: "Ensuring universal access to modern energy services, doubling the global rate of improvement in energy efficiency and sharing renewable energy globally." The International Renewable Energy Agency (2014, http://www.irena.org/Menu/index.aspx?PriMenu ID=13&mnu=Pri) is an intergovernmental membership organization that "encourages governments to adopt enabling policies for renewable energy investments, provides practical tools and policy advice to accelerate renewable energy deployment, and facilitates knowledge sharing and technology transfer to provide clean, sustainable energy for the world's growing population." It is headquartered in Abu Dhabi in the United Arab Emirates. In January 2015 the city is hosting the World Future Energy Summit (2014, http://www.worldfuture energysummit.com/Portal/about-wfes/overview.aspx),

a conference meeting and exhibition that is "dedicated to renewable energies, energy efficiency and clean technologies."

RENEWABLE INNOVATIONS FOR THE FUTURE

As of October 2014, numerous other renewable energy sources and technologies were being investigated for their potential to provide thermal power and/or electricity generation. Some innovative projects had reached the commercial stage. For example, in 2012 the Ocean Renewable Power Company (ORPC; http://www.orpc.co/ content.aspx?p=h3jCHHn6gcg%3D) began operating the first commercial tidal power system to be connected to the U.S. electricity grid. The system is located in the Bay of Fundy between Maine and Canada. It uses the tidal movement of the sea as it ebbs and flows to generate power. According to ORPC, 100 billion tons (91 billion t) of water flow in and out of the bay each day with the changing of the tides.

Other renewable energy sources of interest include:

- Wave energy—ocean wave power plants capture energy directly from wind-driven surface waves or from pressure changes below the surface to generate electricity.

- Ocean thermal energy conversion—this source uses the temperature difference between warm surface water and the cooler water in the ocean's depths to power a heat engine into producing electricity. Ocean thermal energy conversion systems can be installed on ships, barges, or offshore platforms with underwater cables that transmit electricity to shore.

- Hydrogen—hydrogen is the lightest and most abundant chemical element, and an interesting fuel from an environmental point of view. Its combustion produces only water vapor, and it is entirely carbon free. Three-quarters of the mass of the universe is hydrogen, so in theory the supply is ample. However, the combustible form of hydrogen is a gas and is not found in nature. It must be made from other energy sources, such as fossil fuels. Hydrogen can be split from water, but the processes are either quite costly, require a great deal of energy, or both.

In addition, technology developments for existing renewable sources could render them more effective and useful in the future. In "Inflatable Turbines: The Windfarms of the Future?"(Telegraph.co.uk, April 18, 2014), Olivia Yallop describes an inflatable wind turbine that researchers say could be tethered to a ground station and catch the much stronger winds that circulate thousands of feet above the earth's surface. This could greatly increase wind energy production. Matthew Kelly notes in "Full Steam Ahead on Key Solar Discovery" (Herald.com, June 2, 2014) that Australian researchers reported in 2014 they had used solar energy to generate "the hottest supercritical steam ever achieved outside of fossil fuel sources." (Supercritical steam is steam heated to a high temperature and subjected to high pressure to improve the thermodynamic performance of certain power generating turbines.) The new technology could make electricity generation from solar power more efficient and cost effective.

CHAPTER 7

ENERGY RESERVES—OIL, GAS, COAL, AND URANIUM

Energy resources are not the same as energy reserves. Energy resources are all deposits that exist, whereas energy reserves have a much narrower definition. Energy reserves are deposits about which some specific information is known or can be estimated. Reserves are quantified using specific criteria that are technologically and/or economically based. One problem is that there are many different terms used by U.S. government agencies to refer to reserves, such as *proved*, *unproved*, *technically recoverable*, *undiscovered*, *conventional*, and *continuous*. Thus, one must be careful to specify what types of reserves are being discussed. At the federal level, there are two primary agencies that estimate and publish energy reserve amounts:

- U.S. Geological Survey (USGS)—according to the USGS, in "About the Energy Program" (August 7, 2014, http://energy.usgs.gov/GeneralInfo/Aboutthe EnergyProgram.aspx), its Energy Resources Program "conducts research and assessments on the location, quantity, and quality of mineral and energy resources, including the economic and environmental effects of resource extraction and use."

- U.S. Energy Information Administration (EIA) within the U.S. Department of Energy—the EIA collects data about reserves from a variety of sources, including other federal and state agencies, industry, and academia.

OIL AND NATURAL GAS

As explained in earlier chapters, the United States is highly dependent on oil and natural gas as energy sources. Combined, these two fuels accounted for 44.1 quadrillion Btu of the United States' 81.7 quadrillion Btu primary energy consumption in 2013, or 54% of the total. (See Table 1.2 in Chapter 1.) Thus, sufficient domestic reserves of these fuels are vitally important to the nation's economic well-being.

PROVED RESERVES

In *U.S. Crude Oil, Natural Gas, and Natural Gas Liquids Proved Reserves, 2012* (April 2014, http://www.eia.gov/naturalgas/crudeoilreserves/pdf/uscrudeoil.pdf), the EIA defines proved reserves as "volumes of oil and natural gas that geological and engineering data demonstrate with reasonable certainty to be recoverable in future years from known reservoirs under existing economic and operating conditions." This definition encompasses both technical and economic considerations. Proved reserves are not simply deposits that are technically viable to extract, they must also be economically viable to extract. Changing economic conditions affect proved reserves estimates in that rising market prices push proved reserves estimates upward, whereas falling market prices push estimates downward.

The EIA provides reserves estimates for crude oil and lease condensate and for wet natural gas. As noted in Chapter 2, lease condensate is a liquid recovered from natural gas at the well (the extraction point) and is generally blended with crude oil for refining. In *U.S. Crude Oil, Natural Gas, and Natural Gas Liquids Proved Reserves, 2012*, the EIA defines wet natural gas as including both natural gas and natural gas plant liquids (NGPL), which are liquid compounds recovered during processing.

According to the EIA, proved reserves of the fuels at year-end 2012 were:

- Crude oil and lease condensate—33.4 billion barrels (see Table 7.1)

- Wet natural gas—322.7 trillion cubic feet (tcf; 9.1 trillion cubic m [tcm]) (see Table 7.2)

Figure 7.1 shows historical data for proved U.S. reserves of crude oil and lease condensate dating back to 1982. The total fell from around 30 billion barrels during the early 1980s to 21 billion barrels in 2008. Subsequent

TABLE 7.1

Proved reserves of crude oil and lease condensate, 2002–12

[Million barrels]

Year	Adjustments (1)	Net revisions (2)	Revisions[a] and adjustments (3)	Net of sales[b] and acquisitions (4)	Extensions (5)	New field discoveries (6)	New reservoir discoveries in old fields (7)	Total[c] discoveries (8)	Estimated production (9)	Proved[d] reserves 12/31 (10)	Change from prior year (11)
Crude oil and lease condensate (million barrels)											
2002	423	682	1,105	51	600	318	187	1,105	2,082	24,023	180
2003	192	−9	183	−416	530	717	137	1,384	2,068	23,106	−917
2004	80	444	524	37	731	36	159	926	2,001	22,592	−514
2005	237	558	795	327	946	209	57	1,212	1,907	23,019	427
2006	109	43	152	189	685	38	62	785	1,834	22,311	−708
2007	21	1,275	1,296	44	865	81	87	1,033	1,872	22,812	501
2008	318	−2,189	−1,871	187	968	166	137	1,271	1,845	20,554	−2,258
2009	46	2,008	2,054	95	1,305	141	95	1,541	1,929	22,315	1,761
2010	188	1,943	2,131	667	1,766	124	169	2,059	1,991	25,181	2,866
2011	207	1,414	1,621	537	3,107	481	88	3,676	2,065	28,950	3,769
2012	137	912	1,049	415	5,191	55	129	5,375	2,386	33,403	4,453

[a]Revisions and adjustments = Col. 1 + Col. 2.
[b]Net of sales and acquisitions = acquisitions − sales.
[c]Total discoveries = Col. 5 + Col. 6 + Col. 7.
[d]Proved reserves = Col. 10 from prior year + Col. 3 + Col. 4 + Col. 8 − Col. 9.
Notes: Old means discovered in a prior year. New means discovered during the report year. One barrel = 42 U.S. gallons.

SOURCE: Adapted from "Table 5. Total U.S. Proved Reserves of Crude Oil and Lease Condensate, Crude Oil, and Lease Condensate, 2002–12,"in *U.S. Crude Oil and Natural Gas Proved Reserves, 2012*, U.S. Energy Information Administration, April 2014, http://www.eia.gov/naturalgas/crudeoilreserves/pdf/ uscrudeoil.pdf (accessed July 11, 2014)

TABLE 7.2

Proved reserves of wet natural gas, 2001–12

[Billion cubic feet]

Revisions Year	Adjustments (1)	Net revisions (2)	Revisions[a] and adjustments (3)	Net of sales[b] and acquisitions (4)	Extensions (5)	New field discoveries (6)	New reservoir discoveries in old fields (7)	Total[c] discoveries (8)	Estimated production (9)	Proved[d] reserves 12/31 (10)	Change from prior year (11)
Wet natural gas (billion cubic feet)											
2001	1,849	−2,438	−589	2,715	17,183	3,668	2,898	23,749	20,642	191,743	5,233
2002	4,006	1,038	5,044	428	15,468	1,374	1,752	18,594	20,248	195,561	3,818
2003	2,323	−1,715	608	1,107	17,195	1,252	1,653	20,100	20,231	197,145	1,584
2004	170	825	995	1,975	19,068	790	1,244	21,102	20,017	201,200	4,055
2005	1,693	2,715	4,408	2,674	22,069	973	1,243	24,285	19,259	213,308	12,108
2006	946	−2,099	−1,153	3,178	22,834	425	1,197	24,456	19,373	220,416	7,108
2007	990	15,936	16,926	452	28,255	814	1,244	30,313	20,318	247,789	27,373
2008	271	−3,254	−2,983	937	27,800	1,229	1,678	30,707	21,415	255,035	7,246
2009	5,923	−1,899	4,024	−222	43,500	1,423	2,656	47,579	22,537	283,879	28,844
2010	1,292	4,055	5,347	2,766	46,283	895	1,701	48,879	23,224	317,647	33,768
2011	2,715	−112	2,603	3,298	47,635	987	1,260	49,882	24,621	348,809	31,162
2012	−810	−45,614	−46,424	−1,859	47,053	780	408	48,241	26,097	322,670	−26,139

[a]Revisions and adjustments = Col. 1 + Col. 2.
[b]Net of sales and acquisitions = acquisitions − sales.
[c]Total discoveries = Col. 5 + Col. 6 + Col. 7.
[d]Proved reserves = Col. 10 from prior year + Col. 3 + Col. 4 + Col. 8 − Col. 9.
Notes: Old means discovered in a prior year. New means discovered during the report year. Natural gas is measured at 60 degreesFahrenheit and atmospheric pressure base of 14.73 pounds per square inch absolute (psia).

SOURCE: "Table 9. Total U.S. Proved Reserves of Wet Natural Gas, 2001–12," in *U.S. Crude Oil and Natural Gas Proved Reserves, 2012*, U.S. Energy Information Administration, April 2014, http://www.eia.gov/naturalgas/crudeoilreserves/pdf/uscrudeoil.pdf (accessed July 11, 2014)

estimates indicate far greater reserve amounts. The uptick since 2008 reflects additional reserves estimated for onshore reservoirs in the lower 48 states. Figure 7.2 shows proved reserves volumes in 2012 by geographical area.

Texas had the largest volume (11,101 million barrels), followed by the Gulf of Mexico federal offshore area (4,956 million barrels), North Dakota (3,773 million barrels), and California (2,976 million barrels).

FIGURE 7.1

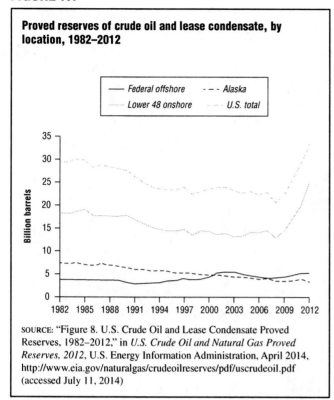

Proved reserves of crude oil and lease condensate, by location, 1982–2012

SOURCE: "Figure 8. U.S. Crude Oil and Lease Condensate Proved Reserves, 1982–2012," in *U.S. Crude Oil and Natural Gas Proved Reserves, 2012*, U.S. Energy Information Administration, April 2014, http://www.eia.gov/naturalgas/crudeoilreserves/pdf/uscrudeoil.pdf (accessed July 11, 2014)

Historical proved reserves data for wet natural gas are shown in Figure 7.3. The overall U.S. total was relatively flat or slightly declining from 1980 through the 1990s. A tremendous upswing then occurred. Proved reserves increased from around 175 tcf (5 tcm) in 1999 to nearly 349 tcf (9.9 tcm) in 2011. The total decreased in 2012 to 323 tcf (9.1 tcm). All of the increase was due to greater proved reserves in natural gas reservoirs in the lower 48 states. Figure 7.4 shows proved reserves of wet natural gas in 2012 by geographical area. Texas had the largest volume, at 93,475 billion cubic feet (bcf; 2,647 billion cubic m [bcm]). Wyoming was the second largest, at 31,636 bcf [895.8 bcm], followed by Oklahoma, at 28,714 bcf (813.1 bcm); Louisiana, at 22,135 bcf (626.9 bcm); and Colorado, at 21,674 bcf (613.7 bcm).

The calculations involved in estimating proved reserves of both fuels between 2002 and 2012 are shown in Table 7.1. The EIA notes that "reserves estimates change from year to year as new discoveries are made, existing fields are more thoroughly appraised, existing reserves are produced, and prices and technologies change."

The EIA indicates that recent reserves gains reflect higher estimates for unconventional geological sources (e.g., shale and tight formations). These sources are described in detail in Chapter 2 for oil and Chapter 3 for natural gas. Technological advancements, such as horizontal drilling and hydraulic fracturing, have allowed operators greater access to fuels that are trapped in formerly inaccessible geological sources. In addition, the agency indicates that proved oil reserves have increased partly because of higher market prices for oil. By contrast, decreasing natural gas prices between 2011 and 2012 reduced proved natural gas reserves between those two years. As noted earlier, economic viability is a key consideration when estimating proved reserves volumes.

Some of the terms listed in Table 7.1 require more explanation. The column labeled "Total discoveries" is the sum of the columns labeled "Extensions," "New field discoveries," and "New reservoir discoveries in old fields." The EIA states that extensions are "additions to reserves that result from additional drilling and exploration in previously discovered reservoirs." As shown in Table 7.1, extensions have accounted for the vast majority of total fuel discoveries.

TECHNICALLY RECOVERABLE RESOURCES

Technically recoverable resources (TRR) are energy resources that are technically recoverable; however, it may or may not be economically viable to recover them. The EIA notes in *Assumptions to the Annual Energy Outlook 2014* (June 2014, http://www.eia.gov/forecasts/aeo/assumptions/pdf/0554(2014).pdf) that TRR is "a common measure of the long-term viability of U.S. domestic crude oil and natural gas as an energy source." The EIA uses TRR estimates to forecast future domestic oil and natural gas production.

TRR include both proved reserves (as defined earlier) and unproved resources, which the EIA says include resources that have been confirmed by exploratory drilling and undiscovered resources (i.e., those assumed to be present based on geological information). TRR estimates are highly uncertain and change as new data are collected and analyzed. EIA estimates of U.S. TRR in 2012 were:

- Crude oil and lease condensate—238 billion barrels
- Wet natural gas—2,266 tcf (64.2 tcm)

It should be noted that the EIA does not include in its TRR estimates any oil and natural gas resources that are located in areas in which drilling is officially prohibited or drilling leases are not expected to be issued.

Off-Limit Areas

As of October 2014, there were several areas around the United States that were off-limits for oil and natural gas drilling for various reasons. Perhaps the most well-known (and most controversial) area is the Arctic National Wildlife Refuge (ANWR) in Alaska. The state's northern region, or North Slope, has long been a prolific production area for oil and natural gas. However, for decades the adjacent ANWR has been closed by federal law to oil and natural gas development. This 19-million-acre

FIGURE 7.2

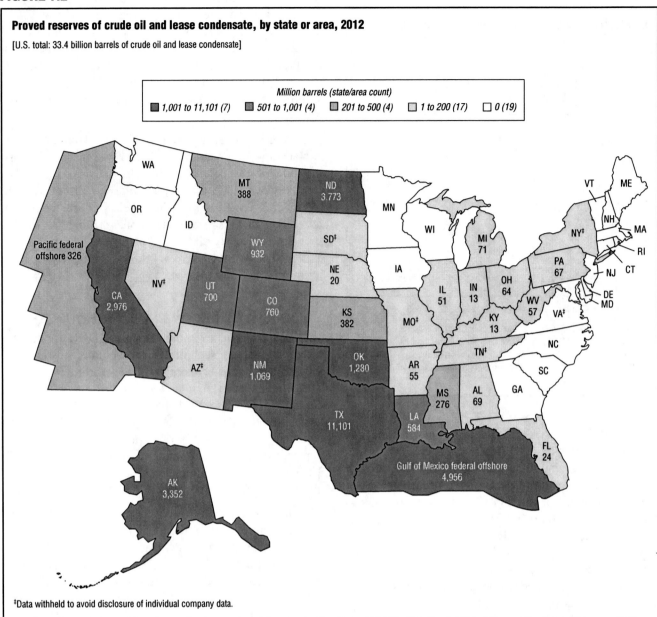

Proved reserves of crude oil and lease condensate, by state or area, 2012

[U.S. total: 33.4 billion barrels of crude oil and lease condensate]

Million barrels (state/area count)

■ 1,001 to 11,101 (7)　■ 501 to 1,001 (4)　■ 201 to 500 (4)　□ 1 to 200 (17)　□ 0 (19)

‡Data withheld to avoid disclosure of individual company data.

SOURCE: "Figure 14. Crude Oil and Lease Condensate Proved Reserves by State/Area, 2012," in *U.S. Crude Oil and Natural Gas Proved Reserves, 2012,* U.S. Energy Information Administration, April 2014, http://www.eia.gov/naturalgas/crudeoilreserves/pdf/uscrudeoil.pdf (accessed July 11, 2014)

(7.7-million-ha) area of pristine wilderness lies along the Alaskan-Canadian border. The USGS believes that there are substantial volumes of oil and natural gas beneath ANWR. Oil from the North Slope is transported via the Trans-Alaska Pipeline System to the port city of Valdez in southern Alaska. Over the years there have been numerous calls (mostly from Republican politicians) for ANWR to be opened to oil and gas drilling. However, as of October 2014, no federal legislation had been passed that would permit such development.

As explained in Chapter 1, the federal and state governments control resource leases for public lands within their jurisdictions, including offshore areas. Although oil and natural gas drilling are prolific in the Gulf of Mexico,

the same is not true for areas offshore the Atlantic and Pacific coasts. For decades, these areas have been off-limits to resource development. New offshore drilling along the West Coast was banned by the federal government and the coastal states decades ago. In 2010 President Barack Obama (1961–) announced a controversial plan to open the Atlantic Outer Continental Shelf to drilling. However, the plan was put on hold only months later after the BP (formerly British Petroleum) oil spill occurred in the Gulf of Mexico. (See Chapter 2 for a description of the spill and its aftermath.) Thus, as of October 2014, no new oil and natural gas leases were in effect within U.S. waters off the Atlantic and Pacific coasts. In addition, the federal government's lease sale

FIGURE 7.3

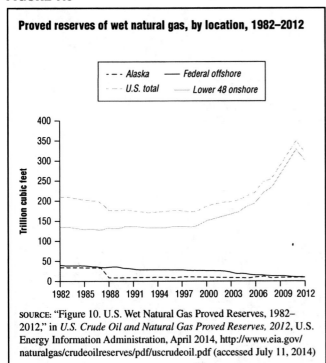

Proved reserves of wet natural gas, by location, 1982–2012

Legend:
- – – Alaska
- Federal offshore
- U.S. total
- Lower 48 onshore

SOURCE: "Figure 10. U.S. Wet Natural Gas Proved Reserves, 1982–2012," in *U.S. Crude Oil and Natural Gas Proved Reserves, 2012*, U.S. Energy Information Administration, April 2014, http://www.eia.gov/naturalgas/crudeoilreserves/pdf/uscrudeoil.pdf (accessed July 11, 2014)

schedule through 2017 (2014, http://www.boem.gov/Oil-and-Gas-Energy-Program/Leasing/Five-Year-Program/Lease-Sale-Schedule/2012---2017-Lease-Sale-Schedule.aspx) showed no lease sales planned for the Atlantic or Pacific coasts.

Exploration and Development

Finding oil and gas usually takes two steps. First, geological and geophysical exploration identifies areas where oil and gas are most likely to be found. Much of this exploration is seismic, in which shock waves are used to determine the formations below the surface of the earth. Different rock formations transmit shock waves at different velocities, so they help determine if the geological features most often associated with oil and gas accumulations are present. After the seismic testing has been completed—and if it has been successful—exploratory wells are drilled.

In *Annual Energy Review 2011* (September 2012, http://www.eia.gov/totalenergy/data/annual/pdf/aer.pdf), the EIA notes that exploratory wells are drilled for three purposes: to find crude oil or natural gas in an area previously considered to be unproductive, to find a new reservoir in a field that has previously produced crude oil or natural gas in another reservoir, and to extend the limit of a crude oil or natural gas reservoir that has previously been productive. By contrast, the agency indicates that development wells are drilled within proved areas of reservoirs to depths that are known to be productive. Figure 7.5 shows the number of wells drilled by fuel type

between 1949 and 2010. It also shows the number of wells that were dry. Overall, the majority of the exploratory and development wells were successful.

COAL

Coal supplied 20 quadrillion Btu of the United States' 81.7 quadrillion Btu primary energy consumption in 2013, or 24% of the total. (See Table 1.2 in Chapter 1.) The different ranks of coal (anthracite, bituminous coal, subbituminous coal, and lignite) and the different types of coal mining are described in detail in Chapter 4. The EIA measures three categories of coal reserves (see Table 7.3):

- Demonstrated reserve base (DRB)—coal known from publicly available data to be mapped to measured and indicated degrees of accuracy and found at depths and in coalbed thicknesses considered technologically minable at the time of determinations

- Estimated recoverable reserves—DRB coal considered recoverable after excluding coal estimated to be unavailable due to land use restrictions and after applying assumed mining recovery rates

- Recoverable reserves at producing mines—the quantity of coal that can be recovered (i.e., mined) from existing coal reserves at reporting mines

In 2012 the nation's total DRB was 481.4 billion tons (436.7 billion t). (See Table 7.3.) Most of the DRB requires underground mining, rather than surface mining, to be extracted. The five states with the largest DRB quantities in 2012 were:

- Montana—118.9 billion tons (107.8 billion t)
- Illinois—104 billion tons (94.3 billion t)
- Wyoming—60 billion tons (54.4 billion t)
- West Virginia—31.3 billion tons (28.4 billion t)
- Kentucky—28.7 billion tons (26.1 billion t)

URANIUM

As explained in Chapter 5, uranium is the resource used to produce nuclear power for electricity generation. Nuclear electric power supplied 8.3 quadrillion Btu of the United States' 81.7 quadrillion Btu primary energy consumption in 2013, or 10% of the total. (See Table 1.2 in Chapter 1.)

The world's natural uranium supply is enormous because the element is present at low levels throughout the earth's crust and oceans. Uranium is most highly concentrated in uranium ores, which are mined as described in Chapter 5. The recovered uranium is processed into a powder called yellowcake, which has the chemical formula U_3O_8.

FIGURE 7.4

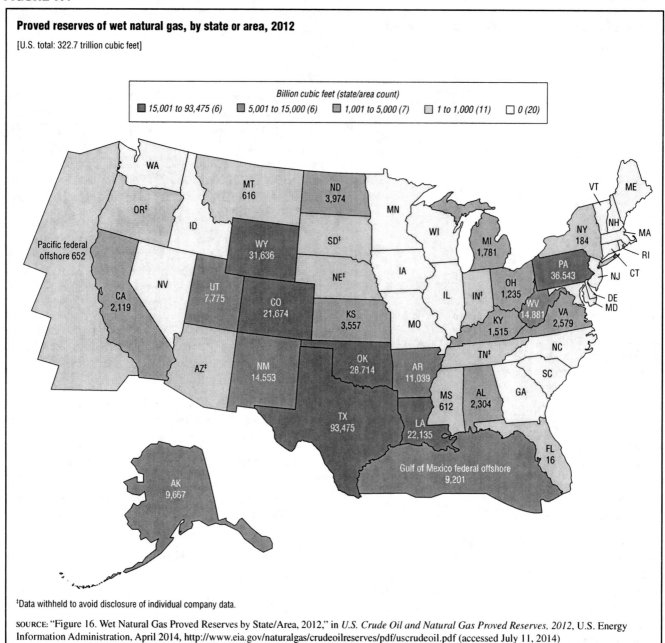

Proved reserves of wet natural gas, by state or area, 2012

[U.S. total: 322.7 trillion cubic feet]

Billion cubic feet (state/area count)

☐ 15,001 to 93,475 (6) ☐ 5,001 to 15,000 (6) ☐ 1,001 to 5,000 (7) ☐ 1 to 1,000 (11) ☐ 0 (20)

‡Data withheld to avoid disclosure of individual company data.

SOURCE: "Figure 16. Wet Natural Gas Proved Reserves by State/Area, 2012," in *U.S. Crude Oil and Natural Gas Proved Reserves, 2012*, U.S. Energy Information Administration, April 2014, http://www.eia.gov/naturalgas/crudeoilreserves/pdf/uscrudeoil.pdf (accessed July 11, 2014)

In *2013 Domestic Uranium Production Report* (May 2014, http://www.eia.gov/uranium/production/annual/pdf/dupr.pdf), the EIA provides U.S. uranium reserve estimates at year-end 2013. (See Table 7.4). These are the amounts believed to be present at 74 mines and properties that could be extracted at various cost levels. Overall, the total reserves were estimated at 337.6 million pounds U_3O_8. According to the EIA, exploration and development drilling for uranium totaled 3.8 million feet (1.2 million m) in 2013.

Besides uranium ores, natural uranium can also be extracted from so-called unconventional sources, which are described by Susan Hall and Margaret Coleman in *Critical Analysis of World Uranium Resources*

(2013, http://pubs.usgs.gov/sir/2012/5239/sir2012-5239.pdf). These sources include seawater (which has not yet been commercially exploited due to high costs) and deposits of phosphate rock, lignite, and black shale. These deposits are found around the world (including in the United States) and have provided uranium in the past under favorable economic conditions. Hall and Coleman note "the extraction of uranium from phosphates is receiving the most attention, because it can potentially tap into a vast resource." Technical innovations have improved the cost effectiveness of uranium extraction from phosphate deposits. The United States, in particular, contains uranium-rich phosphate deposits in Florida. (See Figure 7.6.)

FIGURE 7.5

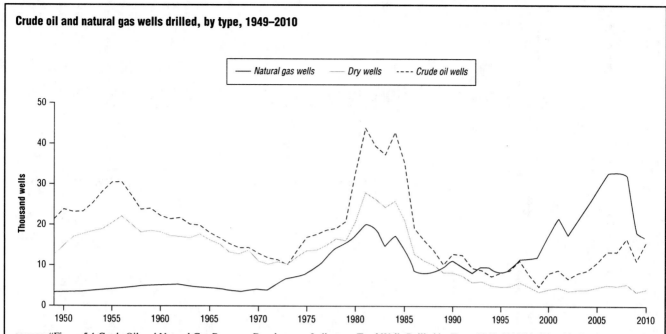

Crude oil and natural gas wells drilled, by type, 1949–2010

SOURCE: "Figure 5.1 Crude Oil and Natural Gas Resource Development Indicators: Total Wells Drilled by Type, 1949–2010," in *Monthly Energy Review: June 2014*, U.S. Energy Information Administration, June 25, 2014, http://www.eia.gov/totalenergy/data/monthly/archive/00351406.pdf (accessed June 27, 2014)

INTERNATIONAL RESERVES

When considering energy reserves outside of the United States, it is important to understand that many different terms are used internationally to refer to reserve volumes and to categorize them based on technological and economic criteria.

The EIA provides worldwide estimates of proved reserves of several fuels through its "International Energy Statistics" (http://www.eia.gov/cfapps/ipdbproject/IED Index3.cfm). However, data are not available for all fuels, countries, or regions for every year.

Crude Oil and Natural Gas

According to the EIA (2014, http://www.eia.gov/cfapps/ipdbproject/IEDIndex3.cfm?tid=5&pid=57&aid=6) , world proved reserves of crude oil totaled 1.6 trillion barrels in 2014. The countries with the largest reserves were Venezuela (297.7 billion barrels), Saudi Arabia (268.4 billion barrels), Canada (173.2 billion barrels), Iran (157.3 billion barrels), and Iraq (140.3 billion barrels).

The EIA (2014, http://www.eia.gov/cfapps/ipdb project/IEDIndex3.cfm?tid=3&pid=3&aid=6) indicates that proved reserves of natural gas totaled 6,845.6 tcf (193.8 tcm) in 2013. The countries with the largest reserves were Russia (1,688 tcf [47.8 tcm]), Iran (1,187 tcf [33.6 tcm]), Qatar (890 tcf [25.2 tcm]), the United States (308.4 tcf [8.7 tcm]), and Saudi Arabia (287.8 tcf [8.1 tcm]).

Coal

The EIA (2014, http://www.eia.gov/cfapps/ipdb project/IEDIndex3.cfm?tid=1&pid=7&aid=6) reports worldwide proved recoverable reserves of coal at 979.8 billion tons (888.9 billion t) in 2011. The largest reserves were held by the United States (258.6 billion tons [234.6 billion t]), Russia (173.1 billion tons [157.1 billion t]), China (126.2 billion tons [114.5 billion t]), Australia (84.2 billion tons [76.4 billion t]), and India (66.8 billion tons [60.6 billion t]).

Uranium

The Organisation for Economic Co-operation and Development (OECD) is a collection of dozens of mostly Western nations (including the United States) that are devoted to global economic development. Every two years the OECD's Nuclear Energy Agency, in collaboration with the International Atomic Energy Agency, publishes a report on the worldwide uranium industry. As of October 2014, the most recent report was *Uranium 2011: Resources, Production and Demand* (2012, http://www.iaea.org/OurWork/ST/NE/NEFW/Technical-Areas/NFC/uranium-production-cycle-redbook.html#RedBook). The Nuclear Energy Agency and International Atomic Energy Agency estimate total world identified uranium resources at 8.3 million tons (7.5 million t) of contained uranium metal in 2011.

As explained in Chapter 5, nuclear fuel can also be made from plutonium (a by-product of uranium fission), from the by-products and waste materials resulting from

TABLE 7.3

Coal reserves, by type and mining method, by state, 2012

[Million short tons]

Coal-resource state	Underground-minable coal			Surface-minable coal			Total		
	Recoverable reserves at producing mines	Estimated recoverable reserves	Demonstrated reserve base	Recoverable reserves at producing mines	Estimated recoverable reserves	Demonstrated reserve base	Recoverable reserves at producing mines	Estimated recoverable reserves	Demonstrated reserve base
Alabama	209	425	844	56	2,230	3,130	265	2,655	3,974
Alaska	—	2,335	5,423	w	487	672	w	2,821	6,094
Arizona	w	—	—	w	—	—	w	—	—
Arkansas	w	127	272	—	101	144	w	228	416
Colorado	w	5,811	11,073	—	3,744	4,759	300	9,555	15,832
Georgia	—	—	2	—	1	2	—	1	4
Idaho	—	2	4	—	—	—	—	2	4
Illinois	w	27,792	87,493	w	10,044	16,502	2,215	37,835	103,995
Indiana	252	3,544	8,556	348	318	544	600	3,862	9,100
Iowa	—	807	1,732	—	320	457	—	1,127	2,189
Kansas	—	—	—	—	680	971	—	680	971
Kentucky total	1,071	6,947	16,130	192	7,266	12,583	1,263	14,213	28,713
Kentucky (east)	w	360	644	w	5,030	9,008	644	5,390	9,652
Kentucky (west)	w	6,587	15,486	w	2,236	3,574	619	8,823	19,061
Louisiana	—	—	—	w	288	388	w	288	388
Maryland	w	309	564	w	33	48	34	342	612
Michigan	—	55	123	w	3	5	—	58	128
Mississippi	—	—	—	—	—	—	—	—	—
Missouri	—	689	1,479	w	3,155	4,507	w	3,844	5,986
Montana	w	35,906	70,925	w	38,738	47,927	960	74,644	118,851
New Mexico	w	2,763	6,073	w	4,075	5,819	497	6,838	11,892
North Carolina	—	5	11	—	—	—	—	5	11
North Dakota	—	—	—	1,128	6,711	8,797	1,128	6,711	8,797
Ohio	w	7,614	17,306	w	3,717	5,679	235	11,331	22,985
Oklahoma	w	571	1,225	w	221	315	11	791	1,540
Oregon	—	6	15	—	2	3	—	9	17
Pennsylvania total	355	10,337	22,522	199	985	4,155	554	11,322	26,677
Pennsylvania (anthracite)	w	340	3,841	w	418	3,341	131	758	7,183
Pennsylvania (bituminous)	w	9,997	18,681	w	567	814	423	10,564	19,495
South Dakota	—	—	—	—	277	366	—	277	366
Tennessee	w	274	500	w	171	253	4	445	753
Texas	—	—	—	751	9,252	12,019	751	9,252	12,019
Utah	w	2,365	4,825	w	211	267	199	2,576	5,091
Virginia	234	517	920	49	312	488	283	829	1,408
Washington	—	674	1,332	505	6	8	505	681	1,340
West Virginia total	1,337	14,949	28,010	w	2,064	3,271	1,842	17,013	31,281
West Virginia (northern)	w	NA	NA	w	NA	NA	480	NA	NA
West Virginia (southern)	w	NA	NA	w	NA	NA	1,362	NA	NA
Wyoming	w	22,926	42,456	w	14,487	17,495	6,932	37,413	59,951
U.S. total	**6,656**	**147,750**	**329,814**	**12,008**	**109,898**	**151,571**	**18,664**	**257,648**	**481,385**

TABLE 7.3

Coal reserves, by type and mining method, by state, 2012 [CONTINUED]

[Million short tons]

— = No data reported.
w = Data withheld to avoid disclosure.
NA = Not available.

Notes: Recoverable coal reserves at producing mines represent the quantity of coal that can be recovered (i.e. mined) from existing coal reserves at reporting mines. EIA's estimated recoverable reserves include the coal in the demonstrated reserve base considered recoverable after excluding coal estimated to be unavailable due to land use restrictions, and after applying assumed mining recovery rates. This estimate does not include any specific economic feasibility criteria. The effective date fo the demonstrated reserve base, as customarily worded, is 'Remaining as of January 1, 2013.' These data are contemporaneous with the Recoverable Reserves at Producing Mines, customarily presented as of the end of the reporting year's mining, that is in this case, December 31, 2012. The demonstrated reserve base includes publicly available data on coal mapped to measured and indicated degrees of accuracy and found at depths and in coalbed thicknesses considered technologically minable at the time of determinations. All reserve expressions exclude silt, culm, refuse bank, slurry dam, and dredge operations. Reserves at Producing Mines exclude mines producing less than 25,000 short tons, which are not required to provide reserves data.

SOURCE: "Table 15. Recoverable Coal Reserves at Producing Mines, Estimated Recoverable Reserves, and Demonstrated Reserve by Mining Method, 2012," in *Annual Coal Report 2012*, U.S. Energy Information Administration, December 2013, http://www.eia.gov/coal/annual/pdf/acr.pdf (accessed July 7, 2014)

TABLE 7.4

Uranium reserves, year-end 2013

[Million pounds U₃O₈]

Uranium reserve estimates[a] by mine and property status, mining method, and state(s)	End of 2013		
	Forward cost[b]		
	$0 to $30 per pound	$0 to $50 per pound	$0 to $100 per pound
Properties with exploration completed, exploration continuing, and only assessment work	W	W	130.7
Properties under development for production and development drilling	W	31.8	W
Mines in production	W	19.6	W
Mines closed temporarily, closed permanently, and mined out	W	W	135.2
In-situ leach mining	W	W	124.1
Underground and open pit mining	W	W	213.5
Arizona, New Mexico and Utah	0	W	189.1
Colorado, Nebraska and Texas	W	W	40.6
Wyoming	W	W	107.9
Total	**46.6**	**W**	**337.6**

W = Data withheld to avoid disclosure of individual company data.
[a]Reserve estimates on 71 mines and properties for end of 2012 and on 74 mines and properties for end of 2013. These uranium reserve estimates cannot be compared with the much larger historical data set of uranium reserves that were published in the July 2010 report U.S.
[b]Forward Cost: The operating and capital costs still to be incurred in the production of uranium from in-place reserves. By using forward costing, estimates for reserves for ore deposits in differing geological settings and status of development can be aggregated and reported for selected cost categories. Included are costs for labor, materials, power and fuel, royalties, payroll taxes, insurance, and applicable general and administrative costs. Excluded from forward cost estimates are prior expenditures, if any, incurred for property acquisition, exploration, mine development, and mill construction, as well as income taxes, profit, and the cost of money. Forward costs are neither the full costs of production nor the market price at which the uranium, when produced, might be sold.
Note: Totals may not equal sum of components because of independent rounding.
U₃O₈ = uranium oxide.

SOURCE: Adapted from "Table 10. Uranium Reserve Estimates at the End of 2012 and 2013," in *2013 Domestic Uranium Production Report*, U.S. Energy Information Administration, May 2014, http://www.eia.gov/uranium/production/annual/pdf/dupr.pdf (accessed July 8, 2014)

uranium mining and processing, and from uranium that was originally processed for use in nuclear weapons. These are considered secondary uranium sources. They are used to meet uranium demand to various degrees around the world. In *Critical Analysis of World Uranium Resources*, the USGS and EIA note that secondary sources (including Russian and U.S. government stockpiles of natural uranium) accounted for 25% of the world's uranium production in 2010.

FIGURE 7.6

Major uranium deposits

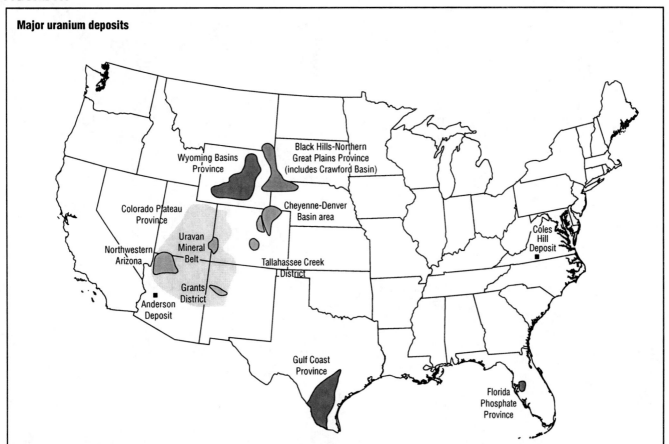

SOURCE: Susan Hall and Margaret Coleman, "Figure 1-23. Uranium Province Map of the United States," in *Critical Analysis of World Uranium Resources*, U.S. Geological Survey and U.S. Energy Information Administration, 2013, http://pubs.usgs.gov/sir/2012/5239/sir2012-5239.pdf (accessed July 11, 2014)

CHAPTER 8
ELECTRICITY

In 1879 Thomas Alva Edison (1847–1931) flipped the first switch to light Menlo Park, New Jersey. Since that time the use of electrical power has become nearly universal in the United States. Electricity is not really an energy source but an energy carrier, because it is generated using primary energy sources, such as fossil fuels. As such, electricity supplies and pricing are highly dependent on the economic factors underlying the fuels and processes that are used to generate electricity. Likewise, the electric power sector is the focal point for environmental concerns that are associated with combusting or otherwise using primary energy sources to produce electricity.

UNDERSTANDING ELECTRICITY

Electricity results from the interaction of charged particles, such as electrons (negatively charged subatomic particles) and protons (positively charged subatomic particles). For example, static electricity is caused by friction: when one material rubs against another, it transfers charged particles. The zap people might feel and the spark people might see when they drag their feet on a carpet and then touch a metal doorknob demonstrate static electricity—electrons being transferred between a hand and the doorknob.

Generating Electricity

As noted in Chapter 1, electricity is not a primary energy source because energy is required to produce electricity. In the United States most electric power is produced by burning fossil fuels. The resulting heat turns water into steam, which can be used as a working fluid to turn the blades of a turbine. The hot gases from the burning fuels can also be used for this purpose. In either case, the turbine rotates a magnet that is nestled within or around coiled wire, which generates an electric current in the wire. Thus, heat is a primary factor in the operation of these plants. The same is true for nuclear power plants.

They rely on the heat that is released from splitting uranium atoms apart to produce steam. (See Chapter 5.) Thermally derived electricity is also obtained from burning wood or waste, from geothermal reservoirs, and through some solar (sunlight-based) systems. These renewable energy sources are described in Chapter 6.

There are also nonthermal means for producing electricity. The most common is hydropower, which is described in Chapter 6. Hydropower relies on water (rather than on steam or hot gases) to be the working fluid that turns turbines. Wind is the working fluid that turns turbines at wind farms. Lastly, some solar systems turn sunlight directly into electrical current using crystalline materials.

Overall, the vast majority of electricity generation methods operated in the United States are thermally based—that is, they convert heat energy to mechanical energy to electrical energy. This conversion process is inherently inefficient because large amounts of energy are lost along the way.

Measuring Electricity

Electric current is the flow of electric charge; it is measured in amperes (amps). Electrical power is the rate at which energy is transferred by electric current. A watt is the standard measure of electrical power, named after the Scottish engineer James Watt (1736–1819). A watt is a very small unit of measure, so electrical power is typically measured in multiples of the watt, such as the kilowatt (kW; 1,000 watts), the megawatt (MW; 1 million watts), or the gigawatt (GW; 1 billion watts). Electrical work is usually measured using the kilowatt-hour (kWh), which is the work done by 1 kW acting for one hour. A 1,000-kW generator running at full capacity for one hour supplies 1,000 kWh of power. That generator operating continuously for an entire year produces nearly 8.8 million kWh of electricity (1,000 kW × 24 hours per day × 365 days per year).

FIGURE 8.1

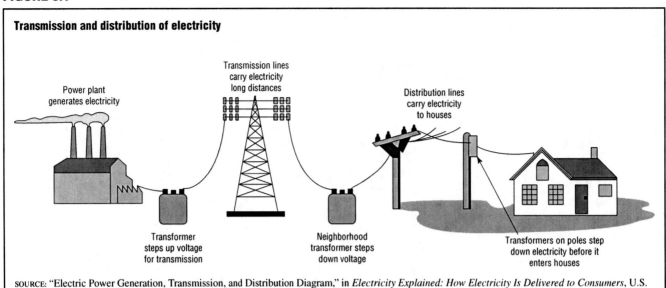

Transmission and distribution of electricity

Power plant generates electricity

Transmission lines carry electricity long distances

Distribution lines carry electricity to houses

Transformer steps up voltage for transmission

Neighborhood transformer steps down voltage

Transformers on poles step down electricity before it enters houses

SOURCE: "Electric Power Generation, Transmission, and Distribution Diagram," in *Electricity Explained: How Electricity Is Delivered to Consumers*, U.S. Energy Information Administration, July 9, 2012, http://www.eia.gov/energyexplained/index.cfm?page=electricity_delivery (accessed July 14, 2014)

Electric Power System/Electrical Grid

An electric power system, or electrical grid, is a network that connects the locations of electrical power generation with the locations of electrical power consumption. Figure 8.1 illustrates the components of a simple electric system. Power plants generate electricity, which is raised to a high voltage for transmission. Voltage is a complicated concept, but basically raising the voltage improves the energy efficiency (i.e., reduces losses) as the transmission lines carry electricity over long distances. The voltage is stepped down (lowered) somewhat before the electricity goes onto the distribution lines that deliver it to neighborhoods, shopping centers, and other clusters of users. Then the voltage is stepped down again for delivery to individual homes and businesses. It should be noted that some industrial facilities can take their electricity at higher voltages than what is delivered to residential and commercial customers.

Electricity is generated and distributed around the country by numerous individual utilities and companies. In "What Is the Electric Power Grid and What Are Some Challenges It Faces?" (September 16, 2014, http://www.eia.gov/energy_in_brief/article/power_grid.cfm), the U.S. Energy Information Administration (EIA), a division of the U.S. Department of Energy, notes that the United States includes more than 7,000 electric generating units, 2,000 electric distribution utilities, and 300,000 miles of transmission and distribution lines. There is no single national grid. The 48 contiguous states have three grids:

- Eastern Interconnection—east of the Rocky Mountains

- Western Interconnection—from the Pacific Ocean to the Rocky Mountains

- Texas Interconnected System—most of Texas

The EIA explains that "these systems operate independently of each other for the most part, although there are limited links between them." Within the grids, substations connect the pieces of the system together, and energy control centers coordinate the operation of all the components. At the federal level the interstate transmission of electricity is regulated by the Federal Energy Regulatory Commission (FERC). The Energy Policy Act of 2005 gave FERC the authority to certify a single organization to enforce mandatory electric reliability standards that are applicable to much of the industry. FERC certified the North American Electric Reliability Corporation for this purpose. It is a nonprofit organization responsible for ensuring the reliability of the electric power system throughout most of Canada and the United States and parts of northern Mexico.

DOMESTIC PRODUCTION AND CONSUMPTION

Electricity is produced on demand (i.e., as it is needed). However, consumer demand varies constantly as people turn on and off air conditioners, light switches, appliances, and other electrical devices. In "Factors Affecting Electricity Prices" (October 7, 2014, http://www.eia.gov/energyexplained/index.cfm?page=electricity_factors_affecting_prices), the EIA indicates that electricity demand on a daily basis is usually highest in the afternoon and early evening. On a seasonal basis, demand is highest during the summer.

There are no large-scale means by which electricity can be efficiently stored for later use. This deficiency profoundly affects the electric power sector and the economics of electricity because it means the system as a whole has to be ready for peak demand at all times. In general, the power industry operates two kinds of

TABLE 8.1

Electricity generation, trade, losses, and end uses, selected years 1950–2013

[Billion kilowatthours]

	Net generation				Trade				End use		
	Electric power sector[a]	Commercial sector[b]	Industrial sector[c]	Total	Imports[d]	Exports[d]	Net imports[d]	T&D losses[e] and unaccounted for[f]	Retail sales[g]	Direct use[h]	Total
1950 Total	329	NA	5	334	2	(s)	2	44	291	NA	291
1955 Total	547	NA	3	550	5	(s)	4	58	497	NA	497
1960 Total	756	NA	4	759	5	1	5	76	688	NA	688
1965 Total	1,055	NA	3	1,058	4	4	(s)	104	954	NA	954
1970 Total	1,532	NA	3	1,535	6	4	2	145	1,392	NA	1,392
1975 Total	1,918	NA	3	1,921	11	5	6	180	1,747	NA	1,747
1980 Total	2,286	NA	3	2,290	25	4	21	216	2,094	NA	2,094
1985 Total	2,470	NA	3	2,473	46	5	41	190	2,324	NA	2,324
1990 Total	2,901	6	131[c]	3,038	18	16	2	203	2,713	125	2,837
1995 Total	3,194	8	151	3,353	43	4	39	229	3,013	151	3,164
2000 Total	3,638	8	157	3,802	49	15	34	244	3,421	171	3,592
2001 Total	3,580	7	149	3,737	39	16	22	202	3,394	163	3,557
2002 Total	3,698	7	153	3,858	37	16	21	248	3,465	166	3,632
2003 Total	3,721	7	155	3,883	30	24	6	228	3,494	168	3,662
2004 Total	3,808	8	154	3,971	34	23	11	266	3,547	168	3,716
2005 Total	3,902	8	145	4,055	44	19	25	269	3,661	150	3,811
2006 Total	3,908	8	148	4,065	43	24	18	266	3,670	147	3,817
2007 Total	4,005	8	143	4,157	51	20	31	298	3,765	126	3,890
2008 Total	3,974	8	137	4,119	57	24	33	287	3,733	132	3,865
2009 Total	3,810	8	132	3,950	52	18	34	261	3,597	127	3,724
2010 Total	3,972	9	144	4,125	45	19	26	265	3,754	132	3,886
2011 Total	3,948	10	142	4,100	52	15	37	255	3,750	133	3,883
2012 Total	3,890	11	146	4,048	59	12	47	263	3,695	138	3,832
2013 Total	3,899	11	148	4,058	64	11	52	279	3,692	139[E]	3,831

[a]Electricity-only and combined-heat-and-power (CHP) plants within the NAICS 22 category whose primary business is to sell electricity, or electricity and heat, to the public. Through 1988, data are for electric utilities only; beginning in 1989, data are for electric utilities and independent power producers.

[b]Commercial combined-heat-and-power (CHP) and commercial electricity-only plants.

[c]Industrial combined-heat-and-power (CHP) and industrial electricity-only plants. Through 1988, data are for industrial hydroelectric power only.

[d]Electricity transmitted across U.S. borders. Net imports equal imports minus exports.

[e]Transmission and distribution losses (electricity losses that occur between the point of generation and delivery to the customer).

[f]Data collection frame differences and nonsampling error.

[g]Electricity retail sales to ultimate customers by electric utilities and, beginning in 1996, other energy service providers.

[h]Use of electricity that is (1) self-generated, (2) produced by either the same entity that consumes the power or an affiliate, and (3) used in direct support of a service or industrial process located within the same facility or group of facilities that house the generating equipment. Direct use is exclusive of station use.

E = Estimate. NA = Not available. (s) = Less than 0.5 billion kilowatthours. T&D = Transmission and distribution.

Notes: Totals may not equal sum of components due to independent rounding. Geographic coverage is the 50 states and the District of Columbia.

SOURCE: Adapted from "Table 7.1. Electricity Overview (Billion Kilowatthours)," in *Monthly Energy Review: June 2014*, U.S. Energy Information Administration, June 25, 2014, http://www.eia.gov/totalenergy/data/monthly/archive/0035l406.pdf (accessed June 27, 2014)

FIGURE 8.2

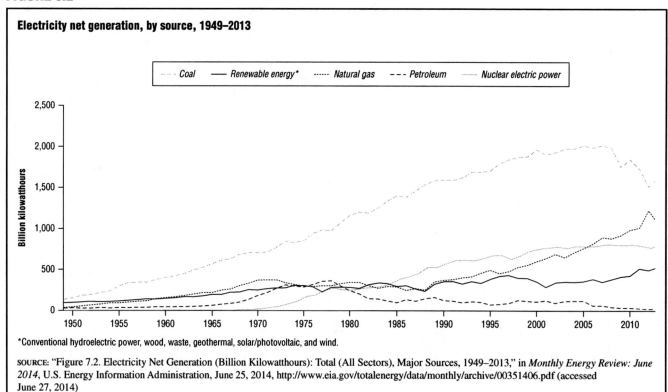

Electricity net generation, by source, 1949–2013

--- Coal   —— Renewable energy*   ⋯⋯ Natural gas   --- Petroleum   ⋯⋯⋯ Nuclear electric power

*Conventional hydroelectric power, wood, waste, geothermal, solar/photovoltaic, and wind.

SOURCE: "Figure 7.2. Electricity Net Generation (Billion Kilowatthours): Total (All Sectors), Major Sources, 1949–2013," in *Monthly Energy Review: June 2014*, U.S. Energy Information Administration, June 25, 2014, http://www.eia.gov/totalenergy/data/monthly/archive/00351406.pdf (accessed June 27, 2014)

generating capacity: baseload and peaking. The EIA explains in "Electric Generators' Roles Vary Due to Daily and Seasonal Variation in Demand" (June 8, 2011, http://www.eia.gov/todayinenergy/detail.cfm?id=1710) that "baseload capacity runs around the clock when it is not down for maintenance. Peaking capacity runs a few times a year for short periods to help electricity systems meet peak demand."

The nation's electricity production has increased over the decades, but its growth has slowed recently. As shown in Table 8.1, net generation (which excludes the electricity used by power plants themselves) increased from 334 billion kWh in 1950 to 4,058 billion kWh in 2013. The vast majority of the nation's electricity is generated by the electric power sector; however, some industrial and commercial facilities operate their own power plants. Electricity produced by these facilities is called direct-use or self-generated electricity. Table 8.1 indicates that very small amounts of electricity are imported or exported across U.S. borders.

Production Sources

Figure 8.2 shows net electricity generation by source between 1949 and 2013. Coal has historically been the largest source. In 2013 it accounted for 1,586 billion kWh, or 39% of the total net generation. Natural gas was second, at 1,113.7 billion kWh, or 27% of the total. It was followed by nuclear power, at 789 billion kWh (19%); renewable energy sources, at 522.5 billion kWh

(13%); and petroleum, at 26.9 billion kWh (1%). According to the EIA, in *Monthly Energy Review: June 2014* (June 2014, http://www.eia.gov/totalenergy/data/monthly/archive/00351406.pdf), other gases derived from fossil fuels accounted for the remainder of the total production.

Coal has long been the fuel of choice because, as explained in Chapter 4, it is abundant domestically and relatively low priced. Nuclear power began playing a larger role during the 1980s, but its use has been rather flat since the late 1990s. (See Figure 8.2.) The biggest movement in fuels has been by natural gas. During the first decade of the 21st century coal's supremacy was seriously challenged by natural gas due to various technological, economic, and legislative factors.

According to the EIA, in "Most Electric Generating Capacity Additions in the Last Decade Were Natural Gas–Fired" (July 5, 2011, http://www.eia.gov/todayinenergy/detail.cfm?id=2070), more than 80% of total generation capacity additions made between 2000 and 2010 were natural gas–fired. This growth reflects market changes that began during the late 1980s:

- Decreasing natural gas prices and increasing domestic supplies.

- Increasing availability of combined-cycle units, which are more efficient than steam-only units. As noted earlier, the working fluid that turns a turbine can be hot gases or steam. In a combined-cycle plant, both

FIGURE 8.3

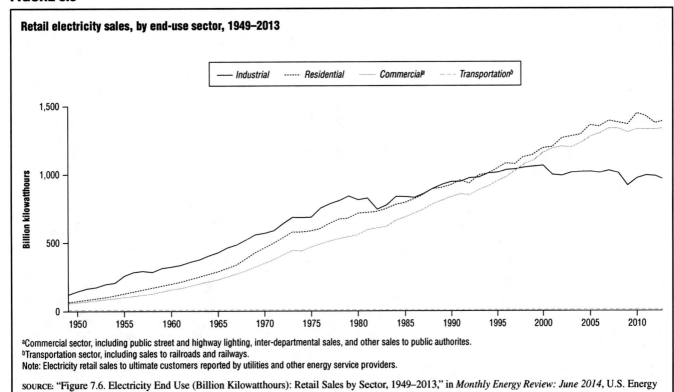

Retail electricity sales, by end-use sector, 1949–2013

aCommercial sector, including public street and highway lighting, inter-departmental sales, and other sales to public authorites.
bTransportation sector, including sales to railroads and railways.
Note: Electricity retail sales to ultimate customers reported by utilities and other energy service providers.

SOURCE: "Figure 7.6. Electricity End Use (Billion Kilowatthours): Retail Sales by Sector, 1949–2013," in *Monthly Energy Review: June 2014*, U.S. Energy Information Administration, June 25, 2014, http://www.eia.gov/totalenergy/data/monthly/archive/00351406.pdf (accessed June 27, 2014)

types of turbines are used, in that hot gases leaving one turbine are used to heat water to produce steam to turn another turbine.

• Repeal of provisions contained in a 1978 law that "discouraged" the use of natural gas for electricity generation.

In addition, natural gas became a favored fuel for power generation because it was cheaper and faster to construct natural gas–fired plants than coal-fired plants.

It is important to understand that fossil fuel–fired power plants do not necessarily use a single fuel for all of their capacity. For example, a plant might use natural gas for its baseload capacity and petroleum for its peaking capacity.

Consumption

Figure 8.3 shows retail electricity sales for various economic sectors. The residential sector was the largest user in 2013, at 1,391.1 billion kWh. It was followed closely by the commercial sector, at 1,338.4 billion kWh, and the industrial sector, at 954.7 billion kWh. The transportation sector was a very small electricity consumer in 2013, accounting for only 7.5 billion kWh.

From 1949 to the mid-1980s the industrial sector was the largest consumer of electricity in the United States, and its usage rate grew quickly. (See Figure 8.3.) That growth slowed through the 1990s, and during the first decade of the 21st century industrial consumption was flat to slightly declining. Meanwhile, residential and commercial consumption continued to grow.

Losses

As noted earlier, energy is lost when thermal energy is converted to mechanical energy and then to electrical energy. Conversion losses are significant. Figure 8.4 shows an energy balance for electricity flows in 2013. Nearly 39.2 quadrillion British thermal units (Btu) of energy was input to electricity generation; however, 24.5 quadrillion Btu (63%) of it was lost during conversion, leaving 14.7 quadrillion Btu of gross generation. An additional 0.9 quadrillion Btu was lost during transmission and distribution of the net generated electricity. Overall, 25.5 quadrillion Btu, or 65% of the incoming energy, was lost.

ELECTRICITY PRICES

Figure 8.5 shows the average retail prices of electricity by sector between 1960 and 2013. Retail prices were quite variable by sector during the 1960s, but prices for all sectors dipped through the early 1970s and then spiked back up through the early 1980s. Prices dropped through the end of the century and then began creeping upward again. The prices shown in Figure 8.5 are nominal, meaning that they do not account for the effects of inflation. By contrast, real prices assume that

FIGURE 8.4

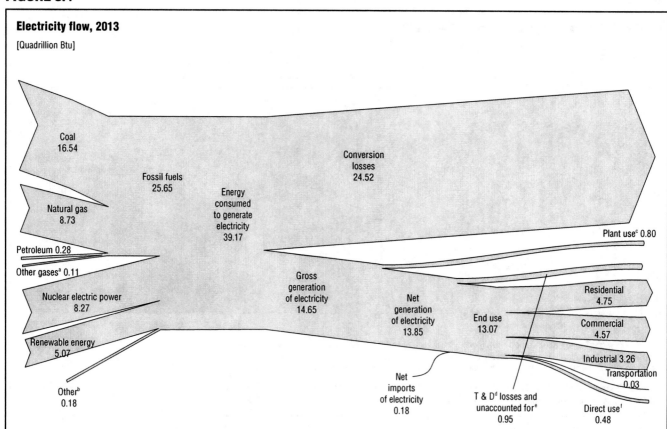

Electricity flow, 2013

[Quadrillion Btu]

Coal 16.54

Natural gas 8.73

Petroleum 0.28

Other gases[a] 0.11

Nuclear electric power 8.27

Renewable energy 5.07

Other[b] 0.18

Fossil fuels 25.65

Energy consumed to generate electricity 39.17

Conversion losses 24.52

Gross generation of electricity 14.65

Net generation of electricity 13.85

Net imports of electricity 0.18

End use 13.07

T & D[d] losses and unaccounted for[e] 0.95

Plant use[c] 0.80

Residential 4.75

Commercial 4.57

Industrial 3.26

Transportation 0.03

Direct use[f] 0.48

[a]Blast furnace gas and other manufactured and waste gases derived from fossil fuels.
[b]Batteries, chemicals, hydrogen, pitch, purchased steam, sulfur, miscellaneous technologies, and non-renewable waste (municipal solid waste from non-biogenic sources, and tire-derived fuels).
[c]Electric energy used in the operation of power plants.
[d]Transmission and distribution losses (electricity losses that occur between the point of generation and delivery to the customer).
[e]Data collection frame differences and nonsampling error.
[f]Use of electricity that is (1) self-generated, (2) produced by either the same entity that consumes the power or an affiliate, and (3) used in direct support of a service or industrial process located within the same facility or group of facilities that house the generating equipment. Direct use is exclusive of station use.
Notes: Data are preliminary. Net generation of electricity includes pumped storage facility production minus energy used for pumping. Values are derived from source data prior to rounding for publication. Totals may not equal sum of components due to independent rounding.
Btu = British thermal units. T & D = Transmission and distribution.

SOURCE: "U.S. Electricity Flow, 2013 (Quadrillion Btu)," in *Diagrams: Energy Flows*, U.S. Energy Information Administration, 2014, http://www.eia.gov/totalenergy/data/monthly/pdf/flow/electricity.pdf (accessed July 14, 2014)

the value of a dollar is constant over time. Thus, changes reflect actual market variations and not inflationary effects. Table 8.2 shows real prices for residential electricity between 1960 and 2013. Real electricity prices for this sector declined through 2004 and then fluctuated through 2013.

Pricing Factors

In "Factors Affecting Electricity Prices," the EIA notes that electricity prices are affected by fuel costs, power plant construction and maintenance costs, and transmission and distribution line costs. Weather also plays a factor. As noted earlier, electricity usage is higher during the summer than during other seasons. Hot summer weather can greatly increase the demand for electricity for air conditioning and drive up prices. Lastly, electricity prices are affected by government regulations and policies, which will be explained later in this chapter.

The prices that are paid by electricity consumers vary by economic sector. According to the EIA, residential and commercial customers pay the most for electricity because delivery to them is the most expensive. By contrast, industrial customers pay the least because they purchase electricity in large amounts and because many industrial facilities do not require their electricity to be stepped down by transformers—that is, their systems can handle electricity at higher voltages than what is delivered to commercial and residential customers.

The EIA indicates in "State Electricity Profiles" (May 1, 2014, http://www.eia.gov/electricity/state) that electricity prices vary considerably state by state. For example, in 2012 the average price was only 6.9 cents per kWh in Louisiana, but 34 cents per kWh in Hawaii. Pricing differences between states are due to various factors, including the number and type of power plants in an area, the availability and price of fuel in local markets, and government regulations and policies that affect pricing.

FIGURE 8.5

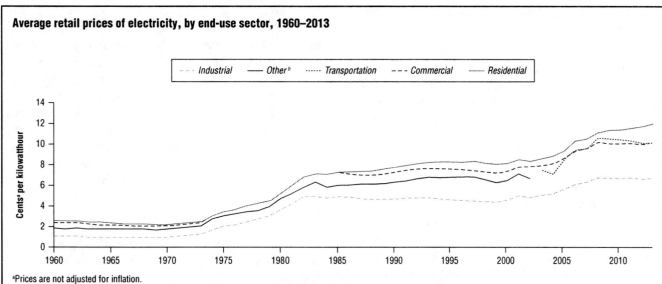

Average retail prices of electricity, by end-use sector, 1960–2013

······ Industrial   —— Other ᵇ   ········ Transportation   – – – Commercial   ········ Residential

ªPrices are not adjusted for inflation.
ᵇPublic street and highway lighting, interdepartmental sales, other sales to public authorities, agricultural and irrigation, and transportation including railroads and railways.
Note: Includes taxes.

SOURCE: "Figure 9.2. Average Retail Prices of Electricity (Cents per Kilowatthour): By Sector, 1960–2013," in *Monthly Energy Review: June 2014*, U.S. Energy Information Administration, June 25, 2014, http://www.eia.gov/totalenergy/data/monthly/archive/00351406.pdf (accessed June 27, 2014)

TABLE 8.2

Real (inflation-adjusted) costs of electricity to residential customers, selected years 1960–2013

	Residential electricity*	
	Cents per kilowatthour	Dollars per million Btu
1960 average	8.8	25.74
1965 average	7.6	22.33
1970 average	5.7	16.62
1975 average	6.5	19.07
1980 average	6.6	19.21
1985 average	6.87	20.13
1990 average	5.99	17.56
1995 average	5.51	16.15
2000 average	4.79	14.02
2001 average	4.84	14.20
2002 average	4.69	13.75
2003 average	4.74	13.89
2004 average	4.74	13.89
2005 average	4.84	14.18
2006 average	5.16	15.12
2007 average	5.14	15.05
2008 average	5.23	15.33
2009 average	5.37	15.72
2010 average	5.29	15.51
2011 average	5.21	15.27
2012 average	5.17	15.17
2013 average	5.20	15.25

Btu = British thermal units.
*Includes taxes.
Notes: Fuel costs are calculated by using the Urban Consumer Price Index (CPI) developed by the Bureau of Labor Statistics. Annual averages may not equal average of months due to independent rounding. Geographic coverage is the 50 states and the District of Columbia.

SOURCE: Adapted from "Table 1.6. Cost of Fuels to End Users in Real (1982–1984) Dollars," in *Monthly Energy Review: June 2014*, U.S. Energy Information Administration, June 25, 2014, http://www.eia.gov/totalenergy/data/monthly/archive/00351406.pdf (accessed June 27, 2014)

GOVERNMENT INTERVENTION. Electricity is considered to be a vital resource for the public. Hence, for decades the government heavily controlled the nation's electricity markets to ensure that this resource was widely available at relatively low costs. As a result, local utility companies developed monopolies in that each company had market control over a specified geographical area. During the 1970s and 1980s the federal government began experimenting with deregulation (breaking up government-supported monopolies). The idea was that competition would keep electricity prices low.

In the electric power sector deregulation has meant allowing consumers to purchase electricity from competing sellers but still receive delivery over existing power lines that are maintained by a local utility. The overall process is known as restructuring. In 1978 Congress passed the Public Utilities Regulatory Policies Act, which required utilities to buy electricity from private companies when doing so was cheaper than building their own power plants. The Energy Policy Act of 1992 gave other electricity generators greater access to the market, which enhanced the states' ability to restructure their systems. Widespread debates occurred regarding regulatory, economic, energy, and environmental policies. State public utility commissions conducted proceedings and crafted rules that were related to competition.

California was a leader in deregulation during the mid-1990s. However, during the summer of 2000 the state experienced rolling electrical blackouts, and electricity bills doubled for many customers. Fearful of similar blackouts and price spikes, most other states slowed or stopped their efforts to deregulate their electricity markets. As a result, as of October 2014 few states had deregulated their electricity markets to any degree. Northeastern states had most fully deregulated, and Texas had competitive markets in most, but not all, of its major cities. However, it is difficult to determine how deregulation has affected electricity pricing because so many different variables are at work.

In the United States the electric power sector includes government entities, such as municipally owned utilities. In addition, the federal government generates electricity for consumers through federally owned corporations, such as the Tennessee Valley Authority. Electricity is also generated by independent power producers (IPPs). In "NRG-GenOn Acquisition Plan Would Create the Largest Independent Power Producer" (September 6, 2012, http://www.eia.gov/todayinenergy/detail.cfm?id=7850), the EIA defines IPPs as "unregulated entities providing electricity into a wholesale electricity market or to another company that provides distribution to the ultimate customers." In 2012 NRG Energy, Inc., merged with GenOn Energy, Inc., and became the largest IPP in the nation. As of October 2014, NRG Energy (http://www.nrg.com/about/who-we-are/our-assets) had dozens of generating plants around the country.

The EIA explains in *State Electricity Profiles 2011* (April 2014, http://www.eia.gov/electricity/state/archive/sep2011.pdf) that electric utilities generated 2,461 million megawatt-hours in 2011, or 62% of the total 3,948 million megawatt-hours generated by the electric power sector. IPPs accounted for 1,331 million megawatt-hours, or 34% of the total. The remaining 156 million megawatt-hours, or 4% of the total, was provided by combined heat and power plants, which typically provide heat to nearby industrial facilities and also provide electricity to the nation's electrical grid.

As described in Chapter 1, the federal government supports the electric power sector via financial incentives, such as tax breaks and subsidies. Whereas these measures put downward pressure on electricity prices, other government activities tend to push prices upward. The primary example is the regulation of emissions and discharges from fuel combustion. As noted earlier, the electric power sector is the biggest end user of coal in the United States. However, coal-fired power plants have been under increasing pressure to reduce their emissions of air pollutants. Stricter standards have forced coal-fired power plants to invest in better control technologies and/or use coal that contains lower sulfur contents. Pollution-control technologies, in particular, can be very expensive.

Additionally, the government has been spearheading a modernization of the nation's electricity system through its Smart Grid initiative. In "Smart Grid" (2014, http://energy.gov/oe/services/technology-development/smart-grid), the Department of Energy's Office of Electricity Delivery and Energy Reliability states that "'Smart grid' generally refers to a class of technology [that] people are using to bring utility electricity delivery systems into the

21st century, using computer-based remote control and automation. These systems are made possible by two-way communication technology and computer processing that has been used for decades in other industries." Modernizing the grid is expected to reap numerous energy-saving benefits and reduce carbon emissions, as shown in Figure 8.6. A more flexible grid will allow consumers greater access to environmentally friendly (or green) power generated with renewable energy sources, such as wind and solar. The most visible Smart Grid innovation has been so-called smart meters, which have been installed at millions of homes and businesses. These computerized meters directly communicate power usage to utility companies and consumers.

Smart Grid projects have been funded by a substantial investment of taxpayer dollars. In *A Policy Framework for the 21st Century Grid: A Progress Report* (February 2013, http://www.whitehouse.gov/sites/default/files/microsites/ostp/2013_nstc_grid.pdf), the administration of President Barack Obama (1961–) notes that $4.5 billion was provided by the American Recovery and Reinvestment Act of 2009. That amount was matched with like funds from the power industry. The Smart Grid initiative is a long-term project that will take years—perhaps decades—to implement across the nation's vast electrical network. Ultimately, it is expected to make the grid more reliable, efficient, and cost effective and empower consumers to make better energy use decisions. In addition, safeguards are being included to help protect the grid from cyberattacks by terrorists or unfriendly foreign governments.

Mohana Ravindranath describes in "As Smart-Grid Funding Winds Down, Energy Leaders Assess Progress" (WashingtonPost.com, February 23, 2014) some of the challenges facing the Smart Grid initiative. They include consumer resistance to change and a lack of universal standards that would ensure interoperability and communication between different electronic systems. Future funding for continued modernization is also a concern given the high costs involved.

THE DOMESTIC OUTLOOK

In *Annual Energy Outlook 2014 with Projections to 2040* (April 2014, http://www.eia.gov/forecasts/aeo/pdf/0383(2014).pdf), the EIA predicts future domestic electricity demand through 2040 for various scenarios. Figure 8.7 shows projected demand for the reference case. Demand growth was less than 1% per year during the first half of the second decade of the 21st century. It is projected to increase by an average rate of 0.8% per year through 2040. The agency forecasts this low growth rate because it believes that increasing demand for electricity from a growing population will

FIGURE 8.6

Expected benefits from the Smart Grid

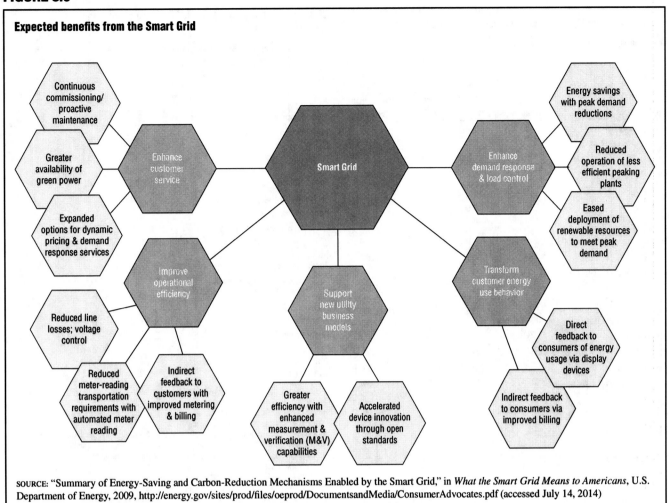

SOURCE: "Summary of Energy-Saving and Carbon-Reduction Mechanisms Enabled by the Smart Grid," in *What the Smart Grid Means to Americans*, U.S. Department of Energy, 2009, http://energy.gov/sites/prod/files/oeprod/DocumentsandMedia/ConsumerAdvocates.pdf (accessed July 14, 2014)

FIGURE 8.7

Electricity demand growth, 1950–2012 and predicted through 2040

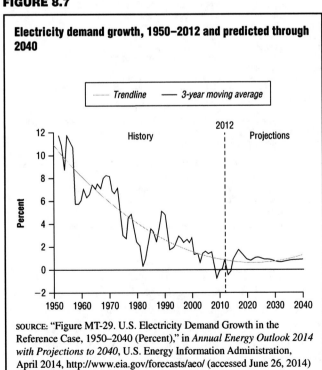

SOURCE: "Figure MT-29. U.S. Electricity Demand Growth in the Reference Case, 1950–2040 (Percent)," in *Annual Energy Outlook 2014 with Projections to 2040*, U.S. Energy Information Administration, April 2014, http://www.eia.gov/forecasts/aeo/ (accessed June 26, 2014)

be offset by energy efficiency improvements in appliances and other electricity-using equipment.

The EIA anticipates that by 2040 natural gas will replace coal as the nation's largest energy source for electricity generation. (See Table 8.3.) The agency predicts that natural gas will supply 1,839 billion kWh in 2040, or 35% of the total. It will be followed by coal, at 1,675 kWh, or 32% of the total. Renewable sources (851 kWh) and nuclear power (811 kWh) will each provide about 16% of the total. Petroleum and other sources will make up the remainder. Overall, fossil fuels are forecast to account for around two-thirds (67%) of electricity generation in 2040.

WORLD ELECTRICITY PRODUCTION AND CONSUMPTION

Net electricity generation worldwide totaled 20.2 trillion kWh in 2010. (See Table 8.4.) Coal provided 8.1 trillion kWh, or 40% of the total. It was followed by natural gas, at 4.5 trillion kWh (22% of the total); renewable sources, at 4.2 trillion kWh (21% of the total); nuclear energy, at 2.6 trillion kWh (13%); and liquids, such as petroleum, at 0.9 trillion kWh (4%).

TABLE 8.3

Electricity generation by fuel, 2012 and predicted for 2040

[Billion kilowatthours, unless otherwise noted]

Supply, disposition, prices, and emissions	Reference case 2012	Reference case 2040	Annual growth 2012–2040 (percent)
Generation by fuel type			
Electric power sector[a]			
Power only[b]			
Coal	1,478	1,635	0.4%
Petroleum	18	16	−0.5%
Natural gas[c]	1,000	1,471	1.4%
Nuclear power	769	811	0.2%
Pumped storage/other[d]	3	3	0.2%
Renewable sources[e]	459	735	1.7%
Distributed generation (natural gas)	0	4	—
Total	**3,727**	**4,675**	**0.8%**
Combined heat and power[f]			
Coal	20	26	0.9%
Petroleum	2	1	−3.6%
Natural gas	133	134	0.0%
Renewable sources	5	8	1.9%
Total	**163**	**169**	**0.1%**
Total electric power sector generation	**3,890**	**4,844**	**0.8%**
Less direct use	13	14	0.3%
Net available to the grid	**3,877**	**4,830**	**0.8%**
End-use sector[g]			
Coal	13	13	0.0%
Petroleum	3	3	−0.4%
Natural gas	95	231	3.2%
Other gaseous fuels[h]	11	18	1.8%
Renewable sources[i]	39	108	3.7%
Other[j]	3	3	0.0%
Total end-use sector generation	**165**	**375**	**3.0%**
Less direct use	127	317	3.3%
Total sales to the grid	**38**	**58**	**1.5%**
Total electricity generation by fuel			
Coal	1,512	1,675	0.4%
Petroleum	23	19	−0.7%
Natural gas	1,228	1,839	1.5%
Nuclear power	769	811	0.2%
Renewable sources[e, i]	502	851	1.9%
Other[k]	19	24	0.7%
Total electricity generation	**4,054**	**5,219**	**0.9%**
Net generation to the grid	**3,915**	**4,888**	**0.8%**
Net imports	**47**	**35**	**−1.1%**
Electricity sales by sector			
Residential	1,375	1,657	0.7%
Commercial	1,324	1,675	0.8%
Industrial	981	1,273	0.9%
Transportation	7	18	3.6%
Total	**3,686**	**4,623**	**0.8%**
Direct use	139	331	3.1%
Total electricity use	**3,826**	**4,954**	**0.9%**
End-use prices			
(2012 cents per kilowatthour)			
Residential	11.9	13.3	0.4%
Commercial	10.1	11.3	0.4%
Industrial	6.7	8.2	0.8%
Transportation	10.7	11.7	0.3%
All sectors average	**9.8**	**11.1**	**0.4%**

TABLE 8.3

Electricity generation by fuel, 2012 and predicted for 2040 [CONTINUED]

[Billion kilowatthours, unless otherwise noted]

Supply, disposition, prices, and emissions	Reference case 2012	Reference case 2040	Annual growth 2012–2040 (percent)
(Nominal cents per kilowatthour)			
Residential	11.9	22.0	2.2%
Commercial	10.1	18.7	2.2%
Industrial	6.7	13.6	2.6%
Transportation	10.7	19.3	2.1%
All sectors average	**9.8**	**18.5**	**2.3%**
Prices by service category			
(2012 cents per kilowatthour)			
Generation	5.7	7.5	1.0%
Transmission	1.1	1.1	0.2%
Distribution	3.1	2.6	−0.6%
(Nominal cents per kilowatthour)			
Generation	5.7	12.4	2.8%
Transmission	1.1	1.8	2.0%
Distribution	3.1	4.3	1.2%
Electric power sector emissions[a]			
Sulfur dioxide (million short tons)	3.34	1.61	−2.6%
Nitrogen oxide (million short tons)	1.68	1.60	−0.2%
Mercury (short tons)	26.35	6.81	−4.7%

[a]Includes electricity-only and combined heat and power plants that have a regulatory status.
[b]Includes plants that only produce electricity and that have a regulatory status.
[c]Includes electricity generation from fuel cells.
[d]Includes non-biogenic municipal waste. The U.S. Energy Information Administration estimates that in 2012 approximately 7 billion kilowatthours of electricity were generated from a municipal waste stream containing petroleum-derived plastics and other non-renewable sources.
[e]Includes conventional hydroelectric, geothermal, wood, wood waste, biogenic municipal waste, landfill gas, other biomass, solar, and wind power.
[f]Includes combined heat and power plants whose primary business is to sell electricity and heat to the public (i.e., those that report North American Industry Classification System code 22 or that have a regulatory status).
[g]Includes combined heat and power plants and electricity-only plants in the commercial and industrial sectors that have a non-regulatory status; and small on-site generating systems in the residential, commercial, and industrial sectors used primarily for own-use generation, but which may also sell some power to the grid.
[h]Includes refinery gas and still gas.
[i]Includes conventional hydroelectric, geothermal, wood, wood waste, all municipal waste, landfill gas, other biomass, solar, and wind power.
[j]Includes batteries, chemicals, hydrogen, pitch, purchased steam, sulfur, and miscellaneous technologies.
[k]Includes pumped storage, non-biogenic municipal waste, refinery gas, still gas, batteries, chemicals, hydrogen, pitch, purchased steam, sulfur, and miscellaneous technologies.
— = Not applicable.
Note: Totals may not equal sum of components due to independent rounding. Data for 2012 are model results and may differ from official EIA data reports.
EIA = Energy Information Administration.

SOURCE: "Table A8. Electricity Supply, Disposition, Prices, and Emissions (Billion Kilowatthours, Unless Otherwise Noted)," in *Annual Energy Outlook 2014 with Projections to 2040*, U.S. Energy Information Administration, April 2014, http://www.eia.gov/forecasts/aeo/ (accessed June 26, 2014)

The EIA examines and predicts electricity generation for countries that are and are not members of the Organisation for Economic Co-operation and Development (OECD). The OECD is a collection of dozens of mostly Western nations that are devoted to global economic development. The total net electricity generation in 2010 was split roughly evenly between OECD members and nonmembers. (See Table 8.4.) OECD members are expected to make small gains in electricity generation, from 10.3 trillion kWh in 2010 to 14.2 trillion kWh in

TABLE 8.4

World net electricity generation, by country category and energy source, 2010, and predicted through 2040

[In trillion kilowatthours]

Region	2010	2015	2020	2025	2030	2035	2040	Average annual percent change, 2010–2040
OECD								
Liquids	0.3	0.3	0.2	0.2	0.2	0.2	0.2	−1.1
Natural gas	2.4	2.7	2.9	3.1	3.5	3.9	4.3	2.0
Coal	3.5	3.3	3.3	3.3	3.3	3.3	3.3	−0.2
Nuclear	2.2	2.1	2.4	2.6	2.7	2.7	2.7	0.7
Renewables	1.9	2.4	2.8	3.0	3.2	3.4	3.7	2.2
Total OECD	10.3	10.8	11.5	12.2	12.9	13.5	14.2	1.1
Non-OECD								
Liquids	0.6	0.6	0.6	0.6	0.5	0.5	0.5	−0.9
Natural gas	2.1	2.3	2.6	3.1	3.7	4.4	5.0	3.0
Coal	4.6	5.9	6.9	8.0	9.0	9.9	10.6	2.9
Nuclear	0.4	0.8	1.3	1.7	2.1	2.5	2.8	6.3
Renewables	2.2	2.9	3.7	4.2	4.7	5.3	5.9	3.3
Total non-OECD	9.9	12.5	15.1	17.6	20.1	22.6	24.8	3.1
World								
Liquids	0.9	0.9	0.8	0.8	0.7	0.7	0.7	−1.0
Natural gas	4.5	5.0	5.5	6.2	7.2	8.3	9.4	2.5
Coal	8.1	9.2	10.1	11.3	12.3	13.2	13.9	1.8
Nuclear	2.6	2.9	3.6	4.3	4.8	5.1	5.5	2.5
Renewables	4.2	5.3	6.5	7.2	7.9	8.8	9.6	2.8
Total world	20.2	23.3	26.6	29.8	33.0	36.2	39.0	2.2

OECD = Organisation for Economic Cooperation and Development.

SOURCE: "Table 13. OECD and Non-OECD Net Electricity Generation by Energy Source, 2010–2040 (Trillion Kilowatthours)," in *International Energy Outlook 2013*, U.S. Energy Information Administration, July 2013, http://www.eia.gov/forecasts/ieo/ (accessed July 11, 2014)

2040, for an annual growth rate of 1.1%. Most of this growth will be from renewables and natural gas. Nonmember electricity generation is projected to grow dramatically, from 9.9 trillion kWh in 2010 to 24.8 trillion kWh in 2040, for an annual growth rate of 3.1%. Nuclear power is expected to fuel most of the capacity additions, particularly in China. (See Figure 8.8).

ENVIRONMENTAL ISSUES

The primary environmental issues involved with electricity generation relate to the underlying fuels and methods that are used to generate power. These issues are briefly described for natural gas in Chapter 3, for coal in Chapter 4, for nuclear power in Chapter 5, and for hydropower and other renewables in Chapter 6.

The electric power sector is regulated for environmental compliance, particularly in regards to air emissions. The combustion of coal, natural gas, and petroleum produces air contaminants, such as sulfur dioxide and carbon dioxide. Coal is especially troublesome because it burns "dirtier" than its counterparts. As shown in Figure 8.2, the United States has long been dependent on coal for its electricity generation. According to the U.S. Environmental Protection Agency (EPA), in "Cleaner Power Plants" (February 11, 2014, http://www.epa.gov/airquality/power planttoxics/powerplants.html), power plants account for at least half of the nation's emissions of certain regulated pollutants:

- Acid gases—77%
- Arsenic—62%
- Sulfur dioxide—60%
- Mercury—50%

However, the EPA notes that sulfur dioxide and mercury emissions from natural gas power plants are "negligible." Likewise, the combustion of natural gas produces only half as much carbon dioxide and less than one-third as much nitrogen oxides as the combustion of coal. Thus, coal-fired power plants are the main culprit when it comes to air emissions from the electric power industry.

Since the Clean Air Act (CAA) was first passed in 1963 the United States has substantially improved its air quality by lowering contaminant emissions from multiple sources. This has been achieved through various programs that target particular pollutants or problems, such as acid rain. The EPA and state environmental agencies require certain emitters to take operational measures and use pollutant control equipment to reduce harmful emissions. For example, coal-burning power plants may be required to burn low-sulfur coal or install expensive

FIGURE 8.8

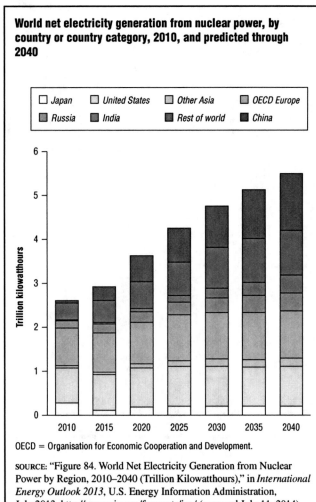

World net electricity generation from nuclear power, by country or country category, 2010, and predicted through 2040

Legend:
☐ Japan ☐ United States ☐ Other Asia ☐ OECD Europe
▨ Russia ▨ India ▨ Rest of world ■ China

Y-axis: Trillion kilowatthours (0 to 6)
X-axis: 2010, 2015, 2020, 2025, 2030, 2035, 2040

OECD = Organisation for Economic Cooperation and Development.

SOURCE: "Figure 84. World Net Electricity Generation from Nuclear Power by Region, 2010–2040 (Trillion Kilowatthours)," in *International Energy Outlook 2013*, U.S. Energy Information Administration, July 2013, http://www.eia.gov/forecasts/ieo/ (accessed July 11, 2014)

scrubbers to wash sulfur and other contaminants from their emissions before discharging them to the air. These requirements have not been applied evenly across the industry because the CAA distinguishes between existing electric generating units (EGUs) and new EGUs. Over the decades many existing EGUs have been exempted from meeting some new and stricter air quality standards through a policy known as "grandfathering."

In 1977, when the CAA was substantially amended to tighten air quality standards on new EGUs, most of the nation's existing EGUs burned coal. These grandfathered EGUs were not required to meet the stricter standards unless and until they made certain major modifications to their infrastructure. It was assumed that the existing EGUs would inevitably make such modifications and hence lose their grandfathered status. However, this has not been the case. Although many companies have since made modifications to their existing EGUs, they have argued in court that the modifications are not major enough to trigger the stricter standards. Numerous court battles have taken place over this highly politicized issue.

When government agencies sue power companies over grandfathering disputes, they are praised by environmentalists but derided by critics for waging a "war" on coal—a domestically produced fuel that is important to the nation's economy.

In 2011 the EPA and the states of Pennsylvania and New York sued the Homer City Generating Station, a large coal-fired power plant in Pennsylvania. In "Homer City Plant Sued on Emissions" (Post-Gazette.com, January 7, 2011), David Templeton and Don Hopey report the plant was constructed in 1969 with two EGUs. A third EGU was later added, and it was equipped with a scrubber as required for new units. However, the two original EGUs were operated for decades without scrubbers because they were able to meet their laxer emissions standards using other means. In the lawsuit, the EPA, Pennsylvania, and New York accused the plant of making major modifications to the two old units during the 1990s and failing to install scrubbers to meet the stricter standards that should have been triggered. However, a judge tossed out the case arguing that too much time had passed since the modifications were made. Environmentalists were sorely disappointed because the Homer City plant is alleged to be one of the nation's dirtiest power plants.

Meanwhile, in late 2011 the EPA finalized new regulations called the Mercury and Air Toxics Standards (MATS). In "Cleaner Power Plants," the agency notes, "These standards level the playing field so that all plants will have to limit their emissions of mercury as newer plants already do." The MATS standards go into effect in 2015 and can be met via use of scrubbers or other specialized equipment. In addition, in 2014 the EPA won a favorable ruling from the U.S. Supreme Court regarding the agency's plan to tighten restrictions on traditional air pollutants, such as sulfur dioxide. The power plant industry, led by the owners of the Homer City plant, had bitterly fought against the new regulations. However, in *Environmental Protection Agency et al. v. EME Homer City Generation, L.P. et al.* (No. 12-1182 [2014]), the U.S. Supreme Court cleared the way for the agency to proceed with its Cross State Air Pollution Rule (http://www.epa.gov/air transport/CSAPR/index.html).

Installing scrubbers or other pollution control equipment, particularly at old power plants, is expensive. In addition, coal has become less economically attractive for power generation. Natural gas has surged in popularity due to domestic abundance and low prices. As a result, some power companies have chosen to retire old coal-fired EGUs rather than renovate them. This was not the case at the Homer City plant. Randy Wells reports in "Upgrade to Power Plant Seen as Boon" (IndianaGazette .com January 11, 2012) that the plant's owners decided to install scrubbers on the two old EGUs to keep them operating.

Historically, CAA regulations have not covered carbon dioxide, which is believed to be a major contributor to global warming and associated climate change. As noted in Chapter 1, President Obama's energy policy focuses heavily on reducing U.S. carbon emissions. A fierce political debate has raged in the United States over what, if any, action the nation should take in this regard. Critics believe that limiting carbon emissions will place an unreasonable financial burden on the electric power industry and irreparably harm the U.S. economy. In March 2012 the EPA proposed limiting carbon emissions from newly constructed power plants. The agency revamped and reissued the proposal in September 2013. In "EPA Fact Sheet: Reducing Carbon Pollution from Power Plants" (2013, http://www2.epa.gov/sites/product ion/files/2013-09/documents/20130920factsheet.pdf), the EPA states, "Because these standards are in line with current industry investment patterns, these standards are not expected to have notable costs and are not projected to impact electricity prices or reliability."

In June 2014 the EPA issued a more controversial proposal to impose carbon limits on existing power plants. The agency explains in "Fact Sheet: Clean Power Plan Overview" (June 14, 2014, http://www2.epa.gov/carbon-pollution-standards/fact-sheet-clean-power-plan-overview) that the new regulations would help lower carbon emissions from the electric power sector by 30% by 2030 compared with 2005 levels. In addition, they would reduce emissions of soot- and smog-forming contaminants by more than 25% by 2030. In *Regulatory Impact Analysis for the Proposed Carbon Pollution Guidelines for Existing Power Plants and Emission Standards for Modified and Reconstructed Power Plants* (June 2014, http://www2.epa.gov/sites/production/files/2014-06/documents/20140602ria-clean-power-plan.pdf), the EPA estimates that compliance with the new regulations could cost the power industry as much as $7.5 billion in 2020. However, net benefits (monetized benefits minus costs) would total up to $50 billion in 2020 due to reduced climate effects and public health improvements from cleaner air. The electric power industry (particularly the coal-burning sector) and its political champions are staunchly opposed to the regulations, which they see as unnecessarily burdensome. It remains to be seen what impacts these regulations will have on electricity prices if they survive expected legal challenges.

CHAPTER 9

ENERGY CONSERVATION

The word *conservation* has different meanings depending on the context in which it is used. When referring to a resource, such as energy, to conserve means to use less of the resource. Of course, energy is a vital resource to a modern society with a growing population and a growing economy. It is a difficult proposition to use less energy and keep growing. One key to achieving this goal is to increase energy efficiency (decrease the amount of energy required to do a certain amount of work). Ever since the start of the Industrial Revolution (1760–1848), innovators have greatly enhanced the efficiency of energy-using vehicles, machines, and processes. Some of these innovations have been driven solely by consumer demand, whereas others have been motivated by government mandates. As will be explained in this chapter, the government plays a major role in pushing energy conservation to further specific goals.

Consumers practice energy conservation in accordance with their budgets. When energy prices rise to an uncomfortable level, consumers cut back their energy spending. The United States uses a mix of energy sources for which prices can vary considerably. In theory, energy consumers can switch from more expensive sources to cheaper sources as prices change. This is difficult in practice, however, because energy-consuming machines tend to be sole-source (e.g., most cars run only on gasoline). Although there is some flexibility for fuel switching in the industrial and electric power sectors, residential and commercial consumers have fewer options in this regard. Nevertheless, they can choose from a variety of efficiency choices within product lines, such as cars, furnaces, air conditioning systems, and even lightbulbs.

Domestic energy self-sufficiency (or energy security) has long been a national goal for the United States. Although domestic production of most energy sources meets domestic demand, the glaring exception is oil. As explained in Chapter 2, the United States imports large amounts of petroleum each year from the Middle East, a region that is riddled with political insecurity and a history of poor relations with the United States. Since the 1970s the United States has greatly reduced its reliance on oil imports from the Middle East. This has been achieved, in part, through persistent government focus on reducing overall petroleum usage by U.S. consumers.

Another motivator for energy conservation lies in environmental concerns about energy sources. The U.S. government enforces numerous regulations that are designed to prevent, reduce, and mitigate the worst environmental impacts from energy production and usage. These measures have had varying levels of success. Historically, the government has focused on air pollutants, such as sulfur dioxide, that result from the combustion of fossil fuels and are known to damage ecosystems and human health. During the 20th century the world became aware of global warming. Scientists believe that the release of large amounts of carbon into the atmosphere has caused the earth's atmosphere to warm unnaturally. (Carbon-containing gases are also known as greenhouse gases.) Anthropogenic (human-caused) warming is occurring at an alarming rate and is precipitating climate and ecosystem changes around the world. Concern about global warming has become a new, and powerful, impetus for reducing fossil fuel combustion.

NATIONAL ENERGY CONSERVATION

At first glance, it appears that the United States has not been successful at conserving energy. Domestic energy consumption increased from 34.6 quadrillion British thermal units (Btu) in 1950 to 97.5 quadrillion Btu in 2013, an increase of 182%. (See Table 1.3 in Chapter 1.) However, this trend is not unexpected, given that the U.S. population and economy grew tremendously during this period.

National energy efficiency can be measured using two indicators. The first is energy consumption per capita (per person). According to the U.S. Energy Information Administration (EIA) within the U.S. Department of Energy (DOE), in *Annual Energy Review 2011* (September 2012, http://www.eia.gov/totalenergy/data/annual/pdf/aer.pdf), energy consumption per capita was 227 million Btu in 1950. The U.S. Census Bureau (2014, http://www.census.gov/popclock) indicates the U.S. population was 317.3 million people at year-end 2013. Given total energy consumption of 97.5 quadrillion Btu, the energy consumption per capita in 2013 was 307 million Btu, a 35% increase from 1950. Thus, energy consumption per capita grew much slower than did total energy consumption.

A second indicator of efficiency is energy consumption per dollar of gross domestic product (GDP; the total market value of final goods and services that are produced within an economy in a given year). The GDP is a measure of national economic well-being; a growing GDP over time indicates a growing and thriving economy. As shown in Figure 9.1, U.S. primary energy consumption per real dollar of GDP decreased from around 16,000 Btu in 1949 to just over 6,000 Btu in 2013, a decrease of 63%.

Clearly, the United States improved its energy efficiency to a great extent between 1949 and 2013. These gains were achieved to varying degrees across all sectors: electric power, transportation, industrial, residential, and commercial. In *Monthly Energy Review: June 2014* (June 2014, http://www.eia.gov/totalenergy/data/monthly/archive/00351406.pdf), the EIA provides the following breakdown of the nation's 97.5 quadrillion Btu consumption of primary energy in 2013:

- Electric power sector—38.4 quadrillion Btu (39% of the total)

- Transportation sector—26.9 quadrillion Btu (28% of the total)

- Industrial sector—21.5 quadrillion Btu (22% of the total)

- Residential sector—6.7 quadrillion Btu (7% of the total)

- Commercial sector—4 quadrillion Btu (4% of the total)

THE ELECTRIC POWER SECTOR

The electric power sector was the largest consumer of primary energy in 2013, accounting for 39% of the total. As explained in Chapter 8, the sector used fossil fuels for around two-thirds of electricity generation that year (39% from coal, 27% from natural gas, and 2% from petroleum and miscellaneous fossil fuel gases). Nuclear energy accounted for another 19% and renewable sources for 13% of the total. The EIA notes that net electricity generation increased from 334 billion kilowatt-hours (kWh) in 1950 to 4,058 billion kWh in 2013. (See Table 8.1 in Chapter 8.) Electricity demand has been driven by growing consumption in the residential, commercial, and industrial sectors.

FIGURE 9.1

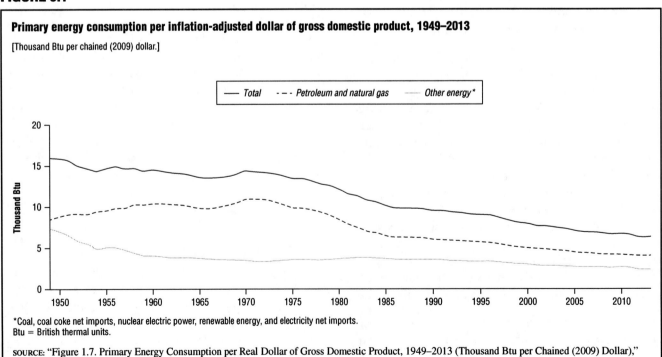

Primary energy consumption per inflation-adjusted dollar of gross domestic product, 1949–2013

[Thousand Btu per chained (2009) dollar.]

*Coal, coal coke net imports, nuclear electric power, renewable energy, and electricity net imports.
Btu = British thermal units.

SOURCE: "Figure 1.7. Primary Energy Consumption per Real Dollar of Gross Domestic Product, 1949–2013 (Thousand Btu per Chained (2009) Dollar)," in *Monthly Energy Review: June 2014*, U.S. Energy Information Administration, June 25, 2014, http://www.eia.gov/totalenergy/data/monthly/archive/00351406.pdf (accessed June 27, 2014)

The electric power sector experiences huge energy losses between inputs and outputs. As explained in Chapter 8, around 65% of the incoming energy in 2013 was lost during generation. The sector has focused its conservation efforts on enhancing the efficiency of individual power plants and their systems. One innovation is the combined-cycle power plant, which reuses the heat leaving one turbine to boil water into steam to turn another turbine. Efficiency gains such as this have allowed the industry to generate more power using less fuel. In addition, the sector as a whole has enhanced its efficiency over time by retiring older less-efficient plants and equipment in favor of newer models.

THE TRANSPORTATION SECTOR

The U.S. transportation system plays a central role in the economy and is a major energy consumer. As noted earlier, the transportation sector accounted for 28% of total primary energy consumption in 2011. As explained in Chapter 1, this sector's energy consumption is for vehicles whose primary purpose is transporting people and/or goods from place to place. Transportation vehicles include automobiles; trucks; buses; motorcycles; trains, subways, and other rail vehicles; aircraft; and ships, barges, and other waterborne vehicles. According to the EIA, in *Monthly Energy Review: June 2014*, Americans used 26.9 quadrillion Btu of energy for transportation in 2013, of which petroleum accounted for 24.9 quadrillion Btu, or 92% of the total.

Historical petroleum consumption by sector is shown in Figure 2.17 in Chapter 2. Between 1949 and 2013 petroleum usage by the industrial, residential and commercial, and electric power sectors was flat to declining. In contrast, petroleum consumption by the transportation sector grew from 3.4 million barrels per day (mbpd) in 1950 to 13.2 mbpd in 2013, a 288% increase. In part, this growth was due to an increasing population and more vehicles on the road. In addition, vehicle types changed dramatically during this period. The DOE's Oak Ridge National Laboratory indicates in *Transportation Energy Data Book, Edition 32* (July 2013, http://info.ornl.gov/sites/publications/files/Pub44660.pdf) that in 1975 cars had an 80.7% market share. By 2012 that percentage had dropped to 63.9% as sport-utility vehicles, minivans, and pickup trucks dominated the market. As shown in Figure 9.2, vehicles with long wheelbases have inherently poorer fuel economy than vehicles with short wheelbases. As explained in Chapter 2, oil prices were historically low from the mid-1980s through the end of the 1990s. During this period Americans bought and drove larger

FIGURE 9.2

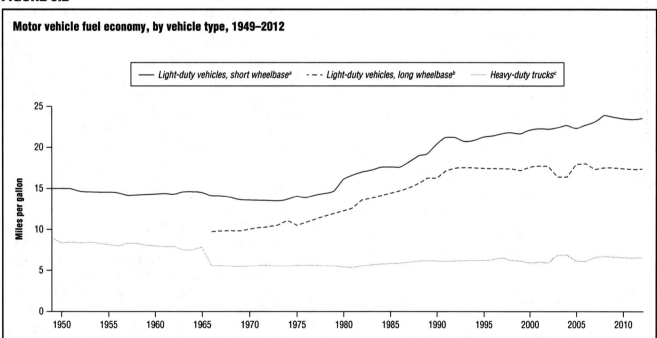

Motor vehicle fuel economy, by vehicle type, 1949–2012

[a]Through 1989, data are for passenger cars and motorcycles. For 1990–2006, data are for passenger cars only. Beginning in 2007, data are for light-duty vehicles (passenger cars, light trucks, vans, and sport utility vehicles) with a wheelbase less than or equal to 121 inches.
[b]For 1966–2006, data are for vans, pickup trucks, and sport utility vehicles. Beginning in 2007, data are for light-duty vehicles (passenger cars, light trucks, vans, and sport utility vehicles) with a wheelbase greater than 121 inches.
[c]For 1949–1965, data are for single-unit trucks with 2 axles and 6 or more tires, combination trucks, and other vehicles with 2 axles and 4 tires that are not passenger cars. For 1965–2006, data are for single-unit trucks with 2 axles and 6 or more tires, and combination trucks. Beginning in 2007, data are for single-unit trucks with 2 axles and 6 or more tires (or a gross vehicle weight rating exceeding 10,000 pounds), and combination trucks.
Note: Geographic coverage is the 50 states and the District of Columbia.

SOURCE: "Figure 1.8. Motor Vehicle Fuel Economy, 1949–2012 (Miles per Gallon)," in *Monthly Energy Review: June 2014*, U.S. Energy Information Administration, June 25, 2014, http://www.eia.gov/totalenergy/data/monthly/archive/00351406.pdf (accessed June 27, 2014)

vehicles to satisfy their personal preferences. This highlights the huge influence that market prices have on consumer demand and shows how difficult it can be to get consumers to conserve oil by their own accord.

Government Intervention

Chapter 2 describes the energy crisis (actually an oil crisis) that stunned the nation during the early 1970s. The political and economic consequences of the United States' dependence on foreign oil spurred government actions to reduce domestic oil consumption, particularly in the transportation sector. In *Saving Energy in U.S. Transportation* (July 1994, http://govinfo.library.unt.edu/ota/Ota_1/DATA/1994/9432.PDF), the Office of Technology Assessment lists the types of conservation measures that government entities have used over the years:

- Require vehicles to have higher fuel economy

- Design highways to optimize traffic flow and reduce fuel consumption

- Impose higher taxes on petroleum fuels and/or low-fuel-economy vehicles

- Use tax credits and subsidies to support research and development devoted to petroleum conservation

- Pass regulations requiring stricter inspection and maintenance programs for vehicles

- Encourage carpooling and working from home

- Add and improve mass transit options

- Mandate the use of alternative-fuel (nonpetroleum) vehicles and alternative fuels

- Offer tax credits and other financial incentives to encourage petroleum conservation by consumers

Not all the measures are mutually supportive. For example, efforts to promote a freer flow of automobile traffic, such as high-occupancy vehicle lanes or free parking for carpools, may sabotage efforts to shift travelers to mass transit or reduce trip lengths and frequency.

FUEL ECONOMY STANDARDS. Of all the measures that the federal government uses to enhance oil conservation, the most well-known and perhaps most controversial are fuel economy standards. These standards represent a high level of government intervention in private markets. In 1975 the Energy Policy and Conservation Act set the initial Corporate Average Fuel Economy (CAFE) standards; since then, the standards have been modified numerous times.

The first CAFE standards required domestic automakers to increase the average mileage of new cars sold to 27.5 miles per gallon (mpg; 8.6 L/100 km) by 1985. Manufacturers could still sell large, less-efficient cars, but to meet the average fuel efficiency rates, they also had to sell smaller, more efficient cars. Automakers that failed to meet each year's standards were fined; those that managed to surpass the rates earned credits they could use in years when they fell below the requirements. Even while keeping some models relatively large and roomy, the manufacturers managed to improve mileage with innovations such as electronic fuel injection, which supplied fuel to an automotive engine more efficiently than its predecessor, the carburetor.

Over the decades more demanding CAFE standards have helped raise the national average fuel economy. As shown in Figure 9.2, highway vehicles are divided by duty and wheelbase. Light-duty vehicles include cars, sport-utility vehicles, and minivans, while heavy-duty vehicles include tractor trailers, buses, and delivery vans. Historically, light-duty vehicles with short wheelbases have achieved the best (highest) fuel economy. In 2012 light-duty vehicles with short wheelbases averaged 23.3 mpg (10.1 L/100 km), compared with 17.1 mpg (13.8 L/100 km) for light-duty vehicles with long wheelbases. By contrast, heavy-duty vehicles averaged 6.4 mpg (36.8 L/100 km) in 2012. In 2010 new CAFE standards were the first to be attribute-based, meaning that they vary depending on specific vehicle attributes, in this case a vehicle's footprint (i.e., the surface area between all of its wheels). Thus, attribute-based CAFE standards vary by vehicle model.

In the press release "Obama Administration Finalizes Historic 54.5 MPG Fuel Efficiency Standards" (http://www.whitehouse.gov/the-press-office/2012/08/28/obama-administration-finalizes-historic-545-mpg-fuel-efficiency-standard), the White House notes that in August 2012 the administration of President Barack Obama (1961–) finalized fuel economy standards that will require model year (MY) 2025 cars and light-duty trucks to achieve the equivalent of 54.5 mpg (4.3 L/100 km).

THE INDUSTRIAL SECTOR

The industrial sector operates facilities and equipment that are devoted to producing, processing, or assembling goods. As noted in Chapter 1, the major energy uses by this sector are for process heat and for cooling and powering machinery. The sector was the third-largest consumer of primary energy in 2013, accounting for 22% of the total. Petroleum and natural gas were the major energy sources used by the sector in 2013. (See Figure 1.5 in Chapter 1.) Electricity, coal, and renewable sources played smaller roles. The annual energy consumption increased dramatically between 1949 and 1970, but has been relatively flat since then. The industrial sector has reduced its energy usage through efficiency improvements to machines and processes. Another major component of industrial energy conservation has been the on-site production of combined heat and power (CHP).

Combined Heat and Power

Many industrial facilities utilize both heat and electricity in their processes. The electricity can be purchased from a local utility, while fuel can be purchased and burned on-site to produce heat, for example, to boil water to make steam. Great efficiency gains can be achieved by performing both these tasks on-site through a CHP plant. A CHP plant is basically a small power plant that burns fuel to generate electricity; the leftover heat can be used to boil water for steam or for other industrial purposes. In *Combined Heat and Power: A Clean Energy Solution* (August 2012, http://energy.gov/sites/prod/files/2013/11/f4/chp_clean_energy_solution.pdf), the DOE and the U.S. Environmental Protection Agency (EPA) indicate that as of 2012 the United States had installed CHP capacity of 82 gigawatts, mostly at manufacturing facilities. According to the agencies, a CHP plant can achieve 65% to 75% efficiency, compared with around 45% efficiency for the separate production of electricity and heat.

In August 2012 President Obama issued the executive order "Accelerating Investment in Industrial Energy Efficiency" (http://www.whitehouse.gov/the-press-office/2012/08/30/executive-order-accelerating-investment-industrial-energy-efficiency), which set a national goal of achieving 40 gigawatts of new CHP capacity over the coming decade. The EIA indicates in *Annual Energy Outlook 2014 with Projections to 2040* (April 2014, http://www.eia.gov/forecasts/aeo/pdf/0383(2014).pdf) that as of April 2014, 11 states (Arizona, Connecticut, Hawaii, Maine, Michigan, New Hampshire, New York, North Carolina, Pennsylvania, Washington, and Wisconsin) included CHP options in their mandatory (enforceable) renewable portfolio standards or similar laws.

THE RESIDENTIAL AND COMMERCIAL SECTORS

The residential and commercial sectors are often lumped together in discussions of energy conservation because their energy consumption is similar. The primary energy uses for both sectors are for space heating, water heating, air conditioning, lighting, refrigeration, cooking, and running appliances and other equipment.

As noted earlier, the two sectors accounted for 11% of primary energy consumption in 2013. Figure 1.4 and Figure 1.6 in Chapter 1 indicate that the sectors mainly consumed natural gas and electricity in 2013. Petroleum, coal, and renewable energy sources were minor energy sources. As shown in both figures, the overall energy consumption for both sectors increased between 1949 and 2013, especially for electricity. Natural gas consumption has been relatively flat for several decades. Figure 8.3 in Chapter 8 shows that the residential and commercial sectors were the largest users of electricity in 2013, accounting for 2,729 billion kWh, or 74% of total electricity retail sales.

Total energy use in these two sectors has increased over the years because the number of people, households, and offices has increased. In addition, people are using ever larger amounts of electronic gadgets, such as computers, printers, televisions, and copiers. However, increased energy demand has been offset somewhat by efficiency gains in equipment and in building efficiency. Also, many people have migrated to the South and West, where their combined use of heating and cooling has generally been lower than in other parts of the country.

Efficiency Gains

Energy conservation in buildings in both the residential and commercial sectors has improved considerably since the early 1980s. Among the techniques for reducing energy use are advanced window designs, "daylighting" (letting light in from the outside by adding a skylight or building a large building around an atrium), solar water heating, landscaping, and planting trees. Residential energy conservation is enhanced by building more efficient new housing and appliances, improving energy efficiency in existing housing, and building more multifamily units.

Efforts to enhance building energy efficiency are driven by various factors, including the desire of building owners to reduce their energy costs. The government also plays a role. The American Recovery and Reinvestment Act, which was passed in 2009, included billions of taxpayer dollars for grants and other programs devoted to improving the energy efficiency of residences and commercial and government buildings. In February 2011 President Obama (http://www.whitehouse.gov/the-press-office/2011/02/03/president-obama-s-plan-win-future-making-american-businesses-more-energy) launched his Better Buildings Initiative with the goal of making commercial and industrial buildings 20 percent more energy efficient by 2020. In *The President's Climate Action Plan* (June 2013, http://www.whitehouse.gov/sites/default/files/image/president27sclimateactionplan.pdf), Obama expanded the Better Buildings Initiative to include multifamily housing. Likewise, the president has set goals to make federal buildings more energy efficient. The White House notes in "Fact Sheet: President Obama Announces Commitments and Executive Actions to Advance Solar Deployment and Energy Efficiency" (May 9, 2014, http://www.whitehouse.gov/the-press-office/2014/05/09/fact-sheet-president-obama-announces-commitments-and-executive-actions-a) that as of 2014 a total of $4 billion in energy efficiency performance contracts were in effect through 2016 for federal buildings.

APPLIANCES AND LIGHTING. In 1987 Congress passed the National Appliance Energy Conservation Act, which gave the DOE the authority to formulate minimum efficiency requirements for 13 classes of consumer products.

It can also revise and update those standards as technologies and economic conditions change. Energy efficiency has increased for all major household appliances but most dramatically for refrigerators and freezers because of better insulation, motors, and compressors. In addition, efficiency labels are now required on appliances, which makes purchasing efficient models easier for consumers.

The Energy Independence and Security Act of 2007 mandated the gradual phasing out of many incandescent lightbulbs. These bulbs feature a wire filament that generates light and heat when an electric current passes through it. They have been in use for decades and are far less efficient than more modern designs, such as compact fluorescent lightbulbs, halogen bulbs, and light-emitting diode bulbs. The EPA provides in "Energy Independence and Security Act of 2007 (EISA): Frequently Asked Questions" (2011, http://www.energy star.gov/ia/products/lighting/cfls/downloads/EISA_Back grounder_FINAL_4-11_EPA.pdf?6bd2-3775) the phase-out schedule and lists the types of incandescent bulbs affected. As of January 1, 2014, the domestic manufacture of 100-watt, 75-watt, 60-watt, and 40-watt incandescent lightbulbs had been discontinued.

TAX PREFERENCES. As shown in Table 1.6 in Chapter 1, the federal government supplied $4.8 billion in tax preferences for energy efficiency in fiscal year (FY) 2013. (The federal government's FY extends from October to September; thus, FY 2013 covered October 1, 2012, to September 2013.) The federal government's tax preferences devoted to energy efficiency accounted for 29% of the total amount allocated to energy that year. (See Figure 1.15 in Chapter 1.) The largest amount within the energy efficiency category was $3 billion, which was directed at incorporating energy-efficiency improvements into existing homes. (See Table 1.6 in Chapter 1.)

THE DOMESTIC OUTLOOK

U.S. total energy consumption is expected to increase at an average annual rate of 0.4% between 2012 and 2040. (See Table 1.8 in Chapter 1.) Increases in demand are projected to be offset in part by efficiency gains. In *Annual Energy Outlook 2014 with Projections to 2040*, the EIA predicts that federal and state mandates and incentives will continue to push more efficient technologies and processes. Energy consumption per capita and energy consumption per dollar of GDP are expected to decrease through 2040 even as the nation's population, GDP, and total energy consumption increase. The EIA mentions several factors that it believes will contribute to energy efficiency through 2040:

- Retirement of older less-efficient power plants that are fired by fossil fuels in response to slower growth in electricity demand and increasing environmental regulatory pressure on the electric power sector

- A shift in the industrial sector from energy-intensive manufacturing (e.g., iron and steel) to less energy-intensive manufacturing (e.g., computers and plastics) and service-providing businesses

- Increasing efficiency for freight vehicles, personal vehicles (e.g., automobiles), and household appliances

INTERNATIONAL COMPARISONS OF CONSERVATION EFFORTS

As noted earlier, one indicator of a country's energy efficiency is the amount of energy it consumes per capita. Table 9.1 shows energy consumption per capita for 1980 and 2011 for the world, by region, and for selected countries. Worldwide, energy consumption per capita increased from 63.6 million Btu per person in 1980 to 74.8 million Btu per person in 2011. Asia and Oceania experienced the largest growth on a regional basis; its consumption per capita increased 163% during this period. In 2011 the United States had a better (lower) energy consumption per capita than did Canada and Saudi Arabia, but a worse (higher) energy consumption per capita than many other nations.

TABLE 9.1

World primary energy consumption per capita, by region and selected country, 1980 and 2011

[Million Btu per person]

	1980	2011	Difference
World	**63.63**	**74.81**	**18%**
Africa	14.31	15.77	10%
Asia & Oceania	19.76	52.04	163%
Central & South America	39.64	57.86	46%
Eurasia	175.70	152.94	−13%
Europe	135.21	134.89	0%
Middle East	61.36	140.07	128%
North America	286.00	257.98	−10%
Australia	187.66	287.99	53%
Canada	398.35	391.08	−2%
China	17.56	78.04	345%
France	152.07	165.93	9%
Germany	—	165.49	N/A
Greece	77.96	121.54	56%
Hong Kong	53.80	175.73	227%
India	5.90	19.85	236%
Iran	39.86	120.67	203%
Iraq	39.60	52.76	33%
Israel	68.83	133.46	94%
Italy	108.36	122.98	13%
Japan	130.11	164.44	26%
Korea, South	46.12	231.87	403%
Mexico	54.41	68.14	25%
Russia	—	209.27	N/A
Saudi Arabia	165.97	325.52	96%
South Africa	93.27	114.51	23%
United Kingdom	156.99	134.68	−14%
United States	343.57	312.79	−9%

Note: N/A = Not applicable. Btu = British thermal units.

SOURCE: Adapted from "Table. Total Primary Energy Consumption per Capita (Million Btu per Person)," in *International Energy Statistics*, U.S. Energy Information Administration, 2014, http://www.eia.gov/cfapps/ipdbproject/iedindex3.cfm?tid=44&pid=45&aid=2&cid=regions&syid=1980&eyid=2011&unit=MBTUPP (accessed July 19, 2014)

Another measure of national energy efficiency is the amount of energy a country consumes for every dollar of goods and services it produces. According to the EIA, in "International Energy Statistics" (2014, http://www.eia.gov/cfapps/ipdbproject/IEDIndex3.cfm?tid=92&pid=46&aid=2), in 2011 the United States lagged behind some industrialized countries in terms of energy efficiency (which is also called energy intensity). The United States consumed 7,328 Btu per dollar (in 2005 U.S. dollars) of GDP, compared with 4,825 Btu per dollar for France, 4,616 Btu per dollar for Japan, 4,447 Btu per dollar for Germany, and 3,610 Btu per dollar for the United Kingdom. That same year, Canada consumed 10,998 Btu per dollar of GDP; Venezuela, 18,144 Btu per dollar of GDP; China, 24,725 Btu per dollar of GDP; and Russia, 31,808 Btu per dollar of GDP.

ENERGY CONSERVATION AND GLOBAL WARMING

Greenhouse Gases

The EPA publishes an annual report on the nation's emissions of greenhouse gases (gases that contribute to global warming). For comparison, the EPA converts the emission amounts of different gases from different sources into units of teragrams of carbon dioxide equivalent (Tg CO_2 Eq.). In *Inventory of U.S. Greenhouse Gas Emissions and Sinks: 1990–2012* (April 15, 2014, http://epa.gov/climatechange/Downloads/ghgemissions/US-GHG-Inventory-2014-Main-Text.pdf), the agency indicates that energy accounted for almost all of U.S. greenhouse gas emissions between 1990 and 2012. (See Figure 9.3.) Figure 9.4 provides a breakdown of the carbon flows for fossil fuels in 2012. Most of the emissions resulted from combustion; small amounts occurred when fossil fuels were used for nonenergy purposes, for example, as feedstock for products such as plastics or asphalt. Overall, the combustion emissions by fossil fuel were:

- Coal—1,606 Tg CO_2 Eq., or 31% of the total

- Natural gas—1,356 Tg CO_2 Eq., or 26% of the total

- Petroleum—2,180 Tg CO_2 Eq., or 42% of the total

As noted earlier, concerns about global warming are driving conservation measures that target fossil fuel combustion. The EIA indicates in "What Are Greenhouse Gases and How Much Are Emitted by the United States?" (August 7, 2014, http://www.eia.gov/energy_in_brief/

FIGURE 9.3

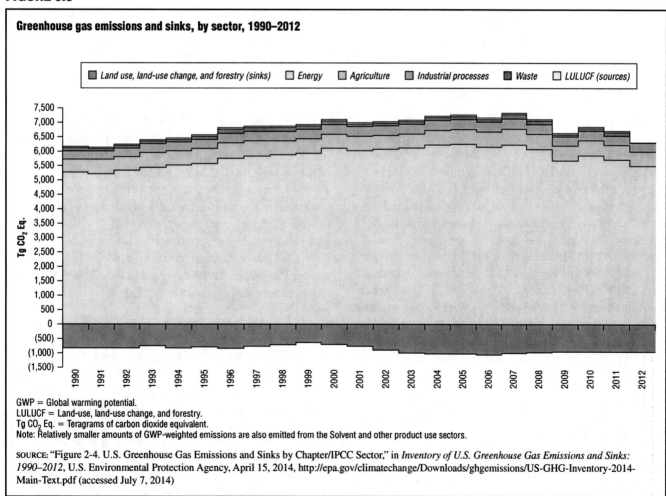

Greenhouse gas emissions and sinks, by sector, 1990–2012

GWP = Global warming potential.
LULUCF = Land-use, land-use change, and forestry.
Tg CO_2 Eq. = Teragrams of carbon dioxide equivalent.
Note: Relatively smaller amounts of GWP-weighted emissions are also emitted from the Solvent and other product use sectors.

SOURCE: "Figure 2-4. U.S. Greenhouse Gas Emissions and Sinks by Chapter/IPCC Sector," in *Inventory of U.S. Greenhouse Gas Emissions and Sinks: 1990–2012*, U.S. Environmental Protection Agency, April 15, 2014, http://epa.gov/climatechange/Downloads/ghgemissions/US-GHG-Inventory-2014-Main-Text.pdf (accessed July 7, 2014)

FIGURE 9.4

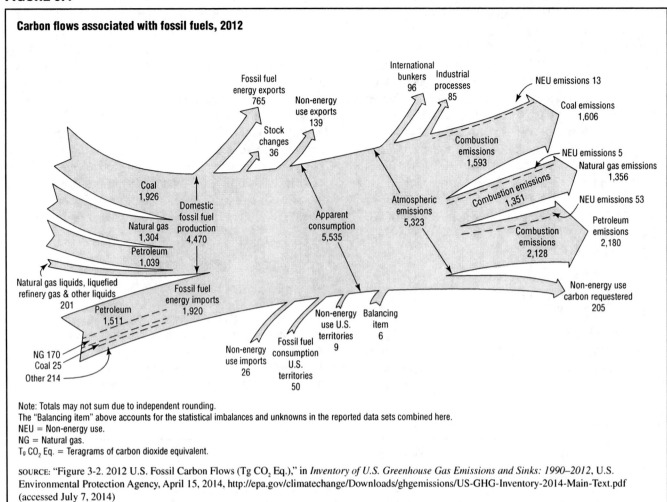

Carbon flows associated with fossil fuels, 2012

Note: Totals may not sum due to independent rounding.
The "Balancing item" above accounts for the statistical imbalances and unknowns in the reported data sets combined here.
NEU = Non-energy use.
NG = Natural gas.
T₉ CO₂ Eq. = Teragrams of carbon dioxide equivalent.

SOURCE: "Figure 3-2. 2012 U.S. Fossil Carbon Flows (Tg CO₂ Eq.)," in *Inventory of U.S. Greenhouse Gas Emissions and Sinks: 1990–2012*, U.S. Environmental Protection Agency, April 15, 2014, http://epa.gov/climatechange/Downloads/ghgemissions/US-GHG-Inventory-2014-Main-Text.pdf (accessed July 7, 2014)

greenhouse_gas.cfm) that in 2013 about 84% of U.S. greenhouse gas emissions were energy-related emissions. The agency explains that 92% of these emissions were carbon dioxide emissions from fossil fuel combustion. Table 9.2 and Figure 9.5 provide breakdowns of U.S. energy-related carbon dioxide emissions by major fuel and economic sector, respectively, between 1973 and 2013. In 2013 petroleum accounted for more of the carbon dioxide emissions (2,501 million tons [2,269 million t]) than did coal (1,898 million tons [1,722 million t]) or natural gas (1,533 million tons [1,391 million t]). The breakdown in Figure 9.5 is for primary energy consumers. It should be noted that emissions from energy consumption in the electric power sector are allocated to the end-use sectors in proportion to each sector's share of total electricity retail sales.

The U.S. government has focused much of its greenhouse gas reduction efforts on the electric power and transportation sectors because they are such large emitters.

THE ELECTRIC POWER SECTOR. Table 9.3 provides a historical breakdown of carbon dioxide emissions from energy consumption by the electric power sector. Coal

has historically accounted for the vast majority of the emissions. In 2013 coal emissions from the electric power sector totaled 1,736 million tons (1,575 million t), or 77% of the sector's total of 2,263 million tons (2,053 million t). Environmental concerns about coal-fired power plants are discussed at length in Chapter 8. That chapter also notes that the EPA proposed in September 2013 limiting carbon emissions from newly constructed power plants. In June 2014 the agency proposed similar limits on existing power plants. The proposals are expected to face fierce resistance from industry and undergo legal challenges in court.

THE TRANSPORTATION SECTOR. Table 9.4 provides a historical breakdown of carbon dioxide emissions from energy consumption by the transportation sector. Petroleum has historically accounted for the vast majority of the emissions. In 2013 petroleum emissions from the transportation sector totaled 1,967 million tons (1,784 million t), or 98% of the sector's total of 2,017 million tons (1,830 million t). Among petroleum products, motor gasoline was responsible for most of the emissions. As noted earlier, ever-tighter CAFE standards have been implemented by the federal government over the decades

TABLE 9.2

Carbon dioxide emissions from energy consumption, by source, selected years 1973–2013

[Million metric tons of carbon dioxide[a]]

	Coal[b]	Natural gas[c]	Aviation gasoline	Distillate fuel oil[d]	Jet fuel	Kerosene	LPG[e]	Lubricants	Motor gasoline[f]	Petroleum coke	Residual fuel oil	Other[g]	Total	Total[h, i]
							Petroleum							
1973 Total	1,207	1,178	6	480	155	32	92	13	911	54	508	100	2,350	4,735
1975 Total	1,181	1,046	5	443	146	24	82	11	911	51	443	97	2,212	4,439
1980 Total	1,436	1,061	4	446	156	24	87	13	900	49	453	142	2,275	4,771
1985 Total	1,638	926	3	445	178	17	87	12	930	54	216	93	2,036	4,600
1990 Total	1,821	1,024	3	470	223	6	67	13	988	70	220	127	2,187	5,039
1995 Total	1,913	1,183	3	498	222	8	80	13	1,044	76	152	121	2,216	5,323
1996 Total	1,995	1,204	3	525	232	9	86	12	1,063	79	152	139	2,300	5,510
1997 Total	2,040	1,210	3	534	234	10	87	13	1,075	80	142	145	2,323	5,584
1998 Total	2,064	1,189	2	538	238	12	82	14	1,107	93	158	128	2,372	5,635
1999 Total	2,062	1,193	3	555	245	11	90	14	1,127	96	148	133	2,422	5,688
2000 Total	2,155	1,243	3	580	254	10	97	14	1,135	86	163	118	2,459	5,868
2001 Total	2,088	1,188	2	598	243	11	88	13	1,151	89	144	135	2,474	5,761
2002 Total	2,095	1,227	2	587	237	6	91	12	1,183	96	125	130	2,470	5,804
2003 Total	2,136	1,193	2	610	231	8	87	11	1,188	96	138	142	2,514	5,855
2004 Total	2,160	1,200	2	632	240	10	87	12	1,214	107	155	144	2,603	5,975
2005 Total	2,182	1,183	2	640	246	10	84	12	1,214	106	165	143	2,623	5,999
2006 Total	2,147	1,167	2	648	240	8	80	11	1,224	106	122	152	2,593	5,919
2007 Total	2,172	1,241	2	652	238	5	83	12	1,227	100	128	150	2,596	6,021
2008 Total	2,140	1,248	2	615	226	2	79	11	1,165	93	110	132	2,436	5,835
2009 Total	1,876	1,225	2	564	204	3	78	10	1,156	87	90	112	2,305	5,417
2010 Total	1,986	1,286	2	590	210	3	79	11	1,145	81	93	122	2,336	5,619
2011 Total	1,876	1,305	2	604	209	2	78	10	1,112	78	79	117	2,291	5,483
2012 Total	1,653	1,362	2	580	206	1	81	9	1,106	78	65	113	2,240	5,267
2013 Total	1,722	1,391	2	588	208	1	87	10	1,114	76	56	126	2,269	5,393

[a]Metric tons of carbon dioxide can be converted to metric tons of carbon equivalent by multiplying by 12/44.
[b]Includes coal coke net imports.
[c]Natural gas, excluding supplemental gaseous fuels.
[d]Distillate fuel oil, excluding biodiesel.
[e]Liquefied petroleum gases.
[f]Finished motor gasoline, excluding fuel ethanol.
[g]Aviation gasoline blending components, crude oil, motor gasoline blending components, pentanes plus, petrochemical feedstocks, special naphthas, still gas, unfinished oils, waxes, and miscellaneous petroleum products.
[h]Includes electric power sector use of geothermal energy and non-biomass waste.
[i]Excludes emissions from biomass energy consumption.
Notes: Data are estimates for carbon dioxide emissions from energy consumption, including the nonfuel use of fossil fuels.
Totals may not equal sum of components due to independent rounding. Geographic coverage is the 50 states and the District of Columbia.

SOURCE: Adapted from "Table 12.1. Carbon Dioxide Emissions from Energy Consumption by Source (Million Metric Tons of Carbon Dioxide)," in *Monthly Energy Review: June 2014*, U.S. Energy Information Administration, June 25, 2014, http://www.eia.gov/totalenergy/data/monthly/archive/00351406.pdf (accessed June 27, 2014)

to improve the nation's average fuel economy (miles per gallon of motor fuel). In 2010 the EPA issued companion standards that limit carbon dioxide emissions from new vehicles. Under these standards MY 2016 automobiles are required to have an average fuel economy of 37.8 mpg (6.2 L/100 km) and emit no more than 225 grams of carbon dioxide per mile.

In 2011 the EPA and the National Highway Traffic Safety Administration (NHTSA) finalized the first fuel economy and carbon dioxide emissions limits for non-light-duty highway vehicles. In *EPA and NHTSA Adopt First-Ever Program to Reduce Greenhouse Gas Emissions and Improve Fuel Efficiency of Medium- and Heavy-Duty Vehicles* (August 2011, http://www.epa.gov/otaq/climate/documents/420f11031.pdf), the agencies indicate that the standards apply to certain large pickup trucks, tractor trailers, buses, and recreational and vocational vehicles. Not all the standards apply to all vehicle

types, and the standards vary based on vehicle attributes, such as engine classifications.

The Domestic Outlook

The EIA predicts in *Annual Energy Outlook 2014 with Projections to 2040* domestic energy-related carbon dioxide emissions through 2040 under three scenarios. (See Figure 9.6.) The agency notes that the reference scenario is a "business-as-usual trend estimate, given known technology and technological and demographic trends." The no sunset scenario assumes that certain subsidies and tax credits that are scheduled to expire during the second decade of the 21st century will remain in place through 2040. The extended policies scenario assumes that the government will put into place more extensive subsidies and tax credits and continue to tighten equipment and building efficiency and fuel economy standards. All three scenarios present a rather flat outlook for energy-related carbon dioxide emissions through 2040.

FIGURE 9.5

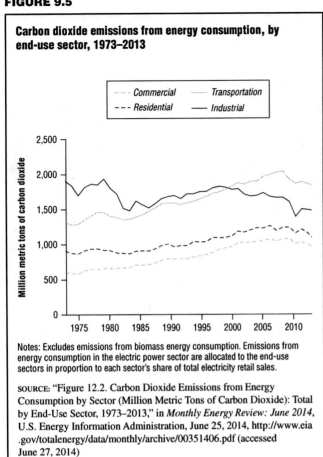

Carbon dioxide emissions from energy consumption, by end-use sector, 1973–2013

Notes: Excludes emissions from biomass energy consumption. Emissions from energy consumption in the electric power sector are allocated to the end-use sectors in proportion to each sector's share of total electricity retail sales.

SOURCE: "Figure 12.2. Carbon Dioxide Emissions from Energy Consumption by Sector (Million Metric Tons of Carbon Dioxide): Total by End-Use Sector, 1973–2013," in *Monthly Energy Review: June 2014*, U.S. Energy Information Administration, June 25, 2014, http://www.eia.gov/totalenergy/data/monthly/archive/00351406.pdf (accessed June 27, 2014)

The Worldwide Outlook

In "International Energy Statistics" (2014, http://www.eia.gov/cfapps/ipdbproject/IEDIndex3.cfm?tid=91&pid=46&aid=31), the EIA calculates the carbon intensity of countries by comparing the metric tons of carbon dioxide they produce per thousand dollars of GDP. As noted earlier, GDP is a measure of economic activity. Thus, countries with low carbon intensities are emitting less carbon dioxide into the atmosphere per unit of economic activity than are countries with higher carbon intensities. In 2011 the carbon intensity of the United States was 0.41. The values for other nations were China, 1.93; Russia, 1.82; Venezuela, 0.95; Canada, 0.45; Germany, 0.26; Japan, 0.26; the United Kingdom, 0.21; and France, 0.17. Therefore, the United States produced less carbon dioxide per thousand dollars of GDP than did China, Russia, Venezuela, and Canada. However, the United States did not perform as well in carbon intensity as did Germany, Japan, the United Kingdom, and France. Each of these nations emitted less carbon dioxide per thousand dollars of GDP than did the United States.

As noted in previous chapters, worldwide energy production is highly dependent on fossil fuel combustion, particularly in developing countries, such as China and India. Therefore, world energy-related carbon dioxide emissions are expected to continue to increase through 2040. (See Figure 9.7.) The EIA predicts that worldwide emissions will grow from 34.4 billion tons (31.2 billion t) in 2010 to 40.1 billion tons (36.4 billion t) in 2040, an increase of 46%. The agency indicates that much of the expected growth is projected to occur in developing countries that are not members of the Organisation for Economic Co-operation and Development (OECD), a collection of dozens of mostly Western nations that are devoted to global economic development. The EIA notes that non-OECD emissions were 38% greater in 2010 than OECD emissions. By 2040 non-OECD emissions are projected to be more than twice as great as OECD emissions.

INTERNATIONAL EFFORTS TO CURB CARBON EMISSIONS. Concern about global warming has spurred many efforts by diplomats and politicians to draw up agreements that would bind countries to certain carbon emissions limits or reductions over time. These efforts date back to 1988, when the United Nations (UN) established the Intergovernmental Panel on Climate Change (IPCC), a group of hundreds of the world's leading scientists. Since that time the IPCC has issued several reports (http://www.ipcc.ch/publications_and_data/publications_and_data_reports.htm) on its findings, including the causes and consequences of global warming and climate change. In addition, it has continually urged governments to move quickly with policies to protect the planet. This has proved to be a near impossible task.

In 1997 the UN convened a 160-nation conference on global warming in Kyoto, Japan, to develop a treaty on climate change that would place binding caps on industrial emissions. The resulting agreement, known as the Kyoto Protocol, bound industrialized nations to reducing their emissions of six greenhouse gases by 2012 to below 1990 levels. The United States refused to be a party to the Kyoto Protocol mostly because the protocol did not apply to developing nations such as China. Some of the nations covered by the agreement have found it impossible to meet their limits, sometimes by wide margins. International meetings convened since the late 1990s have failed to find a solution for this problem or to develop new agreements that are acceptable to developed and developing nations alike.

In 2009 a UN Climate Change Conference that was held in Copenhagen, Denmark, did not produce an agreement for the post-2012 period that would bind all nations to specific emissions limits. The Cancun Climate Change Summit in 2010 and a 2011 UN Climate Change Conference in Durban, South Africa, also proved unsuccessful in this regard. However, during the latter conference the delegates agreed to establish by 2015 a global emissions limit agreement that would take effect in 2020. As of October 2014, it remained to be seen whether the proposed 2015 agreement would actually come to fruition and if the United States would agree to be bound by it.

TABLE 9.3

Carbon dioxide emissions from energy consumption by the electric power sector, selected years 1973–2013

[Million metric tons of carbon dioxide[a]]

	Coal	Natural gas[b]	Petroleum Distillate fuel oil[c]	Petroleum coke	Residual fuel oil	Total	Geothermal	Non-biomass waste[d]	Total[e]
1973 Total	812	199	20	2	254	276	NA	NA	1,286
1975 Total	824	172	17	(s)	231	248	NA	NA	1,244
1980 Total	1,137	200	12	1	194	207	NA	NA	1,544
1985 Total	1,367	166	6	1	79	86	NA	NA	1,619
1990 Total	1,548	176	7	3	92	102	(s)	6	1,831
1995 Total	1,661	228	8	8	45	61	(s)	10	1,960
1996 Total	1,752	205	8	8	50	66	(s)	10	2,033
1997 Total	1,797	219	8	10	56	75	(s)	10	2,101
1998 Total	1,828	248	10	13	82	105	(s)	10	2,192
1999 Total	1,836	260	10	11	76	97	(s)	10	2,204
2000 Total	1,927	281	13	10	69	91	(s)	10	2,310
2001 Total	1,870	290	12	11	79	102	(s)	11	2,273
2002 Total	1,890	306	9	18	52	79	(s)	13	2,288
2003 Total	1,931	278	12	18	69	98	(s)	11	2,319
2004 Total	1,943	297	8	23	69	100	(s)	11	2,352
2005 Total	1,984	319	8	25	69	102	(s)	11	2,417
2006 Total	1,954	338	5	22	28	56	(s)	12	2,359
2007 Total	1,987	372	7	17	31	55	(s)	11	2,426
2008 Total	1,959	362	5	16	19	40	(s)	12	2,374
2009 Total	1,741	373	5	14	14	34	(s)	11	2,159
2010 Total	1,828	399	6	15	12	33	(s)	11	2,271
2011 Total	1,723	409	5	15	7	27	(s)	11	2,171
2012 Total	1,511	493	4	9	6	19	(s)	11	2,035
2013 Total	1,575	442	4	13	6	23	(s)	11	2,053

[a]Metric tons of carbon dioxide can be converted to metric tons of carbon equivalent by multiplying by 12/44.
[b]Natural gas, excluding supplemental gaseous fuels.
[c]Distillate fuel oil, excluding biodiesel.
[d]Municipal solid waste from non-biogenic sources, and tire-derived fuels.
[e]Excludes emissions from biomass energy consumption.
NA = Not available. (s) = Less than 0.5 million metric tons.
Notes: Data are estimates for carbon dioxide emissions from energy consumption.
Data exclude emissions from biomass energy consumption.
Totals may not equal sum of components due to independent rounding. Geographic coverage is the 50 states and the District of Columbia.

SOURCE: Adapted from "Table 12.6. Carbon Dioxide Emissions from Energy Consumption: Electric Power Sector (Million Metric Tons of Carbon Dioxide)," in *Monthly Energy Review: June 2014*, U.S. Energy Information Administration, June 25, 2014, http://www.eia.gov/totalenergy/data/monthly/archive/00351406 .pdf (accessed June 27, 2014)

TABLE 9.4

Carbon dioxide emissions from energy consumption by the transportation sector, selected years 1973–2013

[Million metric tons of carbon dioxide[a]]

	Coal	Natural gas[b]	Petroleum					Motor gasoline[e]	Residual fuel oil	Total	Retail electricity[f]	Total[g]
			Aviation gasoline	Distillate fuel oil[c]	Jet fuel	LPG[d]	Lubricants					
1973 Total	(s)	39	6	163	152	3	6	886	57	1,273	2	1,315
1975 Total	(s)	32	5	155	145	3	6	889	56	1,258	2	1,292
1980 Total	h	34	4	204	155	1	6	881	110	1,363	2	1,400
1985 Total	h	28	3	232	178	2	6	908	62	1,391	3	1,421
1990 Total	h	36	3	268	223	1	7	967	80	1,548	3	1,588
1995 Total	h	38	3	307	222	1	6	1,029	72	1,639	3	1,681
1996 Total	h	39	3	327	232	1	6	1,047	67	1,683	3	1,725
1997 Total	h	41	3	342	234	1	6	1,057	56	1,699	3	1,744
1998 Total	h	35	2	352	238	1	7	1,090	53	1,743	3	1,782
1999 Total	h	36	3	366	245	1	7	1,115	52	1,789	3	1,828
2000 Total	h	36	3	378	254	1	7	1,121	70	1,833	4	1,872
2001 Total	h	35	2	387	243	1	6	1,127	46	1,813	4	1,852
2002 Total	h	37	2	394	237	1	6	1,158	53	1,851	4	1,892
2003 Total	h	33	2	409	231	1	6	1,161	45	1,856	5	1,893
2004 Total	h	32	2	434	240	1	6	1,185	58	1,926	5	1,962
2005 Total	h	33	2	444	246	2	6	1,186	66	1,953	5	1,991
2006 Total	h	33	2	469	240	2	5	1,194	71	1,984	5	2,022
2007 Total	h	35	2	472	238	1	6	1,201	78	1,999	5	2,040
2008 Total	h	37	2	427	226	3	5	1,145	73	1,881	5	1,922
2009 Total	h	38	2	408	204	2	5	1,136	62	1,819	5	1,862
2010 Total	h	38	2	429	210	2	5	1,123	70	1,842	5	1,885
2011 Total	h	39	2	441	209	2	5	1,092	61	1,812	4	1,855
2012 Total	h	41	2	420	206	2	5	1,087	53	1,774	4	1,819
2013 Total	h	42	2	427	208	3	5	1,094	45	1,784	4	1,830

[a]Metric tons of carbon dioxide can be converted to metric tons of carbon equivalent by multiplying by 12/44.
[b]Natural gas, excluding supplemental gaseous fuels.
[c]Distillate fuel oil, excluding biodiesel.
[d]Liquefied petroleum gases.
[e]Finished motor gasoline, excluding fuel ethanol.
[f]Emissions from energy consumption (for electricity and a small amount of useful thermal output) in the electric power sector are allocated to the end-use sectors in proportion to each sector's share of total electricity retail sales.
[g]Excludes emissions from biomass energy consumption. See Table 12.7.
[h]Beginning in 1978, the small amounts of coal consumed for transportation are reported as industrial sector consumption.
(s) = Less than 0.5 million metric tons.
Notes: Data are estimates for carbon dioxide emissions from energy consumption, including the nonfuel use of fossil fuels.
Data exclude emissions from biomass energy consumption.
Totals may not equal sum of components due to in dependent rounding. Geographic coverage is the 50 states and the District of Columbia.

SOURCE: Adapted from "Table 12.5 Carbon Dioxide Emissions from Energy Consumption: Transportation Sector (Million Metric Tons of Carbon Dioxide)," in *Monthly Energy Review: June 2014*, U.S. Energy Information Administration, June 25, 2014, http://www.eia.gov/totalenergy/data/monthly/archive/00351406 .pdf (accessed June 27, 2014)

FIGURE 9.6

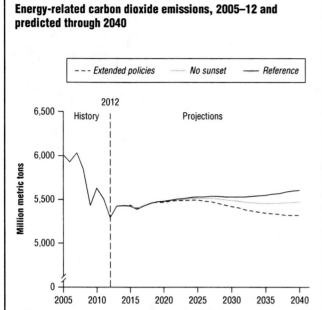

Energy-related carbon dioxide emissions, 2005–12 and predicted through 2040

SOURCE: "Figure IF1-5. Energy-Related Carbon Dioxide Emissions in Three Cases, 2005–40 (Million Metric Tons)," in *Annual Energy Outlook 2014 with Projections to 2040*, U.S. Energy Information Administration, April 2014, http://www.eia.gov/forecasts/aeo/ (accessed June 26, 2014)

FIGURE 9.7

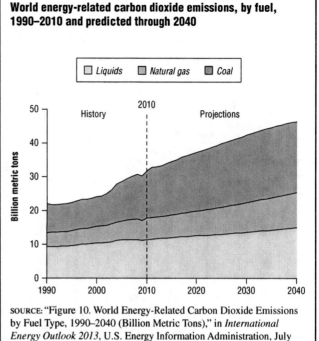

World energy-related carbon dioxide emissions, by fuel, 1990–2010 and predicted through 2040

SOURCE: "Figure 10. World Energy-Related Carbon Dioxide Emissions by Fuel Type, 1990–2040 (Billion Metric Tons)," in *International Energy Outlook 2013*, U.S. Energy Information Administration, July 2013, http://www.eia.gov/forecasts/ieo/ (accessed July 11, 2014)

IMPORTANT NAMES
AND ADDRESSES

American Gas Association
400 N. Capitol St. NW
Washington, DC 20001
(202) 824-7000
URL: http://www.aga.org/

American Petroleum Institute
1220 L St. NW
Washington, DC 20005-4070
(202) 682-8000
URL: http://www.api.org/

American Wind Energy Association
1501 M St. NW, Ste. 1000
Washington, DC 20005
(202) 383-2500
FAX: (202) 383-2505
URL: http://www.awea.org/

Bureau of Land Management
1849 C St. NW, Rm. 5665
Washington, DC 20240
(202) 208-3801
FAX: (202) 208-5242
URL: http://www.blm.gov/

Bureau of Ocean Energy Management
1849 C St. NW
Washington, DC 20240
(202) 208-6474
E-mail: BOEMPublicAffairs@boem.gov
URL: http://www.boem.gov/

Congressional Budget Office
Ford House Office Bldg., Fourth Floor
Second St. and D St. SW
Washington, DC 20515-6925
(202) 226-2602
E-mail: communications@cbo.gov
URL: http://www.cbo.gov/

Congressional Research Service
Library of Congress
101 Independence Ave. SE
Washington, DC 20540
URL: http://www.loc.gov/crsinfo/

Edison Electric Institute
701 Pennsylvania Ave. NW
Washington, DC 20004-2696
(202) 508-5000
URL: http://www.eei.org/

Electric Power Research Institute
3420 Hillview Ave.
Palo Alto, CA 94304
(650) 855-2121
1-800-313-3774
E-mail: askepri@epri.com
URL: http://www.epri.com/

Energy Information Administration
1000 Independence Ave. SW
Washington, DC 20585
(202) 586-8800
E-mail: InfoCtr@eia.gov
URL: http://www.eia.gov/

International Energy Agency
9, rue de la Fédération
Paris Cedex 15, France 75739
33 1 40 57 65 00
FAX: 33 1 40 57 65 09
URL: http://www.iea.org/

National Highway Traffic Safety
Administration
1200 New Jersey Ave. SE, West Bldg.
Washington, DC 20590
1-888-327-4236
URL: http://www.nhtsa.gov/

National Mining Association
101 Constitution Ave. NW, Ste. 500 East
Washington, DC 20001
(202) 463-2600
FAX: (202) 463-2666
URL: http://www.nma.org/

Natural Gas Supply Association
1620 Eye St. NW, Ste. 700
Washington, DC 20006

(202) 326-9300
URL: http://www.ngsa.org/

Natural Resources Defense Council
40 W. 20th St.
New York, NY 10011
(212) 727-2700
FAX: (212) 727-1773
E-mail: nrdcinfo@nrdc.org
URL: http://www.nrdc.org/

Nuclear Energy Institute
1201 F St. NW, Ste. 1100
Washington, DC 20004-1218
(202) 739-8000
FAX: (202) 785-4019
URL: http://www.nei.org/

Oak Ridge National Laboratory
PO Box 2008
Oak Ridge, TN 37831
(865) 576-7658
URL: http://ornl.gov/

Organization of the Petroleum
Exporting Countries
Helferstorferstrasse 17
Vienna, Austria A-1010
43-1 21112-3302
URL: http://www.opec.org/opec_web/en//

Solid Waste Association of
North America
1100 Wayne Ave., Ste. 650
Silver Spring, MD 20910
1-800-467-9262
FAX: (301) 589-7068
URL: http://www.swana.org/

U.S. Bureau of Reclamation
1849 C St. NW
Washington, DC 20240-0001
(202) 513-0501
FAX: (202) 513-0309
URL: http://www.usbr.gov/

U.S. Department of Energy
1000 Independence Ave. SW
Washington, DC 20585
(202) 586-5000
FAX: (202) 586-4403
E-mail: The.Secretary@hq.doe.gov
URL: http://www.energy.gov/

U.S. Environmental Protection Agency
1200 Pennsylvania Ave. NW
Washington, DC 20460
(202) 272-0167
URL: http://www.epa.gov/

U.S. Geological Survey
John W. Powell Bldg.
12201 Sunrise Valley Dr.
Reston, VA 20192

(703) 648-4000
URL: http://www.usgs.gov/

U.S. House of Representatives Committee on Natural Resources
1324 Longworth House Office Bldg.
Washington, DC 20515
(202) 225-2761
FAX: (202) 225-5929
URL: http://resources
committee.house.gov/

U.S. Nuclear Regulatory Commission
Washington, DC 20555-0001
(301) 415-7000
1-800-368-5642
URL: http://www.nrc.gov/

U.S. Senate Committee on Energy and Natural Resources
304 Dirksen Senate Bldg.
Washington, DC 20510
(202) 224-4971
FAX: (202) 224-6163
URL: http://energy.senate.gov/

World Energy Council
62-64 Cornhill
London, United Kingdom EC3V 3NH
44 207734 5996
FAX: 44 207734 5926
URL: http://www.worldenergy.org/

RESOURCES

The U.S. Department of Energy's U.S. Energy Information Administration is the major source of energy statistics in the United States. It publishes weekly, monthly, and yearly statistical collections on most types of energy, which are available in libraries and online at http://www.eia.doe.gov/. The *Annual Energy Review* provides a complete statistical overview, and the *Annual Energy Outlook* projects future developments in the field. The website "International Energy Statistics" presents a statistical overview of the world energy situation, and the *International Energy Outlook* forecasts future industry developments. The Energy Information Administration also provides the *Domestic Uranium Production Report* and the *Monthly Energy Review*. The *U.S. Crude Oil, Natural Gas, and Natural Gas Liquids Proved Reserves* discusses reserves of coal, oil, and gas. The agency's websites "Energy Explained," "Energy in Brief," and "Today in Energy" contain a wealth of technical information about various energy sources.

The Department of Energy's Oak Ridge National Laboratory publishes the annual *Transportation Energy Data Book* and *Biomass Energy Data Book*. In addition, the Department of Energy makes available information on the development of alternative vehicles and fuels, renewable energy sources, and electric industry restructuring.

The U.S. Environmental Protection Agency maintains websites about hydraulic fracturing and global warming and publishes the annual *Inventory of U.S. Greenhouse Gas Emissions and Sinks*. The U.S. Geological Survey maintains extensive data regarding energy reserves. The U.S. Nuclear Regulatory Commission is also an important source of information and publishes the annual *Information Digest*.

INDEX

Nuclear power plants, 82*t*
  accidents, 83–85
  consumption, 92*f*
  domestic production, 79–80
  fuel fabrication, 78(*f*5.6)
  liability limits, 20
  net electricity generated, by state, 84*f*
  nuclear chain reaction, 74
  projections, 85*f*
  reactors, 73, 75
  tax preferences, 17
  trends, 83*f*
  uranium, 74–79, 76, 79*t*, 80*t*, 81*t*
  waste issues, 85–87
  world electricity generation, 128*f*
  world nuclear power production, 82–83
Nuclear Regulatory Commission, 78, 80–81
Nuclear Waste Administration Act, 87
Nuclear Waste Fund, 87
Nuclear weapons, 78
NV Energy, 90

O

Obama, Barack
  building energy efficiency, 135
  carbon emissions, 129
  fuel economy standards, 134
  industrial sector energy efficiency, 135
  Keystone XL Project, 30
  National Energy Policy, 15
  National Nuclear Security
    Administration budget, 79
  offshore resources, 108–109
  renewable energy, 91
  Smart Grid initiative, 124
  tax preferences, 17
Ocean Renewable Power Company, 102
Ocean thermal energy conversion, 102–103
OECD. *See* Organisation for Economic
  Co-operation and Development
Office of Natural Resources Revenue, 19
Offshore resources
  coal, 60, 62
  natural gas, 51
  oil, 26, 27*f*, 28, 28(*f*2.5), 32
  technically recoverable resources,
    108–109
Oil
  consumption, 36–37, 39*f*, 40*f*
  conventional *vs.* unconventional, 25–26
  deposit locations, 26, 27*f*, 28
  distillation fractions, 30*f*
  domestic production, 31–32, 31*f*, 32*t*
  drilling rigs, 28*f*, 28(*f*2.4)
  exploration and development, 109
  exports, 35–36, 39*t*
  extraction, 28
  fuel economy standards, 138–139
  gasoline and diesel fuel prices, 44*t*

imports, 13*f*, 32–34, 34(*f*2.12), 37*t*,
  38(*f*2.15)
international reserves, 111
measurement, 28
natural gas from oil wells, 49
OPEC, imports from, 35*f*
petroleum flow, 36*f*
pipelines, 29–30
prices, 42–45, 42*t*
production, domestic, 34(*f*2.11)
properties, 25
refiner acquisition costs, 42–43, 43*t*
refining, 30–31
renewable energy, "Big Oil" investment
  in, 90
reserves, 105–109, 106(*t*7.1), 107*f*, 108*f*
Strategic Petroleum Reserve, 35,
  38(*f*2.16)
technically recoverable resources,
  107–109
tight oil and shale gas production
  basins, 33*f*
transportation sector, 133–134
traps, 26*f*
underground fields, 25
wells drilled, 111*f*
world consumption and production,
  37–39, 41–42, 41*t*, 42*f*
Oil Pollution Act, 45
Oil Spill Liability Trust Fund, 15, 45
Oil spills
  liability limits, 20
  oil price factors, 45
  targeted taxes, 15
OPEC (Organization of the Petroleum
  Exporting Countries), 32–34, 35*f*
Organisation for Economic Co-operation
  and Development (OECD), 111
  See also Developed countries
Organization of the Petroleum Exporting
  Countries (OPEC), 32–34, 35*f*
Outer continental shelf, 28

P

Pennsylvania, 128
Petroleum. *See* Oil
PG&E, 90
Phosphate deposits, 110
Pipelines
  natural gas, 50, 53
  oil, 29–30, 108
Plutonium, 78, 87, 111, 114
Politics, 14–15, 35
Pollution control equipment, 128
Population, 22
Power grid, 118
Power Marketing Administration, 96
Prices and costs
  coal, 64, 66–68, 70*t*, 71*t*
  electricity, 121–124, 123*f*, 123*t*

energy conservation, 131
energy price estimates, by type, 13*t*
energy price projections, 20, 21*t*–22*t*
external energy costs, 13–14
gasoline and diesel fuel prices, 44*t*
natural gas, 55–56, 56*t*
nuclear power, 87
oil, 42–45, 42*f*, 42*t*, 133–134
refiner acquisition costs, 43*t*
tax preferences, 16–17, 16*f*, 18*t*,
  19(*f*1.15)
uranium, 76–77, 79, 81*t*
Processing
  coal, 58, 60
  natural gas, 49
Production
  biodiesel, 96*t*
  biomass energy, 92
  coal flow, 65(*f*4.3)
  coal production, 60, 62–64
  coal production, by depth, 65(*f*4.4)
  coal production, by location, 66(*f*4.5)
  coal production, by rank, 64*t*
  coal production, by region, 63*f*
  coal production, by state, 62*t*
  coal production, trade, and consumption,
    61*t*, 66(*f*4.6)
  coal production, world, 69(*t*4.5)
  coal production projections, by
    region, 69*f*
  electricity, 118, 120–121, 122*f*, 124–127,
    125(*f*8.7), 127*t*
  energy flow, 12*f*
  energy production, 10(*f*1.9), 20, 21*t*–22*t*,
    22, 23(*t*1.9)
  energy self-sufficiency, 9, 12
  fuel ethanol, 95*t*
  natural gas, 51, 51*t*, 52*f*, 54, 55(*t*3.4), 56
  nuclear power, 79–83
  oil, 31–32, 34(*f*2.11), 41(*t*2.4)
  oil and natural gas plant liquids
    production, 31*f*, 32*t*
  petroleum flow, 36*f*
  renewable energy, 93*t*, 101–102
  by source, 2, 3*t*, 4, 4*f*, 5*f*
  tax preferences, 16–17, 16*f*
  tight oil and shale gas production
    basins, 33*f*
  uranium, 76*f*, 77*f*
Projections
  carbon dioxide emissions, 139, 140,
    143(*f*9.6), 143(*f*9.7)
  coal, 63–64
  domestic energy supply, 21*t*–22*t*
  electricity, 124–125, 125(*f*8.7), 126*t*
  energy conservation, 136
  natural gas, 52(*f*3.5), 56
  nuclear power, 80–82, 85*f*
  oil, 13*f*, 32, 37–39, 41–42
  renewable energy, 99–102, 100*t*–101*t*

CPSIA information can be obtained
at www.ICGtesting.com
Printed in the USA
FFOW05n0445030615

9 781573 026505